W9-APY-291

FROM CURRITUCK TO CALABASH

Living With North Carolina's Barrier Islands

Orrin H. Pilkey, Jr.
William J. Neal
Orrin H. Pilkey, Sr.
Stanley R. Riggs

Duke University Press

The North Carolina Science and Technology Research Center feels that this book contains much useful information for those concerned with coastal development; it also reflects some personal biases of the authors and their associates. The Center has assisted in its publication in an effort to make the information available to developers, property owners (present and potential), and other persons interested in the coastal area.

The views expressed in *From Currituck to Calabash* are those of the authors and do not necessarily reflect the official position of the North Caroina Science and Technology Research Center.

Copyright © 1978, 1980 by Orrin H. Pilkey, Jr., William J. Neal, Orrin H. Pilkey, Sr., Stanley R. Riggs, and the North Carolina Science and Technology Research Center. Reprinted with permission of the North Carolina Science and Technology Research Center by Duke University Press, 1982.

Second Edition 1980

All rights reserved, including the right to reproduce this book or portions thereof in any form.

LCC card 80-52835

ISBN 0-8223-0548-8

Printed in the United States of America

Dedication

To our children and grandchildren with the hope that they too will have a beautiful Carolina shoreline to enjoy.

CONTENTS

TABLES

ILLUSTRATIONS

Foreword

Some 2,500 years ago the citizens of Carthage, a Phoenician people, built a harbor along the shores of the Gulf of Tunis in North Africa. This harbor, from which Hannibal sailed to attack Rome, is still used today by small Arab fishing boats.

A few hundred years later and some twenty miles away, the Romans, a mightier people, built the seaport of Utica. North Africa was the breadbasket of the Roman Empire, and across the docks of Utica flowed huge quantities of food and treasure to be shipped to the motherland. Today, a tourist standing atop the highest column in the ruins of Utica can no longer see the sea. The shoreline has moved 17 kilometers seaward, away from what was once the harbor.

The Carthaginians were careful to design to live with nature. The Romans, the first practitioners of brute-force technology, chose to confront, alter, and destroy nature. What the Romans didn't realize was that in the long run, nature always wins at the shoreline.

The sandy barrier-island shoreline of the U. S. Atlantic and Gulf coasts is a dynamic, ever-changing environment that often does not interact well with the trappings of man. The exploitation of this dynamic coastal area is being carried out at an ever-increasing rate. First came the harbors and ports which required channel maintenance; then came the seashore resorts which attracted construction on the rapidly retreating shorelines. While earlier generations of Americans were like the Carthaginians—either wise enough to locate properly or resigned to watch their homes fall victim to shoreline retreat—modern island-developers are more like the ancient Romans: with money, technology, and political clout, they attempt to stop shoreline retreat so as to extend the lifespans of buildings along the shore. The long-range result of such efforts, however, is economic and environmental calamity. This is visible along the New Jersey and southern Florida shorelines. They attest to the fact that man's success in harnessing nature for his own ends does not necessarily enhance his surroundings or the quality of his life.

We have written this book because we wish to help North Carolinians learn to live in harmony with nature at the shoreline and to understand fully the consequences of doing otherwise. This book is not meant to discourage development; we hope, rather, that it encourages proper, *limited* development. Although certain natural areas warrant protection from development, preservationism is an unrealistic philosophy to follow on all of the coast, especially since a development pattern has already been established on most of it. Unrestricted development, however, endangers coastal residents and island resources. The public should become aware of and concerned about our island resources in order to conserve them.

This book is an outgrowth of the 1975 book *How to Live with an Island*, by Orrin Pilkey, Jr., Orrin Pilkey, Sr., and Robb Turner. Though the first book dealt with development on a single island— Bogue Banks, near Morehead City, North Carolina—many of its principles were applicable to other islands. Thus the book was distributed from Cape Cod, Massachusetts, to Padre Island, Texas. Our primary purpose, however, is to affect development on the North Carolina shoreline. In this book we have applied our understanding of shoreline geology and engineering to every privately owned island in North Carolina—from Currituck to Calabash. William Neal, professor of geology at Grand Valley State College in Allendale, Michigan, spent nine months on sabbatical leave researching and writing much of the manuscript. His work was sponsored by the National Science Foundation Program in Science and Societal Problems. Dr. Stanley Riggs, who teaches geology at East Carolina University, has spent many months and years, "in fair weather and foul," studying the natural forces at work on the Outer Banks. His work has been supported largely by the Sea Grant Program and in part by the N. C. Board of Science and Technology.

Like our earlier book, *From Currituck to Calabash* was published through the interest and efforts of Peter Chenery, director of the North Carolina Science and Technology Research Center. Doris Schroeder, director of communications for the Center, edited the original manuscript, rewriting and rearranging much of the material that we handed her; Betty Zatz, editorial assistant at the Center, then edited it to its final form.

We were also aided by three Lindas: Linda Gerber, administrative secretary of the Duke geology department, who typed the original manuscript; Linda Caulder, secretary at the North Carolina Science and Technology Research Center, who typed the final printer's copy; figures were penned by Jim Hamm and Mark Evans; most of the field photographs were taken by Jim Page, on loan from the N. C. Department of Natural Resources and Community Development.

We are especially grateful for the contributions of Drs. William Cleary and Paul Hosier of the University of North Carolina at Wilmington, Drs. Jay Langfelder and Stan Boc of North Carolina

State University, and Lim Vallianos of the Army Corps of Engineers Wilmington district office.

In gathering data for this book we were helped by many people who live along the shore—so many, in fact, that it would be impossible to list them all here. We are grateful for their cheerful and enthusiastic cooperation, and the new insights and concerns that we acquired from them.

1

A Coastal Perspective

THE RUSH TO THE SHORE:
A HUMAN TIDE

A bumper sticker reads, "The Outer Banks, A Secret Worth Keeping," but someone hasn't kept the secret! On a summer weekend the population of North Carolina's coastal zone may swell by several hundred thousand people. More than 150,000 persons may be on North Carolina's northernmost islands, the Outer Banks, accessible only by two bridges, ferry service, or private boat (Figure 1). Each year more visitors decide to remain on the coast, either as permanent residents or temporary residents of summer cottages.

The development rate of the state's coastal zone can be compared in many ways to an old-fashioned gold rush. The rush is propelled by the good fortunes of the second half of the twentieth century: affluence and leisure time. The main attraction, of course, is the beautiful, richly endowed, 301-mile-long ocean shoreline. Enjoyment of the coast is enhanced by island atmospheres that vary from the bleak desolation of Core Banks to the wild splendor of the Bogue Banks maritime forest.

North Carolina's islands hold something for everyone. On Atlantic Beach one may drink beer to the accompaniment of loud music or ride a ferris wheel, while on Pine Knoll Shores, just a few miles away, one may relax in a serene, forested, island-home development. One may stroll Wrightsville Beach, where condominiums crowd the shore, or neighboring Masonboro Island, yet unaltered by man (Figure 2)!

But all is not going well with our coastal development. We can clearly see where we are heading, since others have been there before us. By studying the histories of other developed shoreline areas with similar oceanographic and geologic characteristics, North Carolina can determine which decisions affecting development were proper and which were not. On the New Jersey and

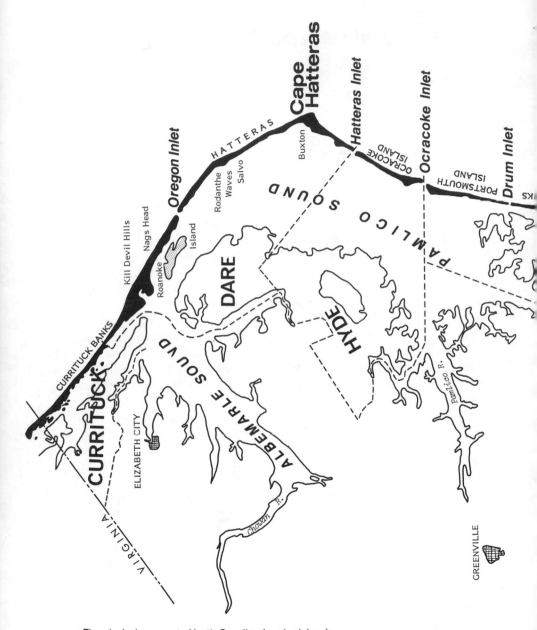

Fig. 1. Index map to North Carolina barrier islands

2

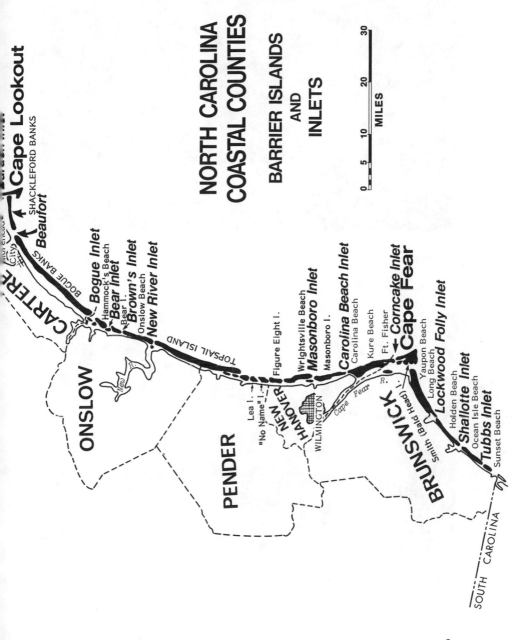

NORTH CAROLINA
COASTAL COUNTIES

BARRIER ISLANDS
AND
INLETS

0 5 10 20 30
MILES

Cape Lookout

SHACKLEFORD BANKS

Beaufort

Morehead City

CARTERET

BOGUE BANKS

Bogue Inlet

Hammock's Beach
Bear I.

Bear Inlet

Brown's Inlet

Onslow Beach

New River Inlet

ONSLOW

New R.

TOPSAIL ISLAND

PENDER

Lea I.
"No Name" I.

Figure Eight I.

Wrightsville Beach

Masonboro Inlet

Masonboro I.

Carolina Beach Inlet

Carolina Beach

Kure Beach

Ft. Fisher

NEW HANOVER

WILMINGTON

Cape Fear R.

Corncake Inlet

Cape Fear

Smith (Bald Head)

Yaupon Beach

Long Beach

Lockwood Folly Inlet

Holden Beach

Shallotte Inlet

Ocean Isle Beach

Tubbs Inlet

Sunset Beach

BRUNSWICK

SOUTH CAROLINA

3

Maritime forest

"Blowout" in a dunefield

Fig. 2. North Carolina islands in their natural state

4

southern Florida coasts, there have been numerous environmental crises and a great deal of property loss because residents have failed to recognize the basic, natural processes of the shoreline. Some good may still come of these losses if they serve to guide today's developers away from past mistakes.

A few years ago, Col. Paul Denison, former Wilmington district chief of the Army Corps of Engineers, stated that "New Jerseyization" was already underway on the North Carolina shore, and he urged citizens of the state to take action to slow the process. ("New Jerseyization" refers to the pattern of development that occurred on the New Jersey shore. This development began in earnest about 1800 and proceeded very rapidly because of the shore's proximity to large population centers.) Col. Denison was not urging that development halt, but rather that it change in intensity and direction. Since then the Coastal Area Management Act has been enacted by the North Carolina Legislature, and a multitude of public hearings have been attended by interested citizens and public officials. A staggering number of hours have been spent on efforts to initiate the planning called for under the law. Yet the New Jerseyization of the North Carolina coast has not perceptibly slowed down.

THE HISTORY OF DEVELOPMENT: THE GOOD, THE BAD, AND THE UGLY

Olden Times

Although the Spanish visited the Cape Fear region in the 1520s, it was not until 1584 that Sir Walter Raleigh began his efforts to explore and colonize the Outer Banks region. The failure of Raleigh's "Lost Colony" is a familiar story; it was only the first of several settlement efforts on the islands to be abandoned.

The early Outer Banks dwellers endured through the 1700s by assuming a variety of occupations, including raising stock, scavenging shipwrecks, processing beached whales, and fishing. Some of these persons, living on the islands in order to escape the laws, taxes, and other requirements of society, may have been considered unsavory by today's standards. Nevertheless, the early islanders were skilled in survival and lived accordingly—in harmony with their islands. Until the late 1700s, homes were built on the sound side of the islands in wooded hammocks that provided some protection

Fig. 3. Nags Head beach (ca. 1930) from site of present-day Wright Brothers Memorial

Source: N. C. Dept. of Cultural Resources,
Division of Archives and History

against wind and flood. The current existence of some of these older Outer Banks villages (such as Hatteras, Ocracoke and Portsmouth) attests to the wisdom of early developers.

Around this time, however, dangerous development began to occur. In 1787, for example, there was a proposal to dig a new inlet on Beacon Island, inside Ocracoke Inlet. Beginning in 1790, a cluster of buildings—which ultimately included wharves, residences, a grist mill, windmill, store, fishery, and tavern—was built on a 60-foot-wide, one-half-mile-long island said to be dry at low tide (Reference 1, Appendix C). Needless to say, hurricanes and inlet changes brought an end to the enterprise and removed all traces of its existence in the early 1800s.

The First Resort

Early development of the barrier islands was slow by today's standards. Access was more limited, and social and political pressure to build bridges to the islands was not strong. Thus, fewer people were able to vacation at the shore.

Although Portsmouth, Ocracoke, and Beaufort were visited by summer vacationers as early as the mid-1700s, Nags Head became the first important seashore resort. The community grew rapidly in the 1830s and was a flourishing resort by the beginning of the Civil War. In consideration of hurricanes, most of the buildings of this resort were built on the sound rather than the ocean side of the island. However, after the Civil War, residents began to build on the beach front.

Morehead City originated in the late 1850s as a resort to rival Nags Head and was built on the mainland to increase accessibility and to better endure the elements. In the late 1800s, the Ocean View Railroad was built from Wilmington to Wrightsville Beach, and another shoreline resort boomed. Atlantic Beach on Bogue Banks began developing with the construction of several dance pavilions in the early 1900s. Construction in 1928 of the first bridge to Bogue Banks hastened its development.

Not all of the towns born on the islands flourished or lived to the present. Diamond City at Cape Lookout was abandoned in 1899 by its 500 inhabitants who were discouraged over continual hurricane damage. The townspeople of Rice Path on Bogue Banks moved because of encroaching sand dunes, and Portsmouth on Portsmouth Island suffered gradual economic death when the adja-

Fig. 4. "New Jerseyization." Note rip-rap seawalls, total lack of beach, and rubble from destroyed engineering structures.

8

cent Ocracoke Inlet—its source of economic growth—was abandoned as a North Carolina port of entry.

Of course, one does not have to delve into ancient history for examples of disappearing towns. Holden Beach and Brunswick County's developing shorelines were completely wiped out in 1954 by Hurricane Hazel, the most devastating storm of this century in North Carolina. Hazel should not have been a surprise, for it was only one of nine such destructive storms to strike the Brunswick County coast since 1740. An Army Corps of Engineers report noted that "hardly a vestige of human habitation (remained) on the Brunswick County shore following Hurricane Hazel." It also noted the "absolute totality of the damage" and the increased potential for storm damage to an area under heavy development. Unfortunately the history lesson went unheeded. Modern technology responded quickly to Holden Beach and other Brunswick County coastal communities, and development there is presently much heavier than before!

World War II brought military occupation of several islands, including Onslow Beach and Topsail Island. Temporary bridges were made permanent and roads were built. When the Army moved out of Topsail Island in the late 1940s, it left behind roads and buildings —seeds of the island's present day development.

The New Jerseyization Phase

The New Jerseyization phase of the North Carolina shore began immediately after World War II. Before 1941 and the coming of the bulldozer, only a few resorts such as Wrightsville Beach and Nags Head were in existence; the rest of the islands were either untouched or hardly touched by man (Figure 3). Today, even the most casual observer can see the results of the New Jerseyization process along the New Jersey coast. A trip there would be worthwhile for every North Carolinian, for the sight of the New Jersey shore conveys a more dramatic message than the pages of any book (Figure 4).

The New Jerseyization problem, in part, is one of destroyed natural beauty. But beauty is in the eyes of the beholder; some prefer to see a hot dog stand on the beach to a dune covered with sea oats. There are, however, non-aesthetic problems as well which stem from New Jerseyization, and which pose a more serious threat to coastal residents:

9

1. **Hurricanes:** Under the constant threat of these storms, lives are endangered by unsafe construction and hazardous building sites. Unfortunately, development on North Carolina islands has not proceeded from the safest to the least safe areas; historically, the most eager builders have often owned the most dangerous stretches of the islands. Construction quality is independent of building-site quality. On Figure Eight Island, for example, some very well built houses are situated on dangerous sites with low elevation, no dunes, and a history of frequent storm overwash. On the other hand, there are trailer parks on Bogue Banks which, though situated at high elevations with good dune protection, are poorly secured to the ground. A single poorly secured mobile home can be detached from its foundation in a storm and render the surrounding area unsafe.

2. **Pollution:** Improper waste disposal threatens the health of coastal citizens and destroys the natural resources that support the local marine fishing industry. Twenty percent of North Carolina's estuarine fishing grounds for crabs, oysters, shrimp, and fish have already been closed because of pollution. Some of North Carolina's more crowded islands have reached a point at which development has essentially halted because of the lack of places to put sewage. For this reason, the State is considering alternative methods of waste disposal. One proposed method is the pumping of treated sewage out to sea. Increasing waste-treatment capacity will engender a new surge of development pressure, and may also cause pollution problems on the continental shelf as it did in New Jersey.

3. **Environmental Destruction:** The beach—the very environment we rush to the island to enjoy—is ultimately destroyed when overdeveloped. Scenic dunes, maritime forests, and marsh habitats gradually disappear. This alteration of the environment is the most striking aspect of New Jerseyization. Beach-saving devices work only temporarily at best. Where seawalls are built, the beach is eventually lost. Old beach resorts in Florida and New Jersey have no beaches at all except where sand has been pumped in. In addition, beach repair is done at great cost to the taxpayer. Miami Beach's latest beach-restoration project, begun in 1977, will erode the public coffers by $64 million.

4. **Reduced Public Access:** Private development inevitably reduces access to the beach for the public that must foot the bills for beach repairs. Access to the beach is prohibited to all but adjacent property owners; others must pay access charges.

The same list of New Jerseyization problems can occur in almost

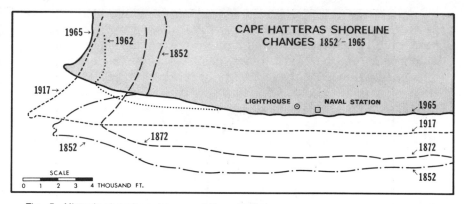

Fig. 5. Historic shoreline changes at Cape Hatteras   *Source: National Park Service*

any developing area. The shore zone, however, is unique in many ways. The rate of development along the shore is extremely rapid and is occurring for the most part on ephemeral, delicate islands that are subject to natural changes (Figure 5). Very little accessible shoreline remains in the state or country. The situation is aggravated by a unique political framework on the islands wherein only a few landowners—the year-round residents—have a voting voice in local affairs. Finally, throughout history the coastal zone of North Carolina has been an economically poor area so that development of almost any kind tends to be welcomed because of its presumed positive economic effect.

HURRICANE HISTORY: A STORMY PAST

In June 1586, Sir Francis Drake arrived off Roanoke Inlet with a shipload of supplies for the Roanoke Island colony. A violent storm—possibly a hurricane—arrived at the same time, and the supply ship was blown out to sea, forcing residents to abandon the settlement. This event marked the beginning of a lively record of hurricane history for North Carolina. Perhaps because of the way the coast protrudes into the hurricane alley of the Atlantic, the state has taken more than its share of hurricane winds, waves, and floods—considerably more than have the neighboring states of Virginia and South Carolina (Table I and Figure 6). Records indicate that North Carolina has a major hurricane on an average of every two to three years. Hurricane occurrence, however, is irregular (References 2 and 3, Appendix C). The 1950s brought considerable

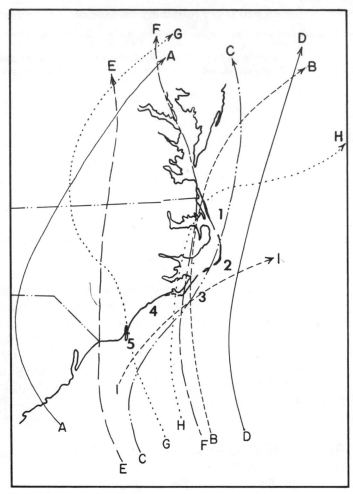

Fig. 6. Hurricane tracks of the '50s

1950s Hurricane Record

A	Able	August 31, 1952
B	Barbara	August 13, 1953
C	Carol	August 30, 1954
D	Edna	September 10, 1954
E	Hazel	October 15, 1954
F	Connie	August 12, 1955
G	Diane	August 17, 1955
H	Ione	September 17, 1955
I	Helene	September 27, 1958

Letters A through I correspond to hurricane tracks shown in Figure 6.

12

TABLE I. Probability of Storms

(Percent probability indicates the number expected to occur over a 100-year period.)

Sector	% Probability Tropical Storm	% Probability Hurricane	% Probability Great Hurricane
1	9	8	4
2	18	11	8
3	14	5	—
4	7	6	2
5	13	6	2

Information adopted from Table 2, p. 16, Reference 75, Appendix C. Sectors 1 through 5 are designated on Figure 6.

destruction by hurricanes, whereas the 1960s brought relative peace and quiet. No one knows what is in store for the late '70s and '80s.

Today, anyone on a North Carolina barrier island during a hurricane is almost certainly there by choice. In the past, however, people were not warned of a hurricane's approach, and were thus not always able to flee their homes before a hurricane struck. The absence of warning made hurricanes even more feared then than they are today, and accentuated the need for safe development. This need was expressed after the August 19, 1879 hurricane, in a quote from the August 20, 1879, Raleigh *Observer:* "Men cannot build houses upon sand and expect to see them stand now anymore than they could in the olden times. . . .summer seaside resorts must be built high enough above the tide line to insure safety as well as patronage. People are wary of making hairbreadth escapes in seeking health and rest."

The effects of 17th-, 18th-, and even 19th-century storms on North Carolina islands were generally not well documented because so few people lived on the islands. We do know that Diamond City at Cape Lookout was abandoned because of an 1899 hurricane which followed a path similar to that of 1954's Hurricane Hazel. The 1879 hurricane referred to in the Raleigh *Observer* quotation also did great damage to Diamond City.

Many accounts of early North Carolina hurricanes were based on observations by shipmasters at sea. The severity of a hurricane was often judged by the number of vessels demasted or lost. Ocracoke accounts typically expressed storm severity in terms of the number of ships sunk or blown aground.

The year 1827, when at least eleven hurricanes came up

13

"Hurricane Alley," may have been the most active hurricane-season ever. The fourth storm of that series was named Calypso, after a sailing vessel that was miraculously saved by its desperate crew. Blown over on its side, the ship righted itself and made landfall in the Cape Fear River. The so-called "great" North Carolina Hurricane of 1827 drove the two-year-old Cape Hatteras lightship ashore onto Ocracoke Island. The captain, his wife, and three daughters were rescued.

The July 12, 1842, hurricane was one of the worst in Carolina history. Apparently passing off the Outer Banks, the storm left only one building in Portsmouth unwrecked, 28 vessels blown aground near Ocracoke, two ships sunk on Diamond Shoals with all hands lost, and a great number of livestock killed. Three months later, a bottle washed ashore in Bermuda with a note dated July 15, 1842, detailing the struggle of the schooner *Lexington* off Cape Hatteras. This scrap of paper was the last trace of the *Lexington* and her crew; they had fallen victim to the storm in full fury.

The origin of something as terrifying and destructive as a hurricane has understandably puzzled many people over the centuries; it still puzzles modern scientists. In 1769 Governor Tryon wrote a letter in which he attributed the hurricane of that year to "the effect of a blazing planet or star that was seen from both Newbern (sic) and here (Brunswick) rising in the east for several nights between the 26th and 31st of August." One hundred years later the problem of hurricane genesis was apparently still unsolved. The "Terrible Storm" of August 19, 1879, was regarded by some Beaufort residents as the wrathful judgment of God which the people of Beaufort had incurred for dancing on Sunday night.

Hurricane chroniclers will note that old-timers have considered each major storm "the worst ever." It's doubtful that storms really are increasing in intensity, but it is certain that as development increases, storm damage increases accordingly. For example, in September 1857, the hurricane that sank the passenger ship *S. S. Central America* (causing the loss of over four hundred lives), swept ashore on Wrightsville Beach to destroy only large stands of oak trees. But the hurricane that struck the beach in October 1899—of apparently less intensity—washed away 16 cottages and damaged all others. By the 1950s the stage had been set for even greater destruction. Hurricane Hazel of October 15, 1954, the most damaging of all hurricanes to strike Wrightsville Beach, destroyed 89 buildings and damaged 530; only 20 escaped intact. Hurricane Diane became the country's first "billion-dollar hurricane" in August

1955. The buildings lost in a hurricane today might include highrise motels and condominiums that were not present in 1955. We may yet witness the time when the property destruction and death toll are even greater per major storm.

The price paid for hurricanes is rising.

2

Shoreline Dynamics

BARRIER ISLANDS: RIBBONS OF SAND

In front of almost every gently sloping coast in the world are narrow strips of sand that we refer to as barrier islands. North Carolina has been blessed with a particularly beautiful and extensive set of barrier islands protecting her mainland shore.

Despite the fact that these islands are found throughout the world, no one has answered the question of *why* they occur so consistently under the circumstances that they do. Though scientists do have some ideas as to *how* they came to exist, there is still active disagreement among them on this subject.

We know that once an island forms, it begins to migrate and change its shape, vegetation, and land forms (Figure 7). Different islands evolve in different ways and at different rates. No two islands are the same.

Understanding island-evolution mechanisms is particularly important for those interested in preventing damage to these ephemeral, dynamic features. Similarly, we must understand island processes if we want to prevent damage to the structures we build on islands.

THE ORIGIN OF BARRIER ISLANDS: HOW THEY BEGAN

In order to understand how our barrier islands formed, it is necessary to understand the recent history of sea-level changes caused by the ice ages. Because large amounts of water have been alternately tied up and released from the massive glacial icecaps (Greenland and Antarctica, for example), sea level as has been go-

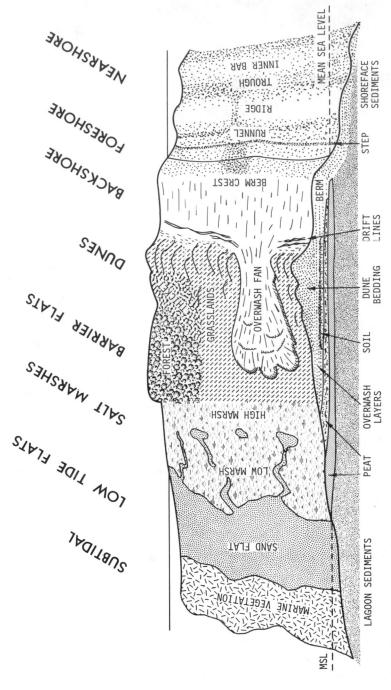

NEARSHORE

FORESHORE

BACKSHORE

DUNES

BARRIER FLATS

SALT MARSHES

LOW TIDE FLATS

SUBTIDAL

MEAN SEA LEVEL

INNER BAR

TROUGH

RIDGE

RUNNEL

STEP

SHOREFACE SEDIMENTS

BERM CREST

BERM

DRIFT LINES

OVERWASH FAN

DUNE BEDDING

GRASSLANDS

FOREST

SOIL

OVERWASH LAYERS

HIGH MARSH

PEAT

LOW MARSH

SAND FLAT

LAGOON SEDIMENTS

MARINE VEGETATION

MSL

Source: Paul Godfrey, University of Massachusetts

Fig. 7. Barrier-island environments

18

ing up and down at an amazing rate since the ice ages began a million or so years ago. The last such rise in sea level began about 19,000 years ago (Figure 8). At that time the sea was 400 feet below its present level, and the shoreline was out beyond the continental-shelf edge, lapping up on the continental slope.

During the ice age, North Carolina had a much larger land area than it has now. A vast forest with marshes and river valleys stretched across the continental shelf (Figure 9). As the sea level rose, the shoreline retreated in response to the rise, and gradually the continental-shelf forest began to disappear. At some point in the history of the sea-level rise, probably when the shoreline was out near the continental-shelf edge, ridges of *sand dunes* began to form parallel to the beaches. These ridges were formed as they are now, by wind blowing sand landward from the beach. In turn, the beach derived sand from the continental shelf by the onshore sweeping action of fair-weather waves. As sea level continued to rise, the line of beach ridges was breached. This breaching may have occurred dur-

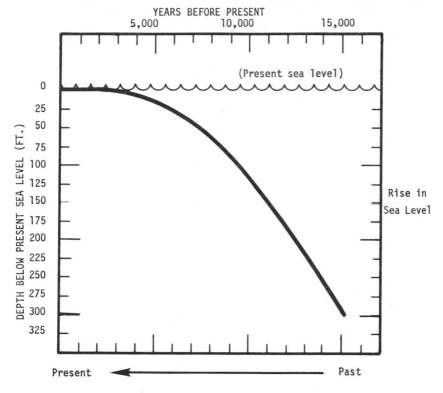

Fig. 8. 15,000 years of sea-level change

19

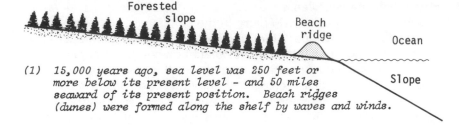

(1) *15,000 years ago, sea level was 250 feet or more below its present level - and 50 miles seaward of its present position. Beach ridges (dunes) were formed along the shelf by waves and winds.*

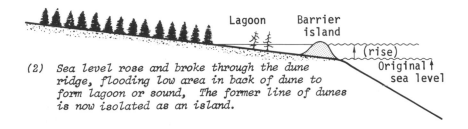

(2) *Sea level rose and broke through the dune ridge, flooding low area in back of dune to form lagoon or sound. The former line of dunes is now isolated as an island.*

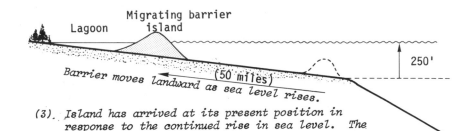

(3) *Island has arrived at its present position in response to the continued rise in sea level. The island will continue to move landward as long as sea level rises and a low slope exists behind the island.*

Fig. 9. Barrier-island formation and migration across the continental shelf

ing major hurricanes. The combination of breaching and the rapid rise in sea level caused the area behind the beach ridges to be flooded; thus the ridges became islands. This theory of barrier-island formation, called "beach ridge drowning," was the product of the fertile mind of the late Dr. John Hoyt of the University of Georgia.

After the islands formed, a whole new set of processes took over and the islands migrated landward as the sea level rose. Needless to say, for the islands to remain islands, the mainland shoreline must have retreated too. Viewed in this context, these narrow strips of sand upon which we build our beach cottages are indeed mobile

20

and ephemeral features.

About 5,000 years ago (Figure 8) the sea-level rise slowed down measurably to perhaps 1 foot per century, and the islands slowed down their migration. One can calculate how rapid the retreat from such a sea-level rise would be. First, make the assumption that the cross-sectional profile across the lagoon (sound), barrier island, and inner continental shelf remains unchanged regardless of the change in sea level (Figure 9). If this is the case, then island migration must be a simple function of the slope of the mainland: the more gentle the slope of the coastal plain, the more rapid the island migration. Accordingly, the horizontal island-migration rate in North Carolina should be 100 to 1,000 times the rate of sea-level rise; that is, for every foot of sea-level rise, the islands retreat 100 to 1,000 feet inland (Figure 10).

The southern part of our state's coastal plain has a much steeper slope than the northern part. Thus, if other factors are equal (and they often are not), our northern islands, the Outer Banks, should be migrating faster than the islands just north and south of Cape Fear. Buxton, for example, should be in more trouble than Wrightsville Beach.

Do you want to prove to yourself that islands migrate? If you're standing on one now, walk to the ocean-side beach and look at the seashells. Chances are that on most North Carolina beaches you will find oyster, clam, or snail shells that once lived behind the barrier island toward the mainland in the lagoon. How did shells on the back side get to the front side? The answer is that the island migrated over the lagoon, and waves attacking and breaking up the old lagoon sands and muds threw the shells up on the present-day beach. Lagoonal oyster shells found on Shackleford Island beach have been radiocarbon-dated at 7,000 years old. In addition, salt-marsh peats that formed in back of the islands at some earlier time are exposed occasionally on ocean-side beaches after storms.

If you haven't guessed already, "island migration" is the term that geologists use for what beach cottage owners call "beach erosion."

THE EVOLUTION OF BARRIER ISLANDS: HOW THEY OPERATE

Every barrier island is unique. Each island evolves by mechanisms that may differ slightly or substantially from those of adjacent islands; each one must be understood separately.

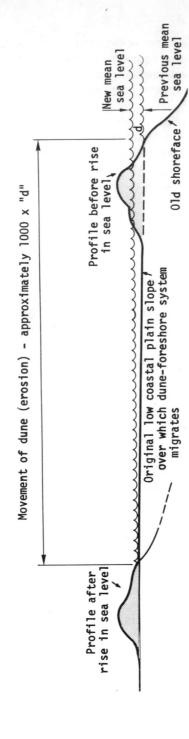

Fig. 10. Ratio of horizontal island migration to the vertical sea-level rise

For years scientists did not realize this. Geologists and biologists studying barrier islands in Texas argued at length with those studying barrier islands in New Jersey. Each group of scientists thought the other group unobservant; what was learned about New Jersey islands, they believed, just didn't apply to Texas islands and vice versa.

However, scientists are beginning to realize that there are fundamental differences among look-alike barrier islands.

Let's compare North Carolina and Texas barrier-island systems on a broad scale. If you dam a river in North Carolina, it should not affect the state's barrier islands at all; North Carolina islands get most of their sand from the adjacent continental shelf. Texas islands, however, are nurtured by rivers such as the Rio Grande and the Brazos, which furnish sand directly to the shoreline during every flood. When this supply is stopped by dams, as it partially has been, the beaches begin to "starve" and retreat more rapidly. Another major difference between Texas and North Carolina barrier islands is in their responses to *overwash.* On Texas barrier islands such as Padre Island, overwash passes—where waves wash sand onto the island—have been flooded again and again during succeeding storms. On North Carolina islands, the sites of major overwash deposition have shifted through time.

Differences among barrier islands off the North Carolina coast alone may be just as great. The most striking example of this is the contrast between Core Banks and Shackleford Bank, two adjacent islands that form the Cape Lookout National Seashore. Shackleford is a high, forested island with extensive *dune formation.* Core Banks, north of Cape Lookout, is a low, narrow island with almost no dunes, and is overwashed by even minor storms. Both are healthy islands, but each exists under somewhat different conditions. The dominant directions of wind on both Shackleford and Core Banks are approximately north or south. Since Core Banks is oriented north and south, the wind usually blows sand coming in from fair-weather waves *up* or *down* the length of the island. Shackleford Bank, in contrast, is oriented east and west. The dominant winds at least part of the year blow sand *across* the island, building up dunes and increasing the height and width of the island.

Drs. William Cleary and Paul Hosier, two scientists from the University of North Carolina at Wilmington, have been engaged in work that illustrates another difference between North Carolina barrier islands. On Masonboro Island south of Wrightsville Beach, shrubs take years to become established on overwash fans created by

23

Fig. 11. Masonboro Island

storms (Figure 11). This is because the sand brought across Masonboro by storms has a coarse grain size and doesn't hold water well.
On nearby Figure Eight Island the sand is finer grained, better
retains water, and allows vegetation to grow much faster after a
storm. Even various parts of a single island (Oak Island, for example) show great differences in origin and dynamics.

The point we emphasize is that each island has a different story to
tell. The island dweller must learn and respond to the unique traits of
the particular island he inhabits—if he wants to preserve it.

Having discussed differences among barrier islands, let's mention some things they have in common. While the major
mechanisms by which islands move are the same everywhere, the
rates and intensities at which these mechanisms operate differ
widely.

In order for an island to migrate, the front (ocean) side must move
landward by erosion, and the back (sound) side must do likewise by
growth. As it moves, the island must somehow maintain its elevation
and bulk.

Front side moves back by erosion

The beach moves back because the sea level is rising. This sea-level rise is the main worldwide cause of beach erosion, although other local factors such as the lack of sand supply may also cause the problem. The shoreline of the Nile Delta in Egypt, for example, is eroding at an unprecedented rate because the Aswan Dam on the Nile River has cut off the supply of new beach sand.

As the sea level rises, the sandy coastal-plain shoreline of North Carolina retreats. (People living along the shore call this "erosion.") The mechanism of shoreline retreat will be discussed later in the chapter, in a section on beaches. At this point, we need only recognize that the beach retreats horizontally at 100 to 1,000 times the rate of vertical sea-level rise, and the rate of retreat essentially controls the rate of island migration.

Back side moves back by growth

There are several ways by which an island can widen. On the narrow, low North Carolina islands that are backed by a lagoon or sound, a common widening process is that of *inlet formation.* An inlet is the channel of water between adjacent barrier islands. New inlets often form when water breaches the island during a hurricane. Eyewitness accounts and other evidence confirm that water usually breaks through the island from the sound side as the storm subsides and high tides retreat. Over the next few years following inlet formation, sand carried by ocean currents pours through the gap and into the sound. This mass of sand is called a *tidal delta* (Figure 12) and forms the shallows on which ships go aground and through which the Corps of Engineers must dredge in order to maintain channels. In a few years, salt marsh establishes itself on the shallow tidal delta. Salt-marsh grasses cause the land to be built up almost to high-tide level, and when this happens, new land is added to the island. Often the inlet closes or migrates to a new position, and its former position is marked only by a marsh bulging into the sound.

When an inlet migrates laterally to a new position, the tidal delta moves with it. In other words, as the inlet migrates, sand continues to pour into the lagoon, and a series of new tidal deltas continue to form along the entire area of inlet migration. In this way the island is widened over the full distance the inlet shifted. Nearly half of some North Carolina islands mark former inlet positions.

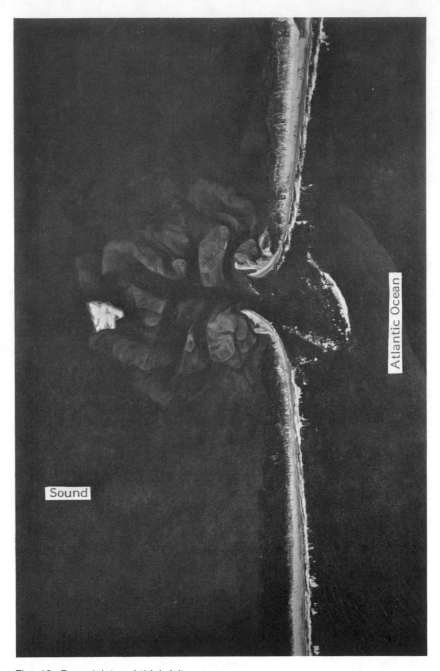

Fig. 12. Drum inlet and tidal delta

Source: N. C. Sea Grant College Program

Another way that islands—especially narrow ones—can be widened is by direct frontal *overwash* of storm waves from the ocean side of the island (Figure 13). All barrier islands receive overwash during storms. On large ones like Bogue Banks, the overwash may barely penetrate the first dune line. On low, narrow ones like most of the Outer Banks north of Cape Lookout, overwash may reach the sound. Overwash waves carry sand which is deposited in tongue- or fan-shaped masses called *overwash fans.* When such fans reach into the sound, the island is widened. If islands are backed by salt marsh, overwash sediment may bury the marsh (Figures 7 and 13). Interestingly enough, some islands need overwash to survive.

It is important to point out that, though in the long run the sound side of an island tends to grow landward, many islands are currently eroding on the sound side. As would be expected, back-side erosion is particularly prominent on islands backed by open water; this includes most of the coastal islands between Bogue Banks and Currituck Bank.

The island maintains its elevation during migration

The remaining problem of a migrating island is how to retain its bulk or elevation as it moves toward the mainland. This problem is solved by two processes: dune formation and overwash fan deposition.

Dunes are formed by the wind, and if a sufficiently large supply of sand comes to the beach from the continental shelf via the waves, a high-elevation island can be formed. Good examples of this type of island in North Carolina are Bogue Banks and the extreme northern Outer Banks in Dare and Currituck Counties.

The reasons for the lack of dune formation on islands of low elevation are the lack of sand supply from the adjacent continental shelf, or dominant wind direction up and down the beach rather than across it. As mentioned previously, this difference in island orientation to wind direction is why Core and Shackleford Banks, two adjacent islands, have such different appearances.

BARRIER-ISLAND ENVIRONMENTS: AN INTEGRATED SYSTEM

At this point you understand how barrier islands develop and operate, and the important principle that each barrier island is

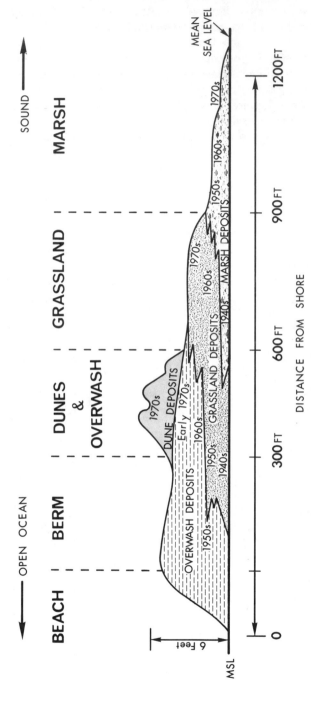

Fig. 13. Cross section of Core Banks

Source: Paul Godfrey, University of Massachusetts

unique. Therefore, if you want expert advice, don't ask the old-timer from Wrightsville Beach to choose your cottage site on Topsail Island.

Another important concept to understand is that barrier-island environments (Figure 7, page 18) are interrelated. Each environment is part of an overall integrated system and to some degree, depends on or affects other environments within the system. Specific environments are discussed in Chapter 4.

Perhaps the best example of one environment affecting others in the system is provided by the role of the ocean-side beach. The beach is important because 1) it alters its shape during storms in such a way as to minimize fundamental damage to the island by waves, and 2) it is the major source of sand for the entire island. Examples of the ways in which man has interfered in the integrated system may best illustrate these functions.

Dr. Paul Godfrey of the University of Massachusetts discovered that the building of the National Park Service's dune-dike system, the long, continuous, artificial dune on the Outer Banks near Cape Hatteras, is causing erosion on the *sound side* of the island. The problem is that the artificial dune prevents overwash fans from crossing the island during storms. Before the dune was built, overwash frequently reached the back side of the island, and new salt marsh was formed on the edge of the new overwash fan. Newly formed low or *Spartina* marsh is an excellent erosion buffer for sound-side waves. By preventing overwash, the frontal dune on the island's ocean side precludes new marsh growth and increases the sound-side erosion rate.

If overwash is not obstructed, the marsh in time (ten years or more) builds up its elevation and essentially chokes itself. The grass thins out and becomes shorter and less healthy-looking. The most casual observer walking along the back side of any marsh-fringed island in its natural state notes that he is walking through alternately tall and short grass. The tall grass is new or fresh grass on recent overwash; the short grass is old grass on an overwash fan. Old marsh is a poor buffer for shoreline erosion and soon begins to give way.

The maritime forest also illustrates the integration of island environments. The large trees are salt-tolerant and form a canopy over the less tolerant undergrowth. The undergrowth, in turn, stabilizes the larger trees by holding down the soil. If trees are thinned or removed, salt spray can attack and eliminate the undergrowth. Loss of vegetation allows sediment to be eroded by wind or other processes, thereby destroying the trees.

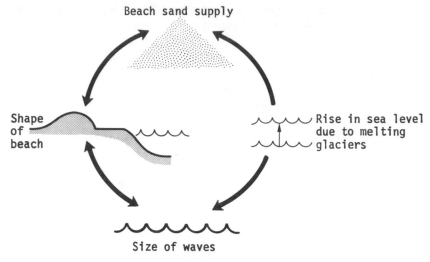

Fig. 14. The Dynamic Equilibrium Model

Much has been said about the damage to islands by dune buggies. This problem further attests to the integration of island environments. Dune buggies can prevent dunes from stabilizing (becoming stationary), and destabilization (moving sand) may result in destroyed dunes and vegetation, and sand-covered maritime forests. Extreme destabilization is visible on Onslow Beach, where the Marine Corps holds maneuvers; overgrazing by horses, goats, sheep, and cows may also cause dune fields to move about as they did, for example, on Currituck Bank. But the most common cause of excessive sand movement on North Carolina barrier islands is construction. The problem is particularly acute during the early stages of construction, and in many instances, has halted further construction altogether.

Just as environments on a single island depend on one another, so do environments on adjacent islands. The beaches on our islands are like flowing rivers of sand. Frequently islands depend on neighboring islands for sand supply. When this supply is cut off (by inlet dredging or construction), the island's frontal erosion rate increases.

The Carolina Beach Inlet was formed artificially by blasting a ditch through the barrier. The inlet stopped the longshore-current flow of sand, and Carolina Beach has since been suffering severe erosion. The jetty at Masonboro Inlet is causing severe erosion at Masonboro Island and making navigation on the channel hazardous. Eventually a second jetty and a dredging program will be needed to correct the problem.

BEACHES: THE SHOCK ABSORBERS

The Dynamic Equilibrium

The beach is one of the earth's most dynamic environments. The beach—or zone or active sand movement—is ever changing and ever migrating, and we now know that it does so in accordance with the earth's natural laws. The natural laws of the beach control a beautiful, logical environment that builds up when the weather is good, and strategically (but only temporarily) retreats when confronted by big storm waves. This system depends on four factors: waves, sea-level rise, beach sand, and shape of the beach. The relationship among these factors is a natural balance referred to as a "dynamic equilibrium" (Figure 14): when one factor changes, the others adjust accordingly to maintain a balance. When man enters the system incorrectly—as he often does—the dynamic equilibrium continues to function in a predictable way, but in a way that is harmful to him.

Answers to the following often-asked questions about beaches may clarify the nature of the dynamic equilibrium. It is important to keep in mind that the beach extends from the toe of the dune to an offshore depth of 40 or 50 feet. The part on which we walk is only the upper beach.

How does the beach respond to a storm?

Old-timers and storm survivors from North Carolina's islands have frequently commented on how beautiful, flat, and broad the beach is after a storm. The flat beach can be explained in terms of the dynamic equilibrium: as wave energy increases and sea level rises, materials move to change the shape of the beach. The reason for this storm response is logical. The beach flattens itself in order to make storm waves expend their energy over a broader and more level surface. On a steeper surface storm-wave energy would be expended on a smaller area, causing greater damage.

Figure 15 illustrates the way in which the beach flattens. Waves take sand from the upper beach or the first dune and transport it to the lower beach. If a hot dog stand or beach cottage happens to be

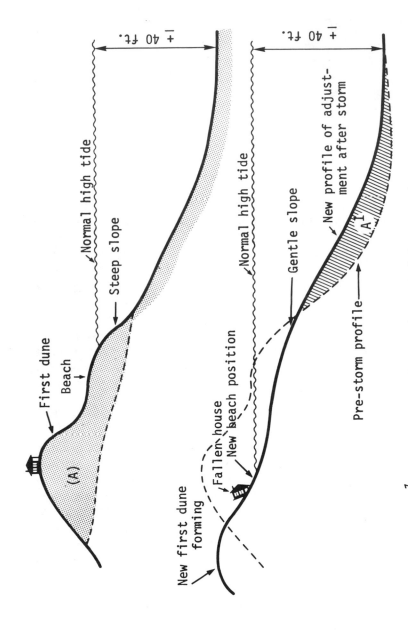

First dune

Beach

(A)

Normal high tide

Steep slope

± 40 ft.

New first dune forming

Fallen house
New beach position

Normal high tide

Gentle slope

New profile of adjust-
ment after storm

Pre-storm profile

A¹

± 40 ft.

(Shaded area A¹ is approximately equal to shaded area A.)

Fig. 15. Beach flattening in response to a storm

32

located on the first dune, it may disappear along with the dune sands.

An island can lose a great deal of sand during a storm. Much of it is replenished, however, gradually pushed shoreward by fair-weather waves. As the sand returns to the beach, the wind takes over and slowly rebuilds the dunes. In order for the sand to be replenished, of course, there should be no man-made obstructions—such as a seawall—between the first dune and the beach.

How does the beach widen?

Beaches grow seaward in several ways, principally by 1) bringing in new sand by the so-called longshore (surf-zone) currents, or 2) bringing in new sand from offshore by forming a "ridge and runnel" system. Actually, these two ways of beach widening are not mutually exclusive.

Longshore currents are familiar to anyone who has swum in the ocean; they are the reason one sometimes ends up somewhere down the beach, away from one's beach towel. Such currents result from waves approaching the shore at an angle; this causes a portion of the breaking waves' energy to be directed along the beach. When combined with breaking waves, the weak current is capable of carrying large amounts of very coarse material for miles along a beach. The sand transported along the shore may be deposited at the end of the island. Since the 1940s, longshore currents have added a full half-mile to the length of Shackleford Banks.

During the summer one frequently sees an offshore bar within a few tens of yards from the beach. This offshore bar or *ridge* is usually where the better swimmers and surfers congregate to catch the big wave (Figure 16B). The trough between the beach and the ridge is called the *runnel*. Ridges and runnels are typically formed during small summer storms. In the quiet weather between storms, the ridge virtually marches onto the shore and is "welded" to the beach. The next time you are at the beach, observe the offshore ridge for a period of a few days, and verify this for yourself. You will find that each day you have to swim out a slightly shorter distance in order to stand on the sand bar.

At low tide during the summer, the beach frequently has a trough filled or partly filled with water. This trough is formed by the ridge

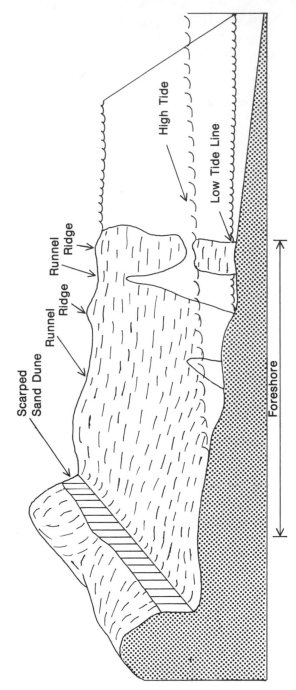

Fig. 16A. Ridge and runnel system

that is in the final stages of welding onto the beach. Several ridges combine to make the *berm* or beach terrace, on which sunbathers loll.

Where does beach sand come from?

In North Carolina, sand is constantly supplied to the beaches at varying rates from the adjacent inner continental shelf. Fair-weather waves push the sand shoreward. Additional sand is carried laterally, parallel to the beach, by the previously mentioned surf-zone current. On a developed island, the sand in front of one beach cottage most likely has come from the front of a neighbor's cottage.

At the present time, rivers do not contribute material directly to North Carolina beaches. The sand carried by rivers is stored in the upper estuaries, miles from the beach. (When sea level was much lower, however, rivers delivered sand to the shelf.)

Where do seashells come from?

Surprisingly, the majority of the shells on North Carolina beaches can be called fossils. Many North Carolina beach shells have radiocarbon ages that fall between 7,000 and 9,000 years. Even some of the shiny-lettered olive and pretty whelk shells are very old.

If you use a shell book (Reference 24, Appendix C) to carefully identify specimens from a North Carolina beach, you will find that sound or lagoon shells are very common on the ocean-side beach. As the islands migrated landward, they ran over the shells that once lived in back-island environments. In a few hundred or thousand years, the lagoon shells were thrust up onto the ocean-side beach.

But as any beach buff knows, not all of North Carolina's beach seashells are fossils. The Coquina clam lives in the upper beach and hastens to rebury itself when exposed by sandcastle builders.

Why do beaches erode?

As we have already pointed out, "beach erosion" is the cottage owner's term for the larger process called island migration. Its principal cause is the sea-level rise—presently judged to be about 1 foot per century along the North Carolina coast. We can be thankful that

Fig. 16B. Ridge and runnel, surf and surfers

we don't have the 3-feet-per-century rise of the New England coast.

A geologist once spoke at a luncheon in Virginia Beach, Virginia, and told the audience that the most serious problem facing their eroding shoreline was the rising sea level. A local reporter, mocking the speech, reported in banner headlines that we must "beware the year 4000" for then our houses will be underwater. The joke is on him, for by then his house actually *may* be underwater—20 miles out at sea and 30 feet deep!

The real problem is not the sea-level rise but rather the horizontal retreat of the strand line caused by the rise. As you remember, the sea level has been going up and down several hundred feet over the last million years because of the alternate formation and melting of glaciers in the higher latitudes. As the sea level rises, nature does not make things hard on herself by constructing a giant sand ridge or some other such feature to hold the sea back. On the contrary, the shoreline smoothly moves back and forth with the sea level. As the shoreline moves up a steep slope (such as the California shelf), the actual movement seems slow. But the same sea-level rise causes a much more rapid shoreline movement if the shelf slope or coastal plain slope is very gentle, as it is in North Carolina. Here lies the problem. North Carolina has a very gentle sea-level rise, but since its land surface has such a slight slope, shoreline movement is much faster—visible within the lifespan of a beach cottage. Normally, the beach simply moves back with the slope of the land and maintains its shape or cross-sectional profile.

If most of the ocean-side shorelines of North Carolina are eroding, what is the long-range future of beach development?

Most of the North Carolina coast is eroding, although locally sands do accumulate and temporary beach growth occurs (for example, Sunset Beach). As frequency of storms and storm tracks vary through time, the local patterns of erosion and growth vary. Available information on erosion and deposition rates is general, and more specific studies are needed for planned use of individual stretches of shoreline. Nevertheless, sufficient information exists to demonstrate that most of the North Carolina coast is experiencing horizontal erosion at the rate of approximately 3 to 5 feet per year (Reference 34, Appendix C). Given the present rate of development and imprudent use of the barrier-island system, we can anticipate extreme losses in the future. Developers must learn to live with the islands to avert such losses (Chapter 3).

Are the shorelines on the back sides of our islands eroding?

Some are; some are not. If a healthy salt marsh is growing on the sound side, there may be no erosion problem. If a sand bluff or surf-zone stumps appear on the back side, beware—erosion is occurring. Rates of erosion for North Carolina's back-island beaches have not been determined, although Drs. Stan Riggs and Michael O'Connor of East Carolina University have begun to gather such information for the Pamlico and Albemarle Sound shorelines.

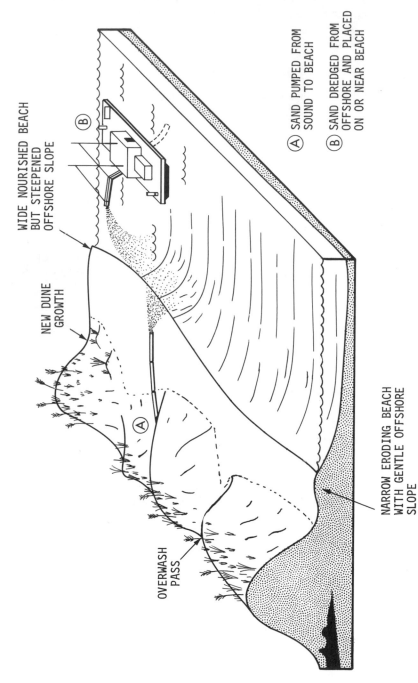

WIDE NOURISHED BEACH BUT STEEPENED OFFSHORE SLOPE

NEW DUNE GROWTH

OVERWASH PASS

Ⓐ

Ⓑ

NARROW ERODING BEACH WITH GENTLE OFFSHORE SLOPE

Ⓐ SAND PUMPED FROM SOUND TO BEACH

Ⓑ SAND DREDGED FROM OFFSHORE AND PLACED ON OR NEAR BEACH

Fig. 17. Beach nourishment

38

3

Man and the Shoreline

SHORELINE ENGINEERING: STABILIZING THE UNSTABLE

Shoreline engineering is a general phrase that refers to any method of changing or altering the natural shoreline system in order to stabilize it. Methods of stabilizing shorelines range from the simple planting of dune grass to the complex emplacement of large seawalls using draglines, cranes, and bulldozers. The benefits of such methods are usually short-lived. Locally, shoreline engineering may actually *cause* shoreline retreat, as evidenced by the beach in front of the Carolina Beach seawall. Beach erosion caused by man may be greater and more spectacular than nature's own.

The ocean-side beaches of North Carolina have fewer engineering mistakes on them than do other states (New Jersey, for example), but this is largely because fewer projects have been carried out; our overall batting average is not too impressive. A few years ago the National Park Service announced that a total of $21 million had been spent to save Outer Banks beaches north and south of Hatteras, but the shoreline continues to retreat (Figure 5, page 11). The economic and environmental price of stabilizing the ocean-side beach is stiff indeed. Public awareness of the magnitude of this problem is essential. (There are, of course, situations in which stabilization is an economic necessity. Channels leading to our state ports at Morehead City and Wilmington, for example, must be maintained.)

There are three major ways by which shorelines are stabilized. These methods are listed below, in decreasing order of environmental safety.

Beach Replenishment

If you must repair a beach, this is probably the most gentle approach. Replenishment consists of pumping sand onto the beach and building up the former dunes and upper beach. Sufficient money is never available to replenish the entire beach out to a depth of 40 feet. Thus, only the upper beach is covered with new sand, so that in effect, a steep beach is created (Figure 17). This new steepened profile often increases the rate of erosion. In beach replenishment, sand is either pumped from the lagoon, a pit on the island, or the shelf, but most often from the lagoon. Lagoon sand, however, tends to be too fine; it quickly washes off the beach, as illustrated at Wrightsville Beach. Furthermore, dredging in the lagoon disturbs the ecosystem, and the hole created in the sound affects waves and currents, sometimes harming the back side of the island. In addition, mining the island leaves an unsightly hole of unusable land, as it did near Cape Hatteras in a 1973 replenishment project. Perhaps the best source of sand environmentally, but the most costly, is the continental shelf. However, Dr. Victor Goldsmith of the Virginia Institute of Marine Science warns that when a hole is dug on the shelf for replenishment sand, wave patterns on the adjacent shoreline will likely be affected. Off the Connecticut coast, wave patterns changed by a dredged hole on the shelf quickly caused the replenished beach to disappear.

In 1965 one of North Carolina's most publicized beach-replenishment projects was undertaken at Wrightsville Beach. Nearly 3 million cubic yards of sand were pumped onto 14 thousand feet of beach. Parts of the beach were replenished in 1966 and in 1970, but much of that sand was later lost. In the summer of 1976 the City was worried because the beach had become very steep. A bulldozer was used to flatten the beach slope by pushing sand from the artificial dune out onto the beach. By the summer of 1977 the beach was again very steep and a scarp had formed (Figure 18).

The real problem with beach replenishment, however, comes with cost and sand supply. The cost of the Wrightsville Beach project was over $1 million in 1966. The 1972-3 appropriation to the National Park Service for beach replenishment in the Cape Hatteras-Buxton area was $4.3 million.

Beach replenishment, then, upsets the natural system, is costly, and temporary, requiring subsequent replenishment projects in order to remain effective. The Corps of Engineers refers to beach replenishment as an "ongoing" project, but "eternal" project is

Fig. 18. Wrightsville Beach scarp

Photo by Jim Page

41

I. SHORELINE EROSION THREATENS POORLY PLACED COTTAGES:

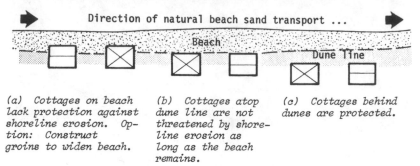

Direction of natural beach sand transport ...

Beach

Dune line

(a) Cottages on beach lack protection against shoreline erosion. Option: Construct groins to widen beach.

(b) Cottages atop dune line are not threatened by shoreline erosion as long as the beach remains.

(c) Cottages behind dunes are protected.

II. INITIAL GROIN CONSTRUCTION INTERRUPTS SAND FLOW:

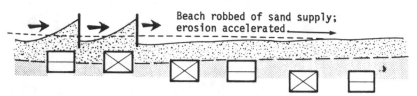

Beach robbed of sand supply; erosion accelerated

(a) Groins disrupt dynamics of beach system. Note portions of beach narrow as widening occurs behind groins.

(b) Beach nourishment cut off so that beach erosion is increased. Cottages now threatened. Option: Construct groins.

(c) Long-term sand supply is cut off, so these cottages will eventually face same conditions as (a) and (b).

III. ULTIMATE FATE OF GROINED SHORELINE:

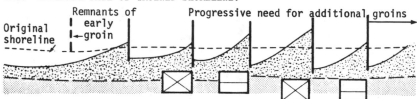

Original shoreline

Remnants of early groin

Progressive need for additional groins

(a) Beach narrow or absent. Dune line receding due to lack of sand nourishment. Cottages lost to erosion in spite of groins. Original groins damaged or destroyed.

(b) Cottages threatened as beach loss continues to move down drift. Dune line retreat creates situation like II-a.

(c) Heavily engineered shoreline. Beach and dune loss approaching II-b condition. Ultimate fate is the same as III-a.

Fig. 19. Evolution of a groined shoreline

Fig. 19. Evolution of a groined shoreline

perhaps a better term. Nevertheless, beach replenishment is usually less harmful to the total dynamic equilibrium than the following methods.

Groins and Jetties

Groins and jetties are walls built perpendicular to the shoreline. A jetty, often very long (sometimes miles), is intended to keep sand from flowing into a ship channel. Groins, much smaller walls built on straight stretches of beach away from channels and inlets, are intended to trap sand flowing in the longshore (surf-zone) current. There are groins present today on many North Carolina beaches, including Cape Hatteras, Cape Lookout, Bogue Banks, Kure Beach, Fort Fisher, and Yaupon Beach. Groins can be made of wood, stone, concrete, steel, or (increasingly in North Carolina) nylon bags filled with sand. Nylon-bag groins are also common in areas where beaches and property are threatened by inlet migration. The ends of Topsail Beach, Bogue Banks, and Long Beach are examples of such areas.

Both groins and jetties are very successful sand traps. If a groin is working correctly, more sand should be piled up on one side of it than on the other. The problem with the groin is that it traps sand that is probably flowing to a neighboring beach. Thus, if a groin on one beach is functioning well, it must be causing erosion elsewhere by "starving" another beach (Figure 19).

Miami Beach, Florida, illustrates the results of groin usage. After one was built, countless others had to be constructed—in self-defense. Prior to the 1977 beach-renourishment project, Miami Beach looked like an Army obstacle course; groins obstructed both pedestrian and vehicular traffic. Groins and other forms of shoreline engineering destroyed Miami Beach. Now, only through an eternal commitment to beach renourishment can the artificial beach be maintained.

Seawalls

Seawalls, built back from and parallel to the shoreline, are designed to receive at least once the full impact of the sea during a tidal cycle. Present in almost every highly developed coastal area, seawalls are fairly common along the North Carolina coast. A more

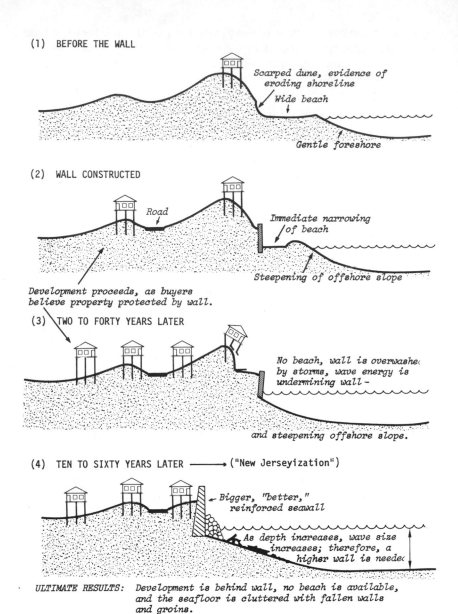

(1) BEFORE THE WALL

Scarped dune, evidence of eroding shoreline

Wide beach

Gentle foreshore

(2) WALL CONSTRUCTED

Road

Immediate narrowing of beach

Steepening of offshore slope

Development proceeds, as buyers believe property protected by wall.

(3) TWO TO FORTY YEARS LATER

No beach, wall is overwashed by storms, wave energy is undermining wall –

and steepening offshore slope.

(4) TEN TO SIXTY YEARS LATER ⟶ ("New Jerseyization")

Bigger, "better," reinforced seawall

As depth increases, wave size increases; therefore, a higher wall is needed

ULTIMATE RESULTS: Development is behind wall, no beach is available, and the seafloor is cluttered with fallen walls and groins.

Fig. 20. Saga of a seawall

44

common type of structure in North Carolina is the bulkhead, a type of seawall placed farther from the shoreline in front of the first dune—or what *was* the first dune—and designed to take the impact of storm waves only.

Building a seawall or bulkhead is a very drastic measure on the ocean-side beach, harming the environment in the following ways:

1. It reflects wave energy, ultimately removing the beach and steepening the offshore profile. (The length of time required for this damage to occur is one to thirty years.) The steepened offshore profile increases the storm-wave energy striking the shoreline; this in turn increases erosion.

2. It increases the intensity of longshore currents, hastening removal of the beach (Figure 20).

3. It prevents the exchange of sand between dunes and beach. Thus, the beach cannot supply new sand to the dunes on the island, nor flatten as it tends to do during storms.

4. It concentrates wave and current energy at the ends of the wall, increasing erosion at these points.

The emplacement of a seawall is an irreversible act with limited benefits. By gradually removing the beach in front of it, every seawall must eventually be replaced with a bigger ("better"), more expensive one. While a seawall may extend the lives of beach-front structures in normal weather, it cannot protect those on a low-lying barrier island from the havoc wrought by hurricanes; it cannot prevent overwash or storm-surge flooding.

The long-range effect of seawalls can be seen in New Jersey and Miami Beach. In Monmouth Beach, New Jersey, the town building inspector told of the town's seawall history. Pointing to a seawall he said, "There were once houses and even farms in front of that wall. First we built small seawalls and they were destroyed by the storms that seemed to get bigger and bigger. Now we have come to this huge wall which we hope will hold." The wall he spoke of, adjacent to the highway, was high enough to prevent even a glimpse of the sea beyond. There was no beach in front of it, but remnants of old seawalls, groins, and bulkheads for hundreds of yards at sea.

A PHILOSOPHY OF SHORELINE CONSERVATION: "WE HAVE MET THE ENEMY AND HE IS US"

In 1801, Postmaster Ellis Hughes of Cape May, New Jersey, placed the following advertisement in the Philadelphia *Aurora*:

> The subscriber has prepared himself for entertaining company who uses sea bathing and he is accommodated with extensive house room with fish, oysters, crabs, and good liquors. Care will be taken of gentlemen's horses. Carriages may be driven along the margin of the ocean for miles and the wheels will scarcely make an impression upon the sand. The slope of the shore is so regular that persons may wade a great distance. It is the most delightful spot that citizens can go in the hot season.

This was the first beach advertisement in America and sparked the beginning of the American rush to the shore.

In the next 75 years, six Presidents vacationed at Cape May. At the time of the Civil War it was certainly the country's most prestigious beach resort. The resort's prestige continued into the 20th century. In 1908, Henry Ford raced his newest model cars on Cape May beaches.

Today, Cape May is no longer found on anyone's list of great beach resorts. The problem is not that the resort is too old-fashioned, but that no beach remains on the cape (Figure 21).

The following excerpts are quoted from a grant application to the federal government from Cape May City. It was written by city officials in an attempt to get funds to build groins to "save the beaches." Though it is possible that its pessimistic tone was exaggerated to enhance the chances of receiving funds, its point was clear:

> Our community is nearly financially insolvent. The economic consequences for beach erosion are depriving all our people of much needed municipal services. . . . The residents of one area of town, Frog Hollow, live in constant fear. The Frog Hollow area is a 12 block segment of the town which becomes submerged when the tide is merely 1 to 2 feet above normal. The principal reason is that there is no beach fronting on this area. . . . Maps show that blocks have been lost, a boardwalk that has been lost. . . . The stone wall, one mile long, which we erected along the ocean front only five years ago has already begun to crumble from the pounding of the waves since there is little or no beach. . . . We have finally reached a point where we no longer have beaches to erode.

Fig. 21. Cape May, N. J., seawall (1976)

47

North Carolina will not have to wait a century and a half for this crisis to reach her shores. The pressure to develop is here and increasing. Like the original Cape May resort, our structures are not placed far back from the shore; nor have we been so prudent as to place structures behind dunes or on high ground. Consequently, North Carolina's coastal development is no less vulnerable to the rising sea than was Cape May's, and no shoreline engineering device will prevent its ultimate destruction. The solution lies in recognizing certain "truths" about the shoreline.

TRUTHS OF THE SHORELINE

Cape May is the country's oldest shoreline resort. Built on a shoreline that migrates much like North Carolina's, it is a classic example of the poorly developed American shoreline, and one from which North Carolina can learn.

From examples of Cape May and other shoreline areas, certain generalizations or "universal truths" about the shoreline emerge quite clearly. These truths are equally evident to scientists who have studied the shoreline and old-timers who have lived there all of their lives. As aids to safe and aesthetically pleasing shoreline development, they should be the fundamental basis of planning on any barrier island.

1. **There is no erosion problem until a structure is built on a shoreline.** Beach erosion is a common, expected event, not a natural disaster. Shoreline erosion in its natural state is not a threat to barrier islands. It is, in fact, an integral part of island evolution (see Chapter 2) and the dynamic system of the entire barrier island. When a beach retreats it does not mean that the island is disappearing; the island is migrating. Many developed islands are migrating at surprisingly rapid rates, though only the few investigators who pore over aerial photographs are aware of it. Whether the beach is growing or shrinking does not concern the visiting swimmer, surfer, hiker, or fisherman. It is when man builds a "permanent" structure in this zone of change that a problem develops.

2. **Construction by man on the shoreline causes shoreline changes.** The sandy beach exists in a delicate balance with sand supply, beach shape, wave energy, and sea-level rise. This is the dynamic equilibrium discussed in Chapter 2. Most construction on or near the shoreline changes this balance and reduces the natural flexibility of the beach (Figure 22). The result is change which often

Photo by Jim Page

Fig. 22. Carolina Beach, N. C. (1977)

threatens man-made structures. Dune-removal, which often precedes construction, reduces the sand supply used by the beach to adjust its profile during storms. Beach cottages—even those on stilts—may obstruct the normal sand exchange between the beach and the shelf during storms. Similarly, engineering devices interrupt or modify the natural cycle. (See Chapter 1 and Figures 13, 14, and 15, pages 28, 30, and 32).

3. **Shoreline engineering protects the interests of a very few, often at a very high cost in federal and state dollars.** Shoreline engineering is carried out to save beach property, not the beach itself. Beach-stabilization projects are in the interest of the minority of beach property owners rather than the public. If the shoreline were allowed to migrate naturally over and past the cottages and hot dog stands, the fisherman and swimmer would not suffer. Yet beach property owners apply pressure for the spending of tax money—public funds—to protect the beach. Since these property owners do not constitute the general public, their personal interests do not warrant the large expenditures of public money required for shoreline stabilization.

Exceptions to this rule are the beaches near large metropolitan areas. The combination of extensive highrise development and heavy beach use (100,000 or more people per day) affords ample economic justification for extensive and continuous shoreline-stabilization projects. The cost of replenishing Wrightsville Beach, for example, is equal to that of replenishing Coney Island, New York, which accommodates tens of thousands more people daily during the summer months. It is more justifiable to spend tax money to replenish the latter beach, since protection of this beach is virtually in the interest of the public that pays for it.

4. **Shoreline engineering destroys the beach it was intended to save.** If this sounds incredible to you, drive to New Jersey or Miami Beach and examine their shores. See the miles of "well protected" shoreline—without beaches! (Figure 23).

5. **The cost of saving beach property through shoreline engineering is usually greater than the value of the property to be saved.** Price estimates are often unrealistically low in the long run for a variety of reasons. Maintenance, repairs, and replacement costs are typically underestimated, because it is erroneously assumed that the big storm, capable of removing an entire beach-replenishment project overnight, will somehow bypass the area. The inevitable hurricane, moreover, is viewed as a catastrophic act of God or a sudden stroke of bad luck for which one cannot plan. The increased

50

Fig. 23. Miami Beachless (1972)

potential for damage resulting from shoreline engineering is also ignored in most cost evaluations. In fact, very few shoreline-engineering projects would be funded at all if those controlling the purse strings realized that such "lines of defense" must be perpetual.

6. **Once you begin shoreline engineering, you can't stop it!** This statement, made by a city manager of a Long Island Sound community, is confirmed by shoreline history throughout the world. Because of the long-range damage caused to the beach it "protects," this engineering must be maintained indefinitely. Its failure to allow the sandy shoreline to migrate naturally results in a steepening of the beach profile, reduced sand supply, and therefore, accelerated erosion. (See Chapter 2.) Thus, once man has installed a shoreline structure, "better"—larger and more expensive—structures must subsequently be installed, only to suffer the same fate as their predecessors (Figure 24).

History shows us that there are two situations that may terminate shoreline engineering. First, a civilization may fail and no longer build and repair its structures. This was the case with the Romans, who built mighty seawalls. Second, a large storm may destroy a shoreline-stabilization system so thoroughly that people decide to "throw in the towel." In America, however, such a storm is usually

51

Fig. 24. Monmouth Beach, N. J., seawall (1976)

regarded as an engineering challenge and thus results in continued shoreline-stabilization projects. As noted in Chapter 2, rubble from two or more generations of seawalls remains off some New Jersey beaches!

THE SOLUTIONS

1. Design to live with the flexible island environment. Don't fight nature with a "line of defense."

2. Consider all man-made structures near the shoreline *temporary.*

3. Accept as a last resort any engineering scheme for beach restoration or preservation, and then, only for metropolitan areas.

4. Base decisions affecting island development on the welfare of the public rather than the minority of shorefront property owners.

5. Let the lighthouse, beach cottage, motel, or hot dog stand fall when its time comes.

4

Selecting a Site on North Carolina's Barrier Islands

ISLAND SAFETY: A PAUSE TO CONSIDER

No locality on a barrier island is safe. Given the right conditions, hurricane, flood, wind and wave erosion, and inlet formation can attack any part of an island. Furthermore, human activity—particularly construction—almost always lessens the relative stability of the natural environment. Man-made structures are static (immobile); when placed in a dynamic (mobile) system, they disrupt the balance of that system. Interference with sand supply, disruption of vegetative cover, topographic alteration, and similar effects of man-made structures actually create conditions favorable to the damage or loss of those structures.

Though some areas on barrier islands are considerably safer for development than are others, all are vulnerable to the natural processes. This fact was recognized in the earliest days of settlement. Governor Dobbs expressed his awareness in a letter of July 1756: "Last summer . . . I found a violent storm of about 5 years ago had carried away Beacon Island, which was near 2 miles long, and all of the banks here in time may be lyable to the like fate. . . ."

Structures placed in the least dynamic zones (stable areas subject to less movement or change) are least likely to incur damage. If we can identify areas, rates, and intensities of natural physical activity, we have a basis for choosing a specific homesite. Consider, for example, an inland river and the floodplain (flat area) next to the river channel. Even casual observation reveals that the river floods. If observed for a long period of time, it may be noted that the time and size of the floods follow a pattern: While the area adjacent to the river is flooded every spring, the entire floodplain is flooded only every 5 to 10 years. Once or twice in a lifetime the flood is devastating, covering an area greater than the floodplain. Detailed stream studies confirm these observations. Thus we can determine and predict the frequency and size of floods in a given area, though we cannot predict *when* one will occur. We may describe an individual flood as a one-in-10-year flood, or a one-in-50-year flood, based on the frequency of a given flood level.

We of course would not want to build a house in a place that is flooded once every year, or even every 10 years; given the choice we might rather locate where the likelihood of flooding is once in 50 to 100 years. Whether to locate in a flood-prone area would be determined by how essential it is to be there and the level of economic loss we are willing to sustain.

TABLE II. Storm stillwater surge levels for one-in-twenty-five-, fifty-, and one-hundred-year storm frequencies.*

SURGE LEVEL(S) (+Ft. MSL)

	1/25	1/50	1/100
Virginia To Cape Hatteras	7.43	8.20	8.80
Cape Hatteras To Cape Lookout	7.10	7.63	8.00
Cape Lookout To New River Inlet	7.63	9.33	10.95
New River Inlet To Cape Fear	8.80	10.55	12.05
Cape Fear To South Carolina	9.67	11.23	12.45

Information adopted from Table 1, p. 9, Reference 36, Appendix C.

*Refers to the level to which the sea rises during a storm, but does not include the height of waves on the sea surface.

We can also predict the frequency and level of storm flooding in coastal areas (Table II; see also Reference 36, Appendix C), though not *when* a given storm will strike. Thus, if one expects a one-in-25-year storm-flood level of 8 to 9 feet for a particular stretch of coast, it would be sensible to build at an elevation of greater than 9 feet above mean sea-level.

The 100-year flood level is a standard used for both inland and coastal areas in determining areas eligible for the National Flood Insurance Program. Flooding in the coastal zone results from a storm-surge rise in sea level accompanied by large, potentially destructive waves. These conditions are generated by exceptionally violent winds during storms.

In addition to storm flood-levels, there are other natural indicators of site safety and stability.

STABILITY INDICATORS:
SOME CLUES FOR THE WISE

On barrier islands a number of environmental attributes indicate the natural history of a given area. In revealing how dynamic an area has been through time, these attributes aid prospective builders in deciding whether a site is safe for development. Natural indicators include vegetation, terrain, land elevation, shells, and soil type.

Vegetation may indicate environmental stability, age, and elevation. In general, the higher and thicker the vegetative growth, the more stable the site and the safer the area for development. Maritime forests grow only at elevations high enough to prevent frequent overwash. In addition, since a mature maritime forest (visible on Bogue Banks, portions of Topsail and Figure Eight Islands, Bald Head Island, and Oak Island) takes at least 100 years to develop, the homeowner can be further assured that forest areas are generally the safest homesites on any island. Bare, unvegetated areas indicate moving sand and hence are unsafe for development.

Terrain and **elevation** are also measures of an area's safety from various adverse natural processes. Low, flat areas are subject to destructive wave attack, overwash, storm-surge flooding, and blowing sand. The flooding of low areas is often from the sound side. (See Chapter 6.) Table II shows expected storm-surge levels for different parts of the North Carolina coast. Experience indicates that most areas under 7 feet in elevation experience relatively frequent, severe flooding. (There were five floods along the North Carolina coast in the 10-year period of the 1950s.) Even areas of 15-foot elevation incurred water damage from Hurricane Hazel in 1954, and during an 1856 hurricane, breakers are said to have struck areas of 30-foot elevation near Wrightsville Beach!

Seashells may also provide clues to the natural process that has historically occurred in a given area. A mixture of brown-stained and natural-colored shells often is washed onshore from the ocean side during storms. Shells of these colors, then, indicate overwash zones. Don't build where overwash occurs.

Mixed black and white shells without brown or natural-colored shells are almost a certain sign that material has been pumped or dredged from the sound. Such material is used to artificially fill low areas on the island or inlets that break through the island during storms, or to nourish an eroding beach. Thus, such a shell mixture may indicate an unstable area where development should be avoided.

Soil profile may give a clue to building-site stability. White-bleached sand overlying yellow sand to a depth of 2 to 3 feet suggests stability, because such a soil profile (often found in forest areas) requires a long period of time to develop. Note soil profile by looking in a road cut, finger canal, or a pit that you have dug. Keep in mind that even formerly stable, forested areas can be eroded by a migrating barrier island, so you may find a "stable" soil profile in an unstable position (as is found on eroding Caswell Beach). Avoid areas where profiles show layers of peat or other organic materials. Such layers have a high water-content and lack the strength to support an overlying structure. The weight of such a structure can compress the layers, causing the structure to sink.

ISLAND ENVIRONMENTS:
BOUNDARIES OF ACTIVITY

Individual islands may be divided into various zones or environments that indicate prevailing physical conditions. These environments include primary dunes, active dune fields, overwash fans, inlets, maritime forests, and marshes (Figure 7, page 18). By identifying and understanding these environments, one can determine the safety of particular island areas for development.

Primary dunes usually are defined as the row of dunes closest to the ocean, although a distinct line or row may be absent. Such dunes serve as a sand reservoir that feeds the beach and back island, and provide elevation as a temporary line of defense against wind and waves.

The primary dune is the natural, main line of defense against erosion and storm damage to man-made structures. This line of defense is "leaky" because of the overwash passes between the dunes. When man interferes with the dune system, both natural and man-made systems suffer. We must recognize the mobility of dune systems—even those stabilized by vegetation such as sea oats or other dune grasses. Dune buggies, foot traffic, drought, and fire destroy vegetation, and therefore, dune stability. By prohibiting vehicles on the dunes, and by building boardwalks and footbridges over them rather than building footpaths through them, we may preserve the dunes. Avoiding the construction of seawalls, groins, and bulkheads also preserves dunes by assuring that the sand flow that feeds them is not interrupted.

If dunes are destroyed or threatened, there are some remedial steps that can be taken to artificially stabilize them. Planting dune grass or sea oats in bare areas serves to stabilize existing dunes and encourages additional dune growth. (See References 44 through 47, Appendix C.) Snow fencing is commonly used to trap sand and to increase dune growth.

The high elevation of a dune does not in itself render a site safe. An area with a high erosion rate is likely to lose its dune protection during the average lifetime of a cottage. Even setback ordinances—which require that structures be placed a minimum distance behind the dune—do not guarantee long-term protection. Furthermore, if you locate on a primary dune you should expect to lose your home during the next major storm. Stilt-house construction is necessary since ground-level floors can suffer flooding, sand accumulation, or destruction in storms.

Dune fields are open, bare-to-grassy sand-dune areas found between the primary dunes and the maritime forest (if present) or sound side of the island. Some of these dunes are active, with the sand and dune positions continually shifting; other dune fields are stable and do not move much at all.

Stable dune fields offer sites that are relatively safe from the hazards of wave erosion, overwash,and storm-surge flooding—if the elevation is sufficiently high. However, digging up the dunes for construction may cause blowing sand, the destabilization of vegetation, and increasing sand movement. (In the past such destabilization was caused by overgrazing.)

Do not build where dunes show bare, unvegetated surfaces; such dunes are active. Not far from Corolla on Currituck Bank, lots on top of 40- to 50-feet-high active dunes have been offered for sale. Houses built there truly become "mobile homes"! In the pre-bulldozer days, houses were either moved or abandoned when

Photo by Jim Page

Fig. 25. Sand migration, Sunset Beach, N.C. (1977)

threatened by dunes. (This occurred on Currituck Bank and Bogue Banks.) On the northern Outer Banks, some houses that were buried during the early part of this century are now reappearing as the sand shifts. In some of the Dare County developments, and in Sunset Beach at the opposite end of the North Carolina coast, sand from active dunes drifts onto, and sometimes covers, roads (Figure 25). When this occurs it is usually best to return it to the area from which it came rather than haul it away as is often done.

Overwash fans develop when water, thrown up by waves and storm surge, flows between and around dunes. Such waters carry sand that is deposited in flat, fan-shaped masses (Figure 7, page 18, and Figure 11, page 24). (They also transport brown, white, and natural-colored shells to the inner island.) These fans provide sand to form and maintain dunes and build up the island's elevation. Where primary dunes are high and continuous, overwash is relatively unimportant and restricted to the beach and near-shore area. (This is illustrated on Bogue Banks, most of Topsail Island, portions of Onslow Beach, and other islands.) Where dunes are absent, low, or discontinuous, overwash fans may extend across the entire island (as they do on Masonboro Island, No Name Island, parts of Lea Island and Figure Eight Island, and most of Core Banks). During severe hurricanes, only the highest elevations (generally above 15 feet) are safe from overwash.

Overwash may damage or bury man-made structures. Roads may be buried (Figure 26) and escape routes blocked. Level roads cut straight to the beach often become overwash passes during storms, especially where roads cut through dunes rather than over them. (See field trip guides, Appendix D, for examples.) Thus the roads built to increase development contribute to its destruction.

Try to avoid building on overwash fans, especially if fresh and unvegetated. Such areas may be difficult to recognize, however, if fans have been destroyed by bulldozing or sand-removal. If no alternative site is available, build on stilts, allow overwash to continue, and build up sand. Use overwash deposits removed from roads and driveways to rebuild adjacent dunes; do not remove the sand from the area.

Inlets, the channels that separate islands, usually form during hurricanes or severe storms (Figure 12, page 26). As a hurricane approaches a barrier island, strong onshore winds drive storm-surge waters and waves against the island and up the estuaries. As the storm passes, the wind either stops blowing or shifts to blow seaward, causing sound waters to return seaward. If existing inlets do not allow the water to escape fast enough, a new inlet is cut from the sound side. Two of North Carolina's more famous inlets, Hatteras and Oregon, are said to have formed in this manner during a September 1846 storm.

Low, narrow island areas lacking extensive salt marsh and opposite river or estuary mouths are likely spots for inlet development. They should therefore be avoided as building sites.

Once formed, an inlet tends to migrate laterally along the barrier island. (See References 38 and 39, Appendix C, for directions and rates of North Carolina inlet migration.) Structures and property in the path of the inlet's migration are destroyed. Sediment carried through the inlet builds an underwater tidal delta in the sound. In time the delta may fill the inlet, closing it naturally. (Today most inlets are dredged to keep the channel open for navigation, so that the natural "healing" process is rare.)

You may recall our saying in Chapter 2 that tidal-delta formation is an important means of island widening. Because of the tidal delta in back of old inlets, the sites of old inlets may be relatively safe areas on which to build. The width promotes dune and vegetation growth, and there is ample room to build far back from the beach. Also, the likelihood of a new inlet forming at the site of an old, naturally closed one is very low. Dr. William J. Cleary of the University of North Carolina at Wilmington has demonstrated that at least 40 percent of the coast between Cape Fear and Cape Lookout consists of old, natural, inlet fills; thus the areas of potential inlet formation are limited.

Artificially filled inlets are unstable areas for development. In 1963 the old inlet between Wrightsville Beach and Shell Island was artificially filled in. Sand was then pumped up from the sound to raise the elevation of Wrightsville Beach prior to construction on the site of the old inlet. The problem was that this sand was taken from the tidal delta. By robbing the island of its natural mechanism to increase its width, man reduced the number of safe areas on which to build. At present, the Wrightsville Beach Holiday Inn rests on the site of the old inlet. The probability of storm damage at this narrow, low point on Wrightsville Beach is high. There is also a strong potential for inlet formation in a major storm; thus some geologists have nicknamed the hotel the "Holiday Inlet."

Maritime forest, thicket and shrub areas are generally the safest places for cottage construction. Under normal conditions, overwash, flooding, and blowing sand are not problems in these environments. The plants stabilize the underlying sediment and offer a

60

Fig. 26. 1973 breaching of Highway 12, route of present
Avon water supply pipeline, Hatteras Island

Source: National Park Service

61

protective screen.

If building in a vegetated area, preserve as much vegetation as possible, including undergrowth. Trees are excellent protection from flying debris during hurricanes. Remove large, dead trees from the construction site, but conserve the surrounding forest to protect your home. Stabilize bare construction-areas as soon as possible with new plantings.

The presence of an active dune field on the margin of a forest may threaten the stability of forest sites. Examples of forests buried by dunes can be seen at the old town of Rice Path on Bogue Banks and on the west end of Shackleford Banks.

Marshes are prolific breeding areas for many fish. Their extensive shallows provide considerable protection against wave erosion of the back side of the island. In the past, however, marshes have been filled to expand land areas on which to build. (Examples are the large back-island area of Bogue Banks at the Atlantic Beach bridge; the finger-canal area near the Onslow-Pender County line on Topsail Island; and the finger-canal areas on Figure Eight Island, Holden Beach and Ocean Isle Beach.) Nature usually takes revenge on those who occupy this land. Buried marsh provides poor support for cottage foundations and destroys the groundwater reservoir. Thus, such building sites typically have an inadequate supply of fresh water and septic systems that do not function properly. In addition, effluent waste from such sites has closed adjacent marshes to shellfishing.

Marshes should not be dredged or filled. (It is also illegal to do so without a permit.) New marsh may indicate overwash being carried into the sound to provide shallows for marsh growth—another clue to active overwash areas. Where sound shorelines are eroding it is possible to create new marshes to stabilize the shoreline. This is being done in experimental work directed by Dr. W. W. Woodhouse, Jr., of North Carolina State University. This method is highly preferable to bulkheading; it not only protects the shoreline, but also allows for the formation of a new habitat for marine plants and animals.

WATER PROBLEMS: AN INVISIBLE CRISIS

One of the more significant hazards to barrier-island living is contaminated water. Although it has not yet caused an epidemic, its potential to do so threatens much of the developed coast, from small villages such as Avon, to wider developments such as Long Beach. Basically the problem revolves around three factors: water supply, waste disposal, and any form of island alteration that affects these two factors. While finger canals are used to illustrate island alteration, keep in mind that dredge-and-fill operations (for example, inlet cutting, the channeling of islands, and the piling of dredge spoil) and other construction activities of man may also alter the groundwater system.

Water Supply: Just as the quality and availability of water determine the plant and animal makeup of an island's ecosystem, they also determine, in part, the island's capacity to accommodate man. Water quality is measured by potability, freshness, clarity, odor, and the presence or absence of pathogens (disease-causing bacteria). Availability implies the presence of an adequate supply.

The only fresh water directly available to a barrier island is that of rainfall over the island. This water seeps through the porous and permeable sands and builds up as a lens or wedge of fresh water. This lens overlies salt water, which seeps into the sediments from the adjacent ocean or sound. The higher the island's elevation above sea level, and the greater the accumulation of fresh water, the greater the thickness of the freshwater lens. The top of the freshwater lens is known as the groundwater table, and on most islands it is this shallow reservoir that supplies domestic fresh water.

If too many wells are dug into the groundwater table, the table drops. Early occupants of a development should not be surprised if their shallow wells "dry up" as the development grows. If wells are overpumped and the groundwater table goes down, saltwater intrusion may occur. Seeking alternative sources of water such as deep aquifiers, or building alternative sources such as municipal water systems (deep wells, pipe lines, filtration plants), is expensive.

Consult the proper authorities about water quantity and quality before you buy (Appendix B, Water Resources)!

Waste Disposal: Wastewater disposal goes hand in glove with water supply. On the majority of North Carolina barrier islands the home septic-system is the primary means of wastewater disposal. This system consists of a holding tank in which solids settle and sewage is biologically broken down, and a drain field that allows water to percolate into the soil. The soil then filters and purifies the water. Unfortunately, the same natural system that is used to cleanse the water is also used to supply high-quality water to residences.

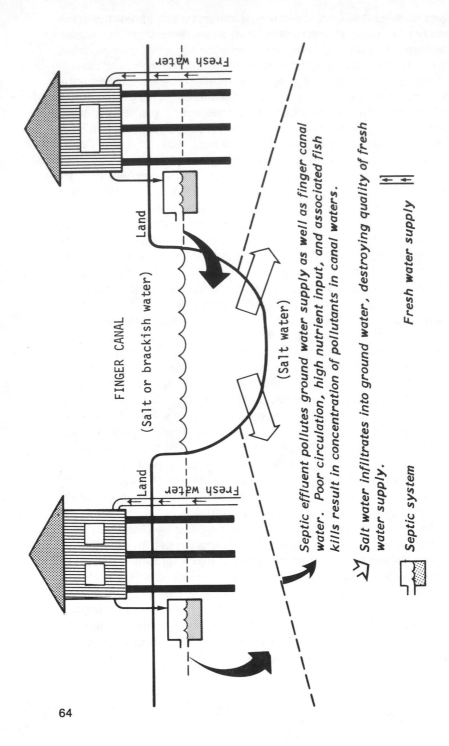

FINGER CANAL

(Salt or brackish water)

Land

Fresh water

Fresh water

Land

Septic effluent pollutes ground water supply as well as finger canal water. Poor circulation, high nutrient input, and associated fish kills result in concentration of pollutants in canal waters.

Salt water infiltrates into ground water, destroying quality of fresh water supply.

(Salt water)

Fresh water supply

Septic system

Fig. 27. Finger-canal problems

Many communities are unaware of the potential water problems they face. Crowded development, improperly maintained systems, and systems installed in soils unsuitable for filtration have resulted in poorly treated or untreated sewage entering the surrounding environment. Polluted water may flood from septic tanks into domestic wells, spreading hepatitis and other diseases. It may also enter sounds and marshes, contaminating shellfish. Septic tanks have been blamed for the pollution and subsequent closing of over 400,000 acres of North Carolina's shellfishing areas.

Municipal waste-treatment plants may be one answer for larger communities, although such plants may become overloaded or inefficient. (A class-action law suit was brought against the city of Wrightsville Beach for dumping excess raw sewage into the sound.) Stricter enforcement of existing codes and policing of existing systems, and proper site-evaluation before issuance of permits should be required by civil officials. In addition, homeowners should learn the mechanics of septic systems in order to prevent malfunctioning or to spot it early. (See Septic System Information and Permits, Appendix B; Reference 51, Appendix C.)

Finger Canals: A common man-made island alteration that causes water problems is the finger canal (Figures 27 and 28). "Finger canal" is the term applied to the ditches or channels dug from the lagoon or sound side of an island into the island proper for the purpose of providing everyone with a waterfront lot. Canals can be made by excavation alone, or by a combination of excavation and infill of adjacent low-lying areas (usually marshes). Finger canals can be found on Bogue Banks, Topsail Island, Holden Beach, Ocean Isle Beach, and Sunset Beach.

The major problems associated with finger canals are the (1) lowering of the groundwater table; (2) pollution of groundwater by seepage of salt or brackish canal water into the groundwater table; (3) pollution of canal water by septic seepage into the canal; (4) pollution of canal water by stagnation due to lack of tidal flushing or poor circulation with sound waters; (5) fish kills generated by higher canal-water temperatures; and (6) fish kills generated by nutrient overloading and deoxygenation of water.

Bad odors, flotsam of dead fish and algal scum, and contamination of adjacent shellfishing grounds are symptomatic of polluted canal water. Thus, finger canals often become health hazards or simply places near which it is too unpleasant to live. Residents along some older Florida finger canals have built walls to separate their cottages from the canal!

65

Fig. 28. Finger canal, Sunset Beach

Photo by Jim Page

Should you consider buying a lot on a canal, remember: canals are not harmful until houses are built along them. Short canals, a few tens of meters long, are generally much safer than long ones. Also, while most canals are initially deep enough for small-craft traffic, sufficient sand movement on the back sides of barrier islands can result in the filling of the canals and subsequent navigation problems. Finally, on narrow islands such as Topsail, finger canals dug almost to the ocean side offer a path of least resistance to storm waters and are therefore potential locations for new inlets.

SITE SAFETY: RULES FOR SURVIVAL

In order to determine site safety on a barrier island it is necessary to evaluate all prevalent dynamic processes on the island. Information on storm surge, overwash, erosion rates, inlet migration, longshore drift, and other processes may be obtained from maps, aerial photographs, scientific literature, or personal observations. Appendix C provides an annotated list of scientific sources; you are encouraged to obtain those of interest to you. Although developers and planners usually have the resources and expertise to utilize such information in making decisions, they sometimes ignore it. In the past the individual buyer was not likely to seek needed information in deciding on the suitability of a given site. Today's buyer should be better informed.

To help the island dweller, we have drawn a series of diagramatic maps (Figures 29 through 42) which summarize information obtained from a cross-section of scientific literature. Our conclusions, as represented on the maps, are based on published data, aerial photographs, and maps, as well as our personal communications and observations. These maps present zones classified as safe, cautionary, or unsafe for development on the basis of the summarized information. Keep in mind, however, that small maps of large areas must be generalized and that every site must still be evaluated individually. Safe sites may exist in "danger" zones, while dangerous sites may exist in "safe" zones.

Following is a list of the properties that are essential to site safety.

Summary Checklist for Site-Safety Evaluation

1. Site elevation is above anticipated storm-surge level (Table II, page 54).

67

2. Site is behind a natural protective barrier such as a line of sand dunes.
3. Site is well away from a migrating inlet.
4. Site is in an area of shoreline growth (accretion) or low shoreline erosion. Evidence of an eroding shoreline includes: a. sand bluff or dune scarp at back of beach, b. stumps or peat exposed on beach, c. slumped features such as trees, dunes, or man-made structures, d. protective devices such as seawalls, groins, or pumped sand.
5. Site is located on a portion of the island backed by salt marsh.
6. Site is away from low, narrow portions of the island.
7. Site is in an area of no or low historic overwash.
8. Site is in a vegetated area that suggests stability.
9. Site drains water readily.
10. Fresh groundwater supply Is adequate and uncontaminated. (There is proper spacing between water wells and septic systems.)
11. Soil and elevation are suitable for efficient septic-tank operation.
12. No compactable layers such as peat are present in soil below footings. (Site is not on a buried salt marsh.)
13. Adjacent structures are adequately spaced and of sound construction.

Escape Routes

Because of the threat of hurricanes, there must exist a route that will permit escape from an island to a safe location inland within a reasonable length of time. The presence of a ready escape route near a building site is essential to site safety, especially in highrise areas where the number of people to be evacuated, transported, and housed elsewhere is greatly increased.

Select an escape route ahead of time. Check to see if any part of it is at a low elevation, subject to blockage by overwash or flooding; if so, seek an alternate route. The exit from Figure Eight Island is an example of a flood-prone route. Note whether there are bridges along the route. Remember that some residents will be evacuating pleasure boats, and that fishing boats will be seeking safer waters; thus, drawbridges will be accommodating both boats and automobiles.

Re-evaluate the escape route you have chosen periodically— especially if the area in which you live has grown. With more people using the route, it may not be as satisfactory as you once thought it was.

Use the escape route early. Be aware that many North Carolina islands have only one route for escape to the mainland. In the event of a hurricane warning, leave the island immediately; do not wait until the route is blocked or flooded. Anyone who has experienced the evacuation of a community knows of the chaos at such bottlenecks. Depend on it: excited drivers will cause wrecks, run out of gas, have flat tires, and cars of frightened occupants will be lined up for miles behind them. Be sure to have plans made as to where you will go. Keep alternative destinations in mind in case you find the original refuge filled or in danger. Otherwise you should start muttering the salute given to Caesar by the Roman gladiators as they entered the arena: *Morituri te salutant,* which, if you have forgotten your high school Latin, means, "We who are about to die salute you."

Hurricane Carmen, which hit the Gulf Coast in September 1974, illustrated the desirability of leaving early to miss the traffic jam. Over 75,000 people are said to have evacuated from what were thought to be the danger areas in Louisiana and Mississippi. The traffic was bumper-to-bumper on the few roads leading north. One accident backed up traffic for 19 miles. Motel lobbies were filled with people looking for a place to stay; all rooms were taken. Weary people were forced to continue traveling north until they found available space. Similar experiences should be anticipated for North Carolina, for island populations have grown considerably since the last major hurricane.

INDIVIDUAL ISLAND ANALYSIS:
"Safe," "Caution," and "Danger" Zones

NORTHERN OUTER BANKS

The Northern barrier islands extend from the Virginia-North Carolina state line southward for about 125 miles to Ocracoke Inlet (Figure 1, pages 2, 3). These Outer Banks occur within Currituck, Dare, and Hyde counties with approximately half of the total coastal property owned privately; the remainder lies largely within the jurisdiction of Cape Hatteras National Seashore and Pea Island National Wildlife Refuge.

North Carolina's barrier islands are both a product of and a response to a multitude of geological and biological processes operating within the coastal zone. Our subdivision of the barrier islands into three major land-use categories—safe, caution, and danger—is based upon three important and essential concepts. First, barriers are a total product of their past geologic history with all parts of their present topography, drainage, soils, dune fields, vegetation, etc., being a consequence of that history. Second, barrier islands are a complex of interacting systems which include the associated inlets, the estuaries behind the barrier, and the nearshore ocean floor in front of the barrier. Third, barriers are extremely dynamic units; here the natural processes and resulting changes operate rapidly in direct response to high energy storms within the coastal zone. To successfully live and work within the framework of this highly dynamic but balanced natural system means that these complex interactions must be recognized and accepted.

Specific factors considered in the category assigned each coastal segment include:

1. average rates of shoreline erosion and build-up, based on data derived from Dr. Robert Dolan, University of Virginia; the N. C. Coastal Resources Commission; and the Cape Hatteras National Seashore;
2. slope and width of the beach and character of the nearshore continental shelf;
3. character of the first (frontal) dune row;
4. degree and extent of overwash;
5. width and height of barrier island;
6. size and extent of dunes on the back side;
7. nature and extent of vegetative cover;
8. size and shape of back barrier estuary;
9. extent of marsh development on back side of island;
10. estuarine (backside) shoreline erosion rates;
11. inlet history and potential for development of new inlets.

Careful study of the maps shows that there is no place on the barrier islands which is totally hazard-free; however, there are definitely some areas (about 28%) which are relatively "safe," with fewer and less severe hazards than other sections. Most of the areas designated as "safe," interestingly enough, are also the locations of the older "native" communities on the barriers! These areas are generally very high, on the wide portions of the barrier, with a fairly heavy vegetative cover of maritime forests. On the other hand, much of the more recent development and that currently taking place occurs in areas of highest hazards. Why? Because most of the "safe" areas have already been developed; areas with serious natural hazards are the last available.

TABLE III. Shoreline "safety" classification for sections of privately-owned Northern Outer Banks

	"Safe"	"Caution"	"Danger"	Totals
Currituck County				
miles	7.9	5.9	10.1	23.9
percent	33	25	42	100%
Dare County				
Currituck County line to Oregon Inlet				
miles	4.2	11.1	17.8	33.0
percent	13	33	54	100%
Rodanthe to Salvo				
miles	1.7	1.2	3.6	6.5
percent	26	19	55	100%
Avon to Cape Point				
miles	2.7	2.4	6.7	11.8
percent	23	20	57	100%
Cape Point to Hatteras				
miles	6.6	2.8	2.8	12.2
percent	54	23	23	100%
Hyde County				
Ocracoke Town area*				
miles	2.2			2.2
percent	100			100%
TOTAL				
miles	25.3	23.4	40.9	89.6
percent	28	26	46	100%

*The town of Ocracoke is located on the back side of the barrier island.

CURRITUCK COUNTY

(Figures 29-30, Segments 1-10)

Although the northernmost portion of North Carolina's Outer Banks lies very near the major population center of southeastern Virginia (Norfolk-Newport News), Currituck Bank has remained largely undeveloped until recently. Considering the map of its coastline today, it is surprising that this 23-mile stretch of beach, with mainland access from two states, could remain so sparsely developed for so long. The reasons were initially related to the presence of abundant historic inlets within this section of the coast and more recently to federal land control in the Virginia coastal area— plus continued inaccessability by road.

Throughout the early history of North Carolina, Currituck Sound was a salt water body, continuously connected to the ocean by a series of inlets. The five historic inlets have occurred alternately but continuously from the days of first discovery through the closure of the last inlet between 1811 and 1828. Old Currituck Inlet on the North Carolina-Virginia border (Segment 1) provided access for trading vessels (especially New Englanders hoping to escape duty payment) until 1729-31 when it closed. Meanwhile, New Currituck Inlet was opened several miles to the south (Segment 4) during a 1713 storm, but closed sometime between 1828 and 1830. The remnants of Musketo Inlet, which closed between 1672 and 1682, can be seen behind the town of Corolla (Segments 5 and 6). Further south are the extensive marsh remnants of Trinity Harbor Inlet which closed sometime in the mid-1600s (Segments 9 and 10). The last inlet into Currituck Sound was Caffey's Inlet (Segment 10) which opened between 1790 and 1798 at the Dare-Currituck County line.

When Caffey's Inlet closed, sometime between 1811 and 1829, Currituck Sound began to freshen. Today it is a freshwater sound and represents an important hunting and fishing resource. If a new inlet were to form, this resource would be modified once again.

The existence of the numerous historic inlets have produced exceptionally wide portions of the barrier. Sand lobes of the inlets' flood tide deltas, which extended well into Currituck Sound, reverted to extensive back barrier marshes upon closure of the inlet. The oldest inlet deltas have been largely lost due to estuarine shoreline erosion and slow submergence over the centuries. Scattered maritime forests have developed with time in front of these old flood tide deltas.

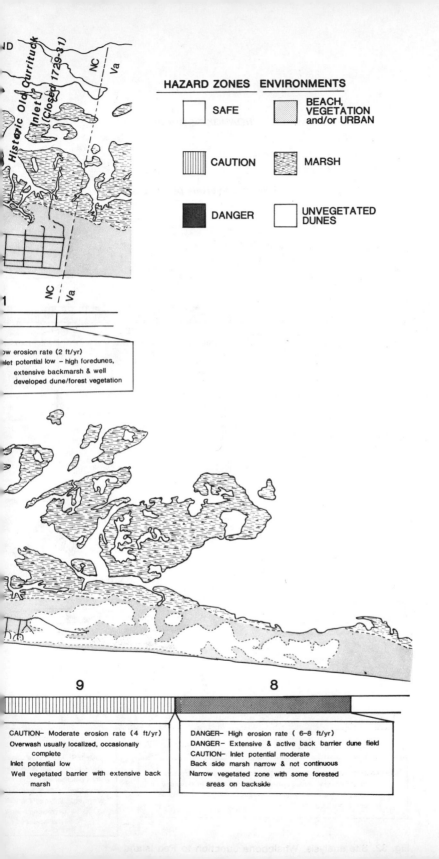

HAZARD ZONES

☐	SAFE
⊞	CAUTION
■	DANGER

ENVIRONMENTS

▦	BEACH, VEGETATION and/or URBAN
▤	MARSH
☐	UNVEGETATED DUNES

Historic Old Currituck Inlet (Closed 1729-31)

NC / Va

NC / Va

1

ᴐw erosion rate (2 ft/yr)
ᴎlet potential low – high foredunes,
   extensive backmarsh & well
   developed dune/forest vegetation

9

8

CAUTION– Moderate erosion rate (4 ft/yr)
Overwash usually localized, occasionally
     complete
Inlet potential low
Well vegetated barrier with extensive back
     marsh

DANGER– High erosion rate (6–8 ft/yr)
DANGER– Extensive & active back barrier dune field
CAUTION– Inlet potential moderate
Back side marsh narrow & not continuous
Narrow vegetated zone with some forested
     areas on backside

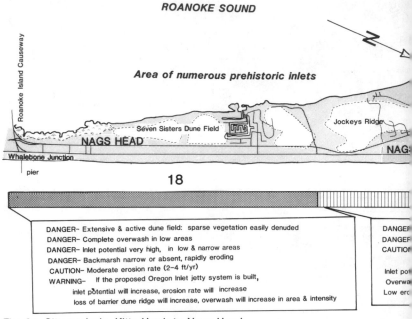

ROANOKE SOUND

Roanoke Island Causeway

Area of numerous prehistoric inlets

Jockeys Ridge

Séven Sisters Dune Field

NAGS HEAD

NAG:

Whalebone Junction

pier

18

DANGER- Extensive & active dune field: sparse vegetation easily denuded
DANGER- Complete overwash in low areas
DANGER- Inlet potential very high, in low & narrow areas
DANGER- Backmarsh narrow or absent, rapidly eroding
CAUTION- Moderate erosion rate (2–4 ft/yr)
WARNING-   If the proposed Oregon Inlet jetty system is built,
                 inlet potential will increase, erosion rate will increase
                 loss of barrier dune ridge will increase, overwash will increase in area & intensity

DANGER
DANGER
CAUTION

Inlet pot
Overwa
Low erc

Fig. 31. Site analysis, Kitty Hawk to Nags Head

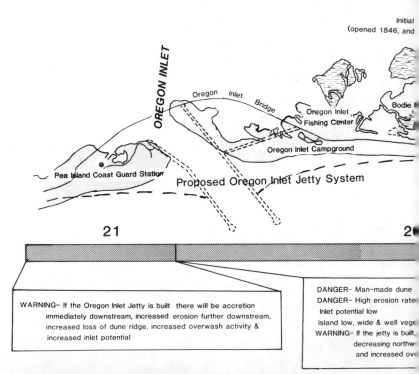

Initial
(opened 1846, and

OREGON INLET

Oregon   Inlet   Bridge

Oregon Inlet
Fishing Center

Bodie

Oregon Inlet Campground

Pea Island Coast Guard Station

Proposed Oregon Inlet Jetty System

21

2

WARNING- If the Oregon Inlet Jetty is built there will be accretion
              immediately downstream, increased erosion further downstream,
              increased loss of dune ridge, increased overwash activity &
              increased inlet potential

DANGER- Man-made dune
DANGER- High erosion rate
Inlet potential low
Island low, wide & well vege
WARNING- If the jetty is built,
            decreasing northw
            and increased ove

Fig. 32. Site analysis, Whalebone Junction to Pea Island

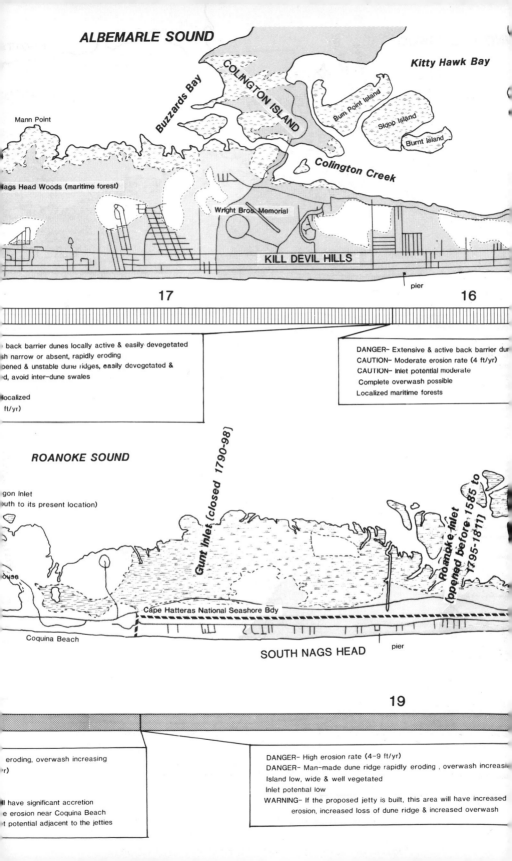

ALBEMARLE SOUND

Kitty Hawk Bay

Buzzards Bay

COLINGTON ISLAND

Burn Point Island

Sloop Island

Mann Point

Burnt Island

Colington Creek

lags Head Woods (maritime forest)

Wright Bros. Memorial

KILL DEVIL HILLS

pier

17   16

back barrier dunes locally active & easily devegetated
sh narrow or absent, rapidly eroding
pened & unstable dune ridges, easily devegetated &
d, avoid inter-dune swales

localized
ft/yr)

DANGER- Extensive & active back barrier dur
CAUTION- Moderate erosion rate (4 ft/yr)
CAUTION- Inlet potential moderate
Complete overwash possible
Localized maritime forests

ROANOKE SOUND

gon Inlet
uth to its present location)

Gunt Inlet (closed 1790-98)

Roanoke Inlet (opened before 1585 to 1795-1811)

ouse

Cape Hatteras National Seashore Bdy

Coquina Beach

SOUTH NAGS HEAD   pier

19

eroding, overwash increasing
r)

l have significant accretion
e erosion near Coquina Beach
t potential adjacent to the jetties

DANGER- High erosion rate (4-9 ft/yr)
DANGER- Man-made dune ridge rapidly eroding , overwash increasi
Island low, wide & well vegetated
Inlet potential low
WARNING- If the proposed jetty is built, this area will have increased
         erosion, increased loss of dune ridge & increased overwash

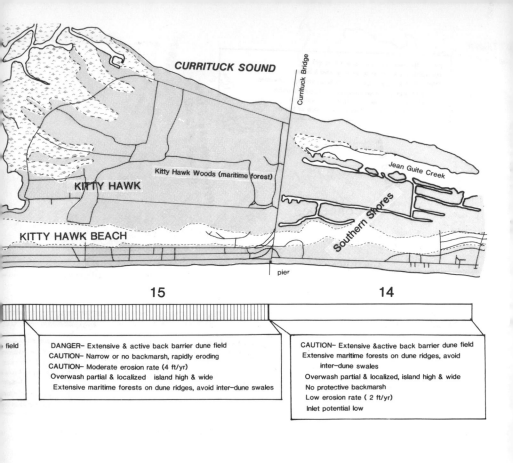

CURRITUCK SOUND

Currituck Bridge

Kitty Hawk Woods (maritime forest)

KITTY HAWK

KITTY HAWK BEACH

Jean Guite Creek

Southern Shores

pier

15

14

field

DANGER– Extensive & active back barrier dune field
CAUTION– Narrow or no backmarsh, rapidly eroding
CAUTION– Moderate erosion rate (4 ft/yr)
Overwash partial & localized   island high & wide
Extensive maritime forests on dune ridges, avoid inter–dune swales

CAUTION– Extensive &active back barrier dune field
Extensive maritime forests on dune ridges, avoid
inter–dune swales
Overwash partial & localized, island high & wide
No protective backmarsh
Low erosion rate (2 ft/yr)
Inlet potential low

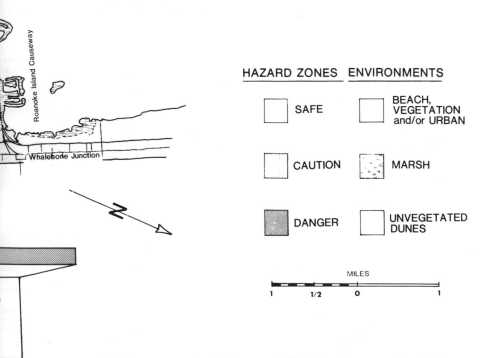

Roanoke Island Causeway

Whalebone Junction

N

HAZARD ZONES   ENVIRONMENTS

SAFE

CAUTION

DANGER

BEACH,
VEGETATION
and/or URBAN

MARSH

UNVEGETATED
DUNES

MILES

1   1/2   0   1

The Currituck Bank is characterized throughout much of its length by an extensive back barrier dune field. This field consists of numerous major dunes (Penny, Lewark, Jones, and Whalehead Hills) with broad and extensive intervening sand sheets. Some of these dune and sand sheets are stabilized with vegetation, but most contain either poor or no vegetative cover. They are, therefore, extremely mobile, with some dunes migrating up to fifty feet per year, burying roads, forests and homes if they were built near these dynamic sand sheets. The more stable vegetated dunes are readily devegetated, becoming mobile in response to both natural and man-induced processes. Major storms and overwash, along with droughts and fires, can devegetate the dune fields. Many people believe that overgrazing by livestock in the early days of the Currituck was largely responsible for dune destabilization. Today, the biggest threat is from development and offroad vehicles (ORVs).

Currituck Bank has an average ocean shoreline recession rate of 5.6 feet per year. It ranges from two feet per year at the North Carolina-Virginia state line, increasing to a maximum of eight feet per year just north of Corolla, and decreasing southward to two feet per year at the Currituck-Dare County line. The rapid rate of shoreline erosion is blatantly obvious along Segments 4 and 5 where abundant tree stumps occur on the beach and in the surf zone; trees cannot grow on a high energy ocean beach!

The U. S. Fish and Wildlife Service manages the Back Bay National Wildlife Refuge within the Virginia coastal system north of Currituck. This major wildlife refuge has historically allowed only limited access across its property from the north by four-wheel-drive vehicles. Southern access north of Duck has also been, until recently, only by four-wheel drive over sand tracks. Massive development plans of the private lands on the Currituck Bank began in the late 1960s and early 1970s. The pressure to develop roads and services on Currituck Bank led to the "Currituck Plan" of 1972, a comprehensive plan to control development of the area (Reference 55, Appendix C). Developers stepped up their activities (subdividing, dune removal, road and canal construction, etc.) to avoid coming under a set of rules that could cut into their profits. More than 6000 lots were platted by large developers, and pressure mounted for improved access from both the north and the south as many of them were put up for sale. Talk of 10,000 or more beach homes on the narrow barrier became common. Subsequently, paved roads have been extended and serious consideration of a North Carolina public highway into the area from the south, as well as bridge and ferry access, has been reactivated.

75

The resulting development explosion forced the U. S. Fish and Wildlife Service finally to terminate access across the refuge from the north at the end of 1979 and to propose the purchase of large portions of the Bank for a new wildlife refuge. The proposal to preserve and protect a large portion of this barrier system is justified by the Department of Interior on two grounds. First, the beach, dunes, and marshlands of this portion of the Outer Banks provide wintering habitat for about 35% of the Atlantic Flyway waterfowl and either year-round or migratory habitat for several endangered and threatened species. Second, the inevitable impact of ongoing and proposed development, including homes and public highways through the area, would result in the modification and destruction of extensive dune fields, maritime forests, and marshlands; cause pollution of the ground water and estuarine water systems; and have an adverse impact upon the waterfowl, the endangered species habitat, and the sport and commercial hunting and fishing industries.

Consideration of the land-use classifications for Currituck Bank (Figures 29, 30; Table III) suggests that two-thirds of the 23 miles is designated "danger" or "caution." At the time of this writing, the following situations had been observed:

1. Minimal-sized ocean front lots, backed by paved roads which would be overwashed and under water during a storm tide, were fronted by a rapidly eroding shoreline with no or minor foredunes. Present setback policies of the North Carolina Coastal Resources Commission would not allow a structure to be built on many of these lots.

2. Many lots on the low vegetated flats have high water tables, and septic tanks could not be permitted. Many areas where lots have been sold or are being put up for sale will have serious problems during storms and heavy rainfall.

3. Building lots on the top and side of major active back barrier dunes are being offered for sale.

4. Etc.

CAUTION: DON'T BUY ANY OF THESE LOTS! If you have to live on Currituck Bank, about 33% is considered "safe." Seek out these areas.

DARE COUNTY

(Figures 30-32, 38-40; Segments 11 through 33)

Approximately four-fifths of the northern Outer Banks lie in Dare County. For our purposes, we have divided the county into six areas. By far the largest and most extensive area of private property lies between the Dare-Currituck County line on the north and the Bodie Island portion of the Cape Hatteras National Seashore on the south (Segments 11-19). This high density area includes the towns and communities of Southern Shores, Kitty Hawk, Kill Devil Hills, Collington Island, Nags Head, and South Nags Head.

The second area is Oregon Inlet (Segments 20, 21). A brief discussion on this inlet is included because of the proposed stabilization project and its potential adverse impact upon private coastal properties in the adjacent areas. The third area is the Cape Hatteras National Seashore which extends from South Nags Head to Ocracoke. This 70-mile stretch of barrier island occurs largely in the National Seashore, and the Pea Island National Wildlife Refuge, but contains numerous isolated pockets of private property.

The fourth area (Segments 22-24) includes the private communities of Rodanthe, Waves, and Salvo. The fifth (Segments 24-29) extends from the village of Avon to Cape Point, including the coastal portion of Buxton. The sixth area is the southeast-facing shoreline, extending from Cape Point on the northeast to the town of Hatteras and Hatteras Inlet on the southwest (Segments 32, 33).

DARE-CURRITUCK COUNTY LINE TO SOUTH NAGS HEAD

(Figures 30, 31, 32: Segments 11 through 19)

This area has a long history of development. In the 1830s, Nags Head became North Carolina's first commercially successful resort. At this time, the "bankers," who lived within the safety and security of the high land and maritime forests of Nags Head Woods on the back side of the island, began to sell "open" land to "outsiders" from the mainland. A thriving tourist community called Old Nags Head sprang up on the sound side of the barrier. Shortly after the Civil War, development began to expand to the ocean side. The arrival of the first set of access bridges in the late 1920s and, 30s, and the second set in the early 1960s connecting the once-remote islands to the mainland, brought major new waves of development. These newcomers began to run into major conflicts almost immediately with the unstable and active dune fields and the very

77

dynamic and actively eroding shoreline. From this time on, storms have wrought extensive and increasing damage to beach-front property. A recent planning study of this portion of Dare County states that this area in 1972 had a permanent resident population of 1742 and a total population of 37,000. The planning projections defined a "maximum holding capacity" of 268,000 people; the "horizon population" or the ideal and more realistic population for this beach system was defined to be 241,300, including a permanent population of 67,000 to be reached in the "horizon year" sometime in the decade between 2010 and 2020. None of these projections is based upon the limits of the natural resources such as usable land, water supplies, or sewage and waste disposal; upon the limits of the different land environments; or, most importantly, the storm processes driving, maintaining and changing the barrier island system. Remember, only 13% of this stretch of barrier island is considered to be "safe," whereas 33% is classified as "caution" zones and 54% is designated as "danger" zones. The past record and the future prognosis are clear; anyone looking at property in this area should very carefully evaluate its location.

Segments 11 and 12 are classified as "danger" areas. This very narrow portion of the island contains broad low flats crossed by common overwash zones. The intervening and extensive back dune field is locally active and, where vegetated, can readily be reactivated. Great caution should be used in the area of the large active dunes. Because of the moderate storm fetch* and the geometry of Currituck Sound, as well as the character of the barrier, these segments have a high potential for the formation of a new inlet, particularly along the very narrow portions of Segment 11. In fact, Caffeys Inlet was located at the northernmost end of this segment between 1790 and 1829.

Segments 13 and 14 are designated as "safe" zones and probably represent some of the "safer" land in the northern half of Dare County. The ocean shoreline is characterized by a very low erosion rate (two feet per year) with moderately wide beaches and healthy foredunes. The back side of the wide island consists of alternating high sand ridges and low swales covered with an extensive and well developed maritime forest. Caution should be used in the high and poorly vegetated dune field which occurs between the beach and

---

* *Fetch* refers to the interaction of wind and waves over long stretches of open water. Strong winds blowing from the same direction for more than a few hours will create waves of damaging height.

the maritime forests. This is a locally mobile sand sheet; the remainder could easily be devegetated. Also, water will collect in the low swales of the maritime forest, and these areas should be avoided.

Segment 15 contains a still more extensive back barrier maritime forest on an ancient sand ridge and swale system. This very wide and high portion of the barrier, called Kitty Hawk Woods, has been the site of a stable community on the Outer Banks since earliest times. The maritime forest affords extensive areas for safe development.

The ocean shoreline in Segments 15 and 16 has only a moderate rate of erosion (four feet per year). However, the beach is narrow and steep with only a very narrow strip of land between the beach and the highway. Consequently, each small storm takes a few more cottages to sea—as evidenced by the numerous driveways and sidewalks that go nowhere (Figure 33). It is just a matter of a short period of time before these lots are completely gone and the highway will be under wave attack. Numerous efforts to build wooden bulkheads in front of cottages has been totally futile (Figure 34). DO NOT BUY ANY WATERFRONT PROPERTY HERE!

Segments 15, 16, 17, and the northern half of 18 are characterized by a broad zone of poorly vegetated to nonvegetated back barrier dunes. The extensive mobile sand dune area occurs between Highway 158 Bypass and either the maritime forest or the estuary. In many places, the dunes are actively encroaching upon and burying the forests; some are even migrating over the estuarine marsh and into the sound. Many developments occur on the tops and sides of these active dunes. ACTIVE DUNES ARE DANGEROUS AND EXPENSIVE PLACES TO BUILD (Figure 35). Wind erosion commonly exposes and breaks sewer and water pipes, houses are undercut, and roads and fire hydrants are regularly buried. Of course, some dunes, such as the Wright Brothers monument on Kill Devil Hill, have been stabilized—but only at very great expense and with difficulty.

The southern portion of Segment 16 has a moderate potential for a new inlet opening in the future. There is a history of overwashing from Kitty Hawk Bay to the ocean during periods of high storm tides from the Albemarle, and the construction of low elevation roads from sound to ocean helps this process.

On the back side of Segment 17 is a vast area of very well developed maritime forest which occurs in Nags Head Woods and on Collington Island. Great caution should be used with any development on the fossil dunes in Nags Head Woods. These

Fig. 33. Arlington Hotel, Nags Head. Shown are the various shoreline positions which eventually led to the demise of the hotel.

80

Stages in the destruction of the Arlington Hotel. Although storms were the immediate cause of its loss, the fundamental reason was the retreat of the shoreline due to sealevel rise.

Fig. 34. The ultimate futility of bulkheads!

Fig. 35. A "lawnmower" near Jockeys Ridge

dunes, unlike the low regular dune ridges in the Kitty Hawk Woods or the Duck Woods at Southern Shores, are very high, extremely steepsided, and therefore very unstable and fragile.

The development history of Collington Island goes back to a land grant in 1663 to establish a plantation here. The plantation itself did not survive, thanks to storms, droughts, and severe water problems; however, a permanent community has survived from the mid-1700s to the present. Similarly, a community was developed in Nags Head Woods in the 1700s. We have much to learn from their sensible construction practices.

Segment 18 is a fairly narrow portion of the barrier island with numerous zones of low topography between and south of the Seven Sisters active dune field. The back side of the barrier faces directly down the long stretch of Albemarle Sound. The waters of the Roanoke River-Albemarle Sound have exited through numerous prehistoric inlets or outlets through the barrier in Segment 18. Most recently these waters discharged through Roanoke Inlet just south of the Roanoke Island causeway. In fact, the marsh islands upon which the causeway is built are the remnants of the Roanoke Inlet sand shoals or flood tide delta (Figure D3, page 212). This was probably the inlet used by the Raleigh Colonists in 1585 and was open until sometime between 1795 and 1811 when it closed. There is a very high probability that a new inlet could open here again in response to a major storm tide coming down the Albemarle Sound. The most vulnerable portions are the very low areas between the dune fields, in developments where canals have been cut well into the barrier, and at the narrow southern end of the segment. If the Oregon Inlet jetties are built, there will be an increased probability of a new inlet forming here.

Segment 19 extends from Whalebone Junction to South Nags Head. All of the private property in this segment occurs in a narrow strip extending from the ocean west to about midway between the coastal highway and Highway 12. Even though the island is very wide and heavily vegetated, the private property along the coast is designated a "danger" zone. This rapidly developing area is characterized by checkerboard developments in which minimal-sized lots are stacked four to six deep between the highway and the ocean. This pattern would be adequate almost any place else in North Carolina but along this segment of barrier island. Here there is a very high erosion rate (four to nine feet per year, increasing from north to south); consequently, the ocean front lots are doomed and going fast: DON'T BUY THEM! A considerable number of cottages built on these lots went to sea in the small storms of March 1980; you can see the new pilings under those whose owners were fortunate enough to have long deep lots. Many of the older developments along the coast have very deep lots where the houses have been moved back numerous times. But where do you move the house in the new checkerboard developments? Walk the beach and notice the houses and lots destined to go to sea in the next storm. It is ironic and sad that these ocean front lots are some of the most expensive real estate in the country, and yet it is the land with the highest hazard. The construction of the proposed Oregon Inlet jetty system will probably increase significantly the rate of erosion along this segment of shoreline.

Oregon Inlet (Segments 20, 21): Oregon Inlet is probably the most dynamic and certainly one of the highest energy inlets of the entire East Coast. It is the only inlet for the entire Albemarle Sound-Roanoke River drainage and much of the Pamlico River-Pamlico Sound drainage systems. The history of the opening, closing, and migration patterns of the northern inlets reflects extreme mobility and dramatic changes in site location. Oregon Inlet is no exception to this. It opened in 1846 approximately two to three miles north of its present location and has been rapidly migrating southward at a rate of between 75 and 125 feet per year (Figure 36). The construction of the Oregon Inlet bridge in 1962 represented a major

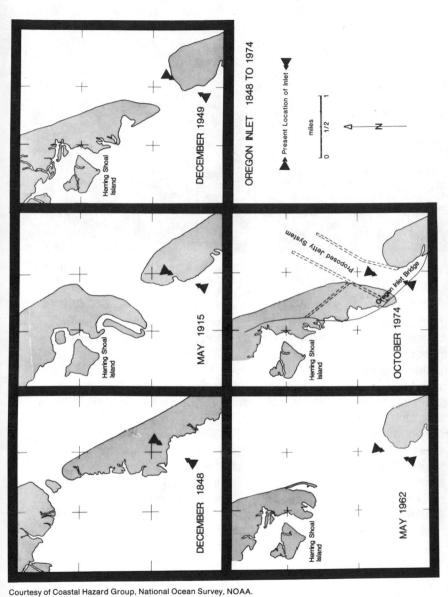

Courtesy of Coastal Hazard Group, National Ocean Survey, NOAA.

Fig. 36. Oregon Inlet, December 1849 to October 1974. The May 1963 inlet was extremely wide due to "blowing out" during the '62 Ash Wednesday storm. What will happen to the proposed jetties in another 1962 storm?

85

Fig. 37. A dragline "gone to sea" at Oregon Inlet after the 1962 Ash Wednesday storm. The dragline was involved in construction of the Herbert C. Bonner bridge.

economic commitment which is not compatible with such a dynamic system (Figure 37). Now, in an effort to protect the bridge as well as increase the usability and reliability of the inlet for commercial fishing vessels, the U. S. Army Corps of Engineers has developed a plan for stabilizing this exceedingly dynamic inlet. The proposed plan calls for an 8,100-foot jetty on the south side and a 10,000-foot jetty along the north side (Figure 32: Segments 20, 21).

The potential geological consequence resulting from the construction of these jetties could be significant. This impact would have a major effect, not only upon the immediately adjacent Seashore and Refuge properties in Segments 20 and 21, but will also impact the adjoining properties in Segments 18, 19, and 22. **WARNING:** If the Oregon Inlet jetty system is built, the following coastal responses will probably take place.

1. The shorelines immediately adjacent to the jetties (up to one to three miles) will accrete sediment both naturally and due to dredge pumping.

2. The shorelines on both sides of the accreted segments (up to five or ten miles) will experience increased rates of shoreline

recession. The increased rate will diminish away from the jetties.

3. There will be an increased rate of loss of barrier dune ridges along the shorelines outlined in (2) along with increased number and extent of overwash zones.

4. There will be increased probability of new inlets opening from the estuaries through low and narrow "weak" zones of the barrier islands in response to high storm tides and flooding. Several localities in Segment 18 are most vulnerable.

5. It is also possible that the restrictions caused by the jetty system could cause a storm tide to flank the jetties producing a new inlet in the adjacent low areas.

State personnel, County Commissioners, local town officials, developers, and present and prospective land owners in the potential impacted areas need to weigh seriously the proposed short-term economic benefits of the jetties against the long-term consequences of barrier island modification. The proposed project could have overwhelming long-term economic ramifications. These problems have not been adequately addressed by the project planners. (See Appendix D1 for further discussion about Oregon Inlet and the proposed jetty system.)

Cape Hatteras National Seashore: This park, the first of many national seashore recreation areas in the U.S., was originally proposed in 1933, authorized by Congress in 1937, and came into existence in 1958. The seashore was established with the intent of preserving a barrier island system in its natural state; however, segments of the seashore are now "managed" as Pea Island National Wildlife Refuge to provide adequate food supplies and habitat for migratory wildfowl. Also, because these islands were generally very low, narrow, and were extensively overwashed, the Civilian Conservation Corps in the 1930s constructed a continuous dune dike along the entire Seashore. This major modification, utilizing sand fencing and dune grasses, produced a barrier dune ridge and a false sense of security for subsequent economic investments such as roads, motels, homes, and government facilities. Storms continuously eroded the dune ridge, periodically breaching large segments and causing extensive flooding, overwash, and damage to the encroaching economic developments behind it. The National Park Service continued rebuilding this vulnerable dune ridge well into the 1970s when they learned that the dune ridges might actually be producing long-term harm to the islands (Chapter 2). For a more detailed discussion of the Cape Hatteras National Seashore, see Reference 57, Appendix C.

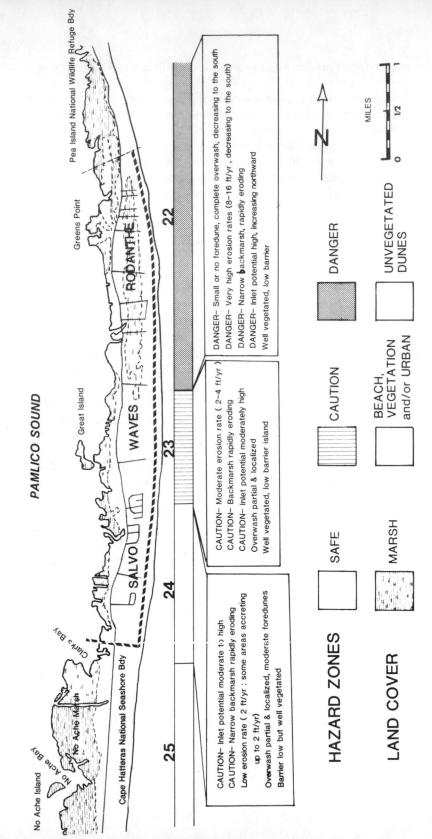

Fig. 38. Site analysis, Rodanthe, Waves and Salvo

Rodanthe, Waves, and Salvo (Figure 38): This five-mile stretch of barrier represents an enclave of small town and private property nestled within the National Seashore. These villages, which date back at least to the 1800s, were originally lifesaving or Coast Guard stations combined with fishing, boat building and farming industries. The map on pages 2 and 3 shows a major change in the direction of the coastline in the region of these villages. This is what's left of a major prehistoric cape along the Outer Banks. The extensive Wimble Shoals, which occur immediately offshore, are also part of this old cape system. The very high shoreline erosion rate (eight to sixteen feet per year) which occurs along Segments 21 and 22 reflects the systematic elimination of this cape structure. Tree stumps are common on the beach; the barrier dune ridge is highly eroded and readily breached; and extensive overwash fans are common. All of these are indicative of a rapid rate of shoreline recession. To the south, along Segments 24 and 25, the beach is fairly broad and shallow with well developed foredunes and low rates of erosion and some actual accretion. This accretion may be due largely to the presence of an offshore sediment supply—eroding Wimble Shoals.

The town of Rodanthe, predating the Revolutionary War, was called Chicamacomico until 1974 when the U. S. Postal Service changed the name. The old cemetery, which dates back to at least 1830, occurs along the edge of the Sound with the old headstones facing west. Much of the original town (as well as the old road) was located west of the cemetery in what is now Pamlico Sound. This is pretty dramatic evidence of the magnitude and extent of the estuarine shoreline erosion problems. Large storm tides and waves resulting from the very large fetch across Pamlico Sound cause (1) extensive erosion of the estuarine shoreline resulting in a narrow back barrier marsh, (2) extensive flooding of the low portions of the barrier, and (3) a moderately high to high potential for the opening of a major inlet or outlet from the Sound across several portions of the relatively narrow and low sections of the barrier.

People interested in buying property in this area should evaluate the location carefully. Only 26% of this barrier is considered "safe," whereas 55% is classified as "danger" zone and 19% as "caution" area. The safest areas appear to be in the southern portion of Segment 23 and in Segment 24.

Avon to Cape Point (Figure 38): The older town of Avon, formerly known as Kinnakeet, was totally nestled among the maritime forest on the back side of the island. In fact, Kinnakeet was noted for the small schooners built from the extensive maritime forests here and

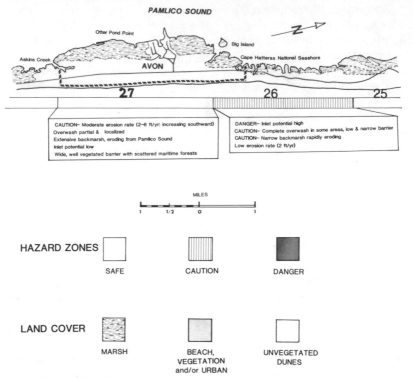

Fig. 39. Site analysis, Avon

at Buxton and Frisco. Today, Avon is a rapidly developing area along the ocean side. The growth and development of this area has already exceeded the island's natural carrying capacity with respect to water supply and sewage disposal. Continued development necessitated the recent construction of a major water pipeline from Frisco. The pipeline was built along the highway across the very vulnerable Buxton Inlet and overwash zone (Segment 28). This portion of the barrier is extensively overwashed every year with the road commonly being washed out. What happens to this vital pipeline and the people who are dependent upon it after the next storm? (See Appendix D1 for further discussion about this water problem.) Thus, even though Avon is classified as a relatively "safe" portion of the barrier, prospective buyers should be aware of the serious water problems during a time of a major storm disaster.

Shoreline erosion rates are a relatively low two feet per year at the northern end of Avon (Segments 25, 26). They systematically increase southward to a maximum of 20 feet per year in the Buxton

90

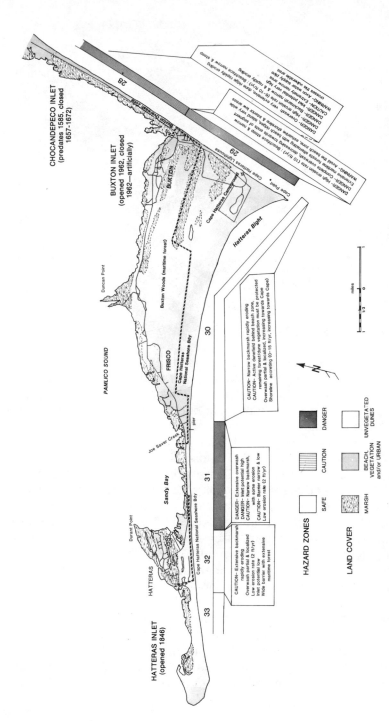

Fig. 40. Site analysis, Buxton overwash area to Hatteras Inlet

91

Fig. 41. An overwash about to happen!

area (Figure 39; Segments 28, 29). The barrier island becomes very low and narrow in Segment 25 with a very high potential for the formation of a new inlet in response to very large storm tides across Pamlico Sound. Indeed, there have been several inlets here in the past. Chacandepeco Inlet predates 1585 and closed between 1657 and 1672. More recently, the 1962 Ash Wednesday storm opened Buxton Inlet (Figures D9 and D10 pages 220, 221) which was artificially closed later that year. There will also be inlets here in the future. The barrier dune ridge is rapidly being eroded, breached, extensively and frequently overwashed (Figure 40). The private property along the ocean front between old Buxton Inlet on the north and the U. S. Naval facility and Cape Hatteras Lighthouse is periodically damaged or destroyed (Figure D12); Highway 12 is regularly flooded, buried, or washed away. This stretch of coastal area is a high hazard zone and should be avoided.

The National Park Service, the U.S. Navy, and the N. C. Department of Transportation have a long history of attempts to stabilize Segments 28 and 29 of the shoreline (for further information see Appendix D1). Extensive beach nourishment projects (Figures D8 and D11, pages 219, 221), nylon sand-bagging (Figure D12, page 222), and the construction of groins (Figure D13, page 224) illustrate many of the shoreline truths of Chapter 3. Following expenditures of over $21 million to "save" this part of the shoreline, the National Park Service made a major policy shift away from continuous and highly expensive engineering solutions (Reference 62, Appendix C). That decision may prove to be one of the wisest in the history of the Outer Banks.

Cape Point to Hatteras: Large portions of this area are among the "safest" on the Outer Banks. Segments 30 and 32 contain the villages of Buxton, Frisco, and Hatteras. These towns are well protected within very high and wide portions of barrier islands composed of a complex series of east-west sand ridges (Figure D14, page 225). The ridges contain one of the most extensive maritime forests on the entire Outer Banks and are characterized by intervening low swampy swales or sedges.

Even though this area is relatively "safe" and contains considerable room for future growth and development, it must be remembered that there are definite limits or carrying capacities even here. Extensive clearing of the forests could reactivate segments of the sand ridges. Increased numbers of septic tanks and demands upon the fresh water resource will have a long-term impact, particularly if the low swales continue to be bulldozed and filled; these fresh ponds and swamps are the water supply! Ocean shoreline erosion is minimal (two feet per year) and is actually accreting (from zero to fifteen feet per year) at Cape Point and at Hatteras Inlet. Estuarine shoreline erosion, however, is relatively high with flooding of the lowlands common in response to high storm tides across the vast Pamlico Sound. A high potential exists for formation of a new inlet or outlet in the narrow and low barrier in the Sandy Bay area (Segment 31) as a result of a major estuarine storm tide. Much of this area is National Seashore; however, some of the private development property on the east and west ends of Sandy Bay (Segment 31) are considered to be "danger" zones and should be evaluated very carefully.

Regardless of whether you are living in or just visiting this "safe" area, remember the following: stormy weather quickly terminates the ferry service; the roads between here and Nags Head flood very rapidly and often are completely overwashed; major storms may even breach the islands with new inlets and wash out existing bridges. In the event of such a storm, don't get stranded. Follow the official instructions for evacuating and seeking safe refuge early.

HYDE COUNTY

Ocracoke Island: This narrow 15.5-mile-long island is part of the Cape Hatteras National Seashore and consists of federal land closed to private development. The island is bounded by Hatteras Inlet on the east and by Ocracoke Inlet on the west. Ocracoke Inlet, separating Ocracoke Island from Portsmouth Island and the recently developed Cape Lookout National Seashore, has been open continuously since it was discovered in 1585. A major inlet, it became a chief port of entry for North Carolina following the establishment of the Town of Ocracoke as an important port in 1715. Ships continued to use it through the Revolutionary War and into the 1820s, but by then extensive dredging was necessary. This proved futile, however, as the channels filled faster than they could be dredged, and the effort was abandoned in the 1830s.

Shipping quickly shifted to Hatteras Inlet after it opened during a hurricane in 1846, but by 1900 commercial shipping through these inlets had been completely replaced by other means of transport. Ocracoke Inlet's greatest notoriety came from Edward Teach, better known as Blackbeard the Pirate, who sailed through her waters until he was beheaded just inside the inlet at Teach's Hole on November 22, 1718.

Ocracoke Island is generally a very narrow and low barrier island flanked by an extensive and major artificial barrier dune ridge. With the exception of a few areas of higher and hummocky back barrier dune fields containing young maritime forests, this island is characterized by extensive overwash zones. Inundation and overwash are natural and characteristic occurrences over most of it; this has considerable impact upon the highway, which is periodically washed out. The narrow marsh development on the back side of the barrier occurs on these overwash fans. The artificial dune ridges along the highway have been constructed in an effort to prevent overwash; however, they are often severely eroded on the ocean side and are just as often washed out during storms. The northeastern half of the island is undergoing severe erosion along the ocean side. Here the shoreline is moving back at an average of six feet per year with erosion rates varying from eight feet per year at the northeast end to two feet per year in the central portions. The southwest half of the island is characterized by a broad and shallow beach resulting from active shoreline accretion.

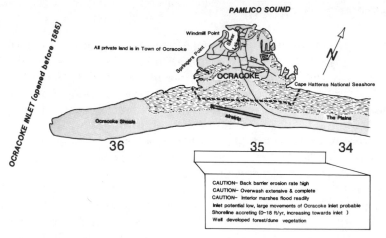

PAMLICO SOUND

OCRACOKE INLET (opened before 1585)

Windmill Point

All private land is in Town of Ocracoke

Springers Point

N

OCRACOKE

Cape Hatteras National Seashore

Ocracoke Shoals

airstrip

The Plains

36

35

34

CAUTION– Back barrier erosion rate high
CAUTION– Overwash extensive & complete
CAUTION– Interior marshes flood readily
Inlet potential low, large movements of Ocracoke Inlet probable
Shoreline accreting (0–18 ft/yr, increasing towards inlet)
Well developed forest/dune vegetation

Fig. 42. Site analysis

Ocracoke Village: (Figure 41) All of the private property is located in the village of Ocracoke. This very old town is located on the back side of the barrier island and is separated from it by an extensive low marsh system. This marsh, along with the other marshes around the village perimeter, floods extensively in response to major storm tides in Pamlico Sound. The largest portion of the village is located on a relatively high and stable series of sand ridges heavily vegetated by a well developed maritime forest. It was an excellent site for the development of a community in the early 1700s by pilots and sailors using Ocracoke Inlet. Ocracoke lighthouse is one of the oldest in the state dating back to 1823.

Because of the very small areal extent of the high land in the Village, there are distinct limits to further development. In addition, the groundwater supply is small and very vulnerable to contamination from septic tanks and saltwater flooding. As you drive around the Village, notice the extensive use of cisterns on all of the older buildings. The limits on land, water, and sewage disposal dictate a very small "carrying capacity" for this area. Great caution should be used by the existing community, the National Park Service, the N. C. Department of Transportation, and any prospective residents or developers to insure that this delicate carrying capacity is not exceeded.

CARTERET COUNTY

The long midsection of the North Carolina coast lies in Carteret County. Here, two types of barrier island have resulted from differences in island orientation to wind and wave action. (See Chapter 2.) The first type consists of 58 miles of beach along Portsmouth Island and Core Banks, oriented northeast-southwest—almost parallel to the prevailing winds. As noted in Chapter 2, this orientation creates low islands that generally lack well developed foredunes or large dune fields. With minimal dune formation, these islands are subject to frequent overwash, and vegetation is generally sparse (Figure 13, page 28). The second section of coast includes the east-west oriented islands of Shackleford Banks and Bogue Banks, with a total of 34 miles of beach. Both of these islands are subjected to onshore winds which provide a ready sand supply. Stable dunes afford protection to the back areas of the islands, nurturing the growth of beautiful maritime forest along the sound.

The Carteret coastline is frequently struck by storms—both hurricanes and northeasters. Since 1585, at least 150 hurricanes and hundreds of storms have hit the entire Outer Banks region. The storms have caused severe shoreline erosion, overwash, flooding, and have brought winds that destroyed vegetation and low dunes. Hurricanes, of course, generated the highest winds, waves, and storm-surge flooding.

Portsmouth Island, Core Banks, and Shackleford Banks make up the Cape Lookout National Seashore. These islands are accessible only by boat, and as federal lands, will be subject to minimal development. Therefore we shall discuss them only briefly.

Portsmouth Island: Like Core Banks, this island is low, frequently ovewashed, and unsuitable for development. It is ironic that Portsmouth, established in 1753 on the back side of the island near Ocracoke Inlet, was the first planned town on the Outer Banks. Although the town grew as a port of entry on the inlet, surviving storms and wars, nature eventually defeated the enterprise. In 1846 a hurricane created Hatteras Inlet and Oregon Inlet to the north. As these inlets became new commerce routes, Portsmouth lost its *raison d'être* and its population declined from a high of 505 in 1850 to a mere handful today.

Core Banks: This low, narrow barrier island extends from Drum Inlet in the north to Barden Inlet west of Cape Lookout, and is separated from the mainland by Core Sound. The subject of several scientific studies, it has served as a natural laboratory for investigations of barrier-island growth, changes and processes. Its shoreline shows high rates of erosion, and much sand has washed across the island to bury the backmarsh.

At least six different inlets have cut the island in the vicinity of present-day Drum Inlet, and tidal deltas in back of the central and southern parts of the island suggest that prehistoric inlets also cut the island. During the eighteenth and nineteenth centuries Old Drum Inlet was opened and closed by storms three times. In 1938 it was necessary for the Corps to dredge the inlet at a cost of more than $50,000. By the late 1950s, the inlet was again closing. In 1971, the Corps opened New Drum Inlet south of its former position and across from the town of Atlantic on the mainland. This artificial inlet interrupted the flow of beach drift, increasing local beach recession. The new inlet has widened and shoaled with time, and sediment has washed into Core Sound to form a tidal delta. Boats are presently unable to use it.

Except for early whalers' camps, the lighthouse, and the Coast Guard and lifesaving stations, Core Banks has remained undeveloped. Yet modern man has made a significant impact on the island. Fishing camps have produced clusters of shacks, poor sanitation conditions, and a solid-waste problem. Fishermen have barged automobiles to the island to use for transportation. Not only were these cars driven at random over the island's ecosystem; they were also "junked" wherever chance dictated that their last run take them. As a result, an estimated 2,500 junk vehicles dot the island. Some have formed sand traps and are building small dunes. The National Park Service plans to remove many of the wrecks.

Cape Lookout, the southern extremity of Core Banks, has migrated to the east and enlarged in area since the late 1800s. The construction in 1945 of a jetty at the northwestern end of the cape peninsula, however, may have reversed this trend by cutting off the sand supply from Barden Inlet. This inlet, which had opened and closed previously, reopened in 1933 and has since been kept open by dredging. The east side of the inlet in the vicinity of the Cape Lookout Lighthouse is eroding fairly rapidly. This raises the question of whether the Park Service will fall into the trap of shoreline engineering to protect the 1859 lighthouse. It seems clear that the location of the artificially dredged channel is responsible for the dangerous position of the lighthouse. Changing the location of the channel may be the most logical way to save the structure.

Shackleford Banks: The establishment of the Cape Lookout National Seashore may ultimately render Shackleford Banks the only North Carolina island "safe" from development. It serves, however, as a historic example of man's failure to learn how to live with an island. Despite its natural, wild appearance, this island is not in its pristine state. In the 1800s, some of the maritime forest that covered the island was cut down for ship timber. The communities of Wade's Hammock and Diamond City developed on opposite ends of the island. In August 1899, a devastating hurricane hit Shackleford Banks. In the three years that followed, all of the residents of Diamond City moved to Harkers Island or the mainland, most of them taking their houses with them. Today, only their graveyards remain.

In the late 1800s, active-dune formation and migration resulted in the loss of more of the island's forest. The old cedars of the forest, re-exposed today, fall to wood collectors for use in lamps and other geegaws. Some maritime forest still remains, however, roamed by the wild descendants of Diamond City's domestic herds; horses, cows, sheep, and goats graze in it at will. Whether these animals should be removed or left to roam the island is subject to debate today. Meanwhile, natural processes continue to operate on the island. Shoreline erosion occurs at moderate to high rates along the front side of the island; overwash occurs regularly on the low eastern end of the island; and accretion has occurred on the western end of the island, which now extends into Beaufort Inlet.

Bogue Banks: Persons interested in specific details on Bogue Banks should obtain a copy of *How to Live with an Island: A Handbook to Bogue Banks, North Carolina* (Reference 64, Appendix C). Figures 43 and 44 summarize much of that information, and data obtained between 1975 and 1977. A brief description of hazard zones on the island follows:

The **Fort Macon to Money Island Beach** shoreline near the Atlantic Beach town limits is a high-hazard zone. Fort Macon State Park will not be developed much beyond its present status, and its dunes, beach, and forest will remain in a relatively natural state. The actual fort area has been damaged by past storms. In fact, the earlier stone Fort Hampton, which protected the inlet during the War of 1812, was destroyed by a severe hurricane of the early 1800s. Private property between the park and town limits also suffered in past storms. The large area subject to either overwash, a high rate of shoreline erosion, storm-surge flooding, or active sand dunes, minimizes the number of sites safe for development. Safe sites are located near the center of the island where shrub stands and maritime woods indicate stability. Any structures above the 100-year storm-surge level (such as the Tar Landing Villa Condominiums, where dunes provide added protection) are safe from flooding.

Atlantic Beach represents that portion of the island most modified by man. The natural contours and environments have been highly altered or obliterated. Marsh fill, finger canals, and septic tanks further detract from the island's natural character.

Potential hazards include damage to beach-front property by hurricanes; overwash along streets perpendicular to the shoreline; storm-surge flooding of lower elevations (especially on the Bogue Sound side of the island); and polluted groundwater. Sites at the higher elevations of 15 or more feet are safe if precautions are taken to minimize wind damage.

West of Atlantic Beach is an area of active sand dunes that should be avoided for development. The maritime forest behind the primary dunes provides safe sites at the higher elevations.

Pine Knoll Shores to Salter Path includes some of the highest, widest, and most stable areas of the island (Figure 43), or, in fact, any island in North Carolina. Much of this area is suitable for development so long as the natural environment—especially the high-forested, middle-to-back area of the island—is maintained. Although the frontal dune is high and continuous, it is narrow and eroding. Therefore, the beach front is not suitable for development. Buildings on the ocean side of the island should be set back from the frontal dune and trough-like depression behind parts of the dune line (as was the John Yancey Motel, whose builders have respected the integrity of the natural topographic and vegetative cover). Sites along the canal in the central portion of the island are of questionable safety because of problems associated with finger canals. The canal is cut rather deep in places, and the sand walls may be prone to slump, requiring the expense of stabilizing the banks through bulkheading or other methods. When development along the canal is complete, septic-tank pollution of the canal may be a problem. Nevertheless, this section of Bogue Banks is generally safe for construction, and exemplifies more reasonable barrier-island development. Looking toward the future, the Pine Knoll Shores community officially adopted a land-use plan in May of 1976 (Reference 66, Appendix C).

The Salter Path settlement (Figure 44) is protected on the ocean side by high dunes and vegetation. Low areas on the Bogue Sound side are subject to flooding.

Indian Beach West has a very high density of mobile homes, and for this reason alone, would suffer extensive damage in a major storm. As a temporary summer recreational campsite, it may be satisfactory to persons who choose to ignore possible water problems and what some call the "rural slum" atmosphere of the area (Reference 64, Appendix C).

Emerald Isle and vicinity, from the town limits of Indian Beach to the west of Emerald Isle, is generally a poor area for development. Most of the island is low, narrow, and lacks protective dunes, vegetation and backmarsh. Consequently, this zone is highly vulnerable to inlet formation. Locally, black and white shell-like lagoon sediment marks former inlets that were cut during hurricanes and later filled with sediment pumped from the lagoon. This sediment is visible on the eastern portion of Emerald Isle, where Hurricane Hazel cut two inlets. Dune removal for development has probably increased the likelihood of inlet formation and complete overwash in some parts of this zone. The combined threats of storm flooding, inlet formation, and overwash burial of roads make this a prime area for evacuation in case of a hurricane warning.

Western Bogue Banks, much like the Pine Knoll section of the island, is relatively safe for development. Well forested dune ridges in the middle and back portions of the island provide good building sites if the forest cover is maintained. The immediate ocean shoreline lacks continuous, protective dunes and should be avoided. This zone widens to the west into an active dune field that is also unsuited for development. Shoreline erosion is more severe in the west, and the last one-half mile of island is completely unsuited for development because of the combination of factors shown in Figure 44. Developers of some shoreline areas on Western Bogue have removed large sand dunes, rendering potentially safe areas dangerous. (The vicinity of the Islander Motel is an example of such an area.) Avoid building near roads cut straight to and level with the beach; they act as overwash passes in major storms.

ONSLOW COUNTY

Four islands—Hammocks Beach, Bear (Shacklefoot) Island, Onslow Beach, and the northeastern part of Topsail Island—make up the Onslow County coast. Hammocks Beach is a state park; Onslow Beach and Bear Island form part of the Camp Lejeune Military Reservation. Only Topsail Island is privately owned and subject to heavy development.

Hammocks Beach State Park: During the summer (Memorial Day

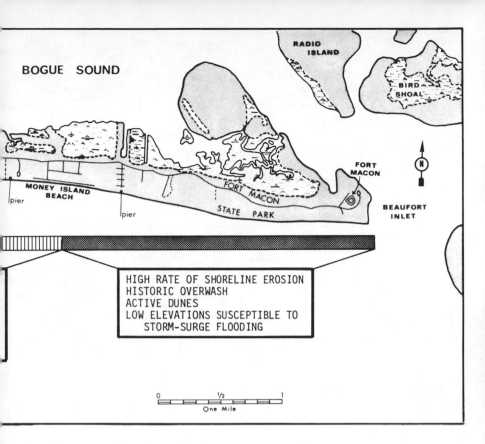

BOGUE SOUND

RADIO ISLAND

BIRD SHOAL

MONEY ISLAND BEACH

pier

pier

FORT MACON

FORT MACON STATE PARK

BEAUFORT INLET

N

HIGH RATE OF SHORELINE EROSION
HISTORIC OVERWASH
ACTIVE DUNES
LOW ELEVATIONS SUSCEPTIBLE TO
    STORM-SURGE FLOODING

0   1/2   1
    One Mile

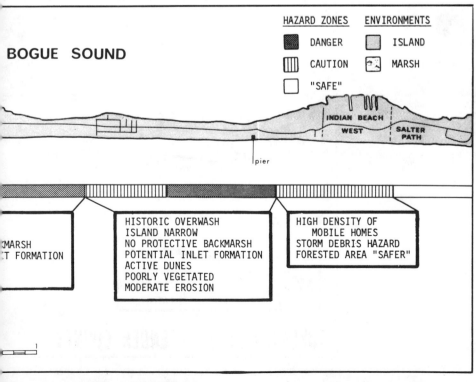

BOGUE SOUND

HAZARD ZONES

DANGER
CAUTION
"SAFE"

ENVIRONMENTS

ISLAND
MARSH

INDIAN BEACH

WEST   SALTER PATH

pier

KMARSH
CT FORMATION

HISTORIC OVERWASH
ISLAND NARROW
NO PROTECTIVE BACKMARSH
POTENTIAL INLET FORMATION
ACTIVE DUNES
POORLY VEGETATED
MODERATE EROSION

HIGH DENSITY OF
    MOBILE HOMES
STORM DEBRIS HAZARD
FORESTED AREA "SAFER"

1

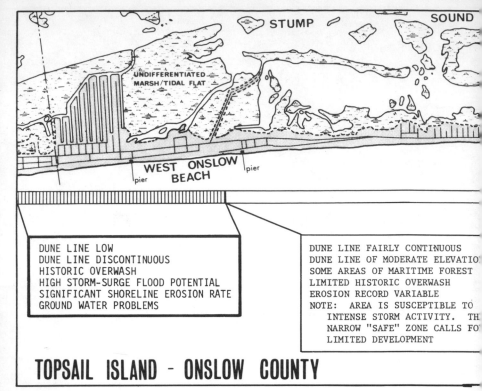

DUNE LINE LOW
DUNE LINE DISCONTINUOUS
HISTORIC OVERWASH
HIGH STORM-SURGE FLOOD POTENTIAL
SIGNIFICANT SHORELINE EROSION RATE
GROUND WATER PROBLEMS

DUNE LINE FAIRLY CONTINUOUS
DUNE LINE OF MODERATE ELEVATIO[N]
SOME AREAS OF MARITIME FOREST
LIMITED HISTORIC OVERWASH
EROSION RECORD VARIABLE
NOTE: AREA IS SUSCEPTIBLE TO
        INTENSE STORM ACTIVITY. TH[E]
        NARROW "SAFE" ZONE CALLS FO[R]
        LIMITED DEVELOPMENT

TOPSAIL ISLAND - ONSLOW COUNTY

Fig. 45. Site Analysis for Topsail Island (Onslow County)

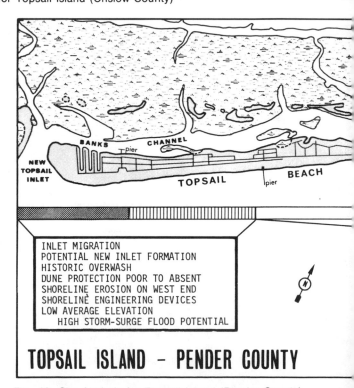

INLET MIGRATION
POTENTIAL NEW INLET FORMATION
HISTORIC OVERWASH
DUNE PROTECTION POOR TO ABSENT
SHORELINE EROSION ON WEST END
SHORELINE ENGINEERING DEVICES
LOW AVERAGE ELEVATION
    HIGH STORM-SURGE FLOOD POTENTIAL

TOPSAIL ISLAND - PENDER COUNTY

Fig. 46. Site Analysis for Topsail Island (Pender County)

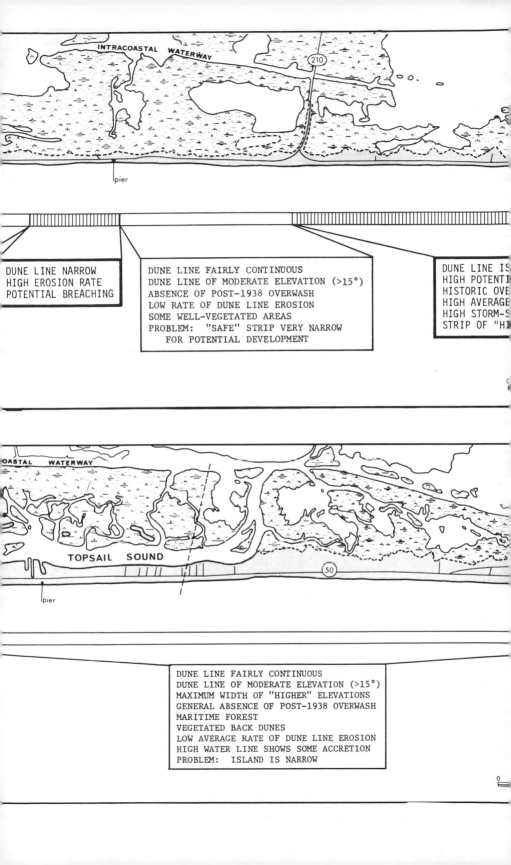

INTRACOASTAL WATERWAY

210

pier

DUNE LINE NARROW
HIGH EROSION RATE
POTENTIAL BREACHING

DUNE LINE FAIRLY CONTINUOUS
DUNE LINE OF MODERATE ELEVATION (>15°)
ABSENCE OF POST-1938 OVERWASH
LOW RATE OF DUNE LINE EROSION
SOME WELL-VEGETATED AREAS
PROBLEM: "SAFE" STRIP VERY NARROW
    FOR POTENTIAL DEVELOPMENT

DUNE LINE IS
HIGH POTENTI
HISTORIC OVE
HIGH AVERAGE
HIGH STORM-S
STRIP OF "HI

OASTAL WATERWAY

TOPSAIL SOUND

50

pier

DUNE LINE FAIRLY CONTINUOUS
DUNE LINE OF MODERATE ELEVATION (>15°)
MAXIMUM WIDTH OF "HIGHER" ELEVATIONS
GENERAL ABSENCE OF POST-1938 OVERWASH
MARITIME FOREST
VEGETATED BACK DUNES
LOW AVERAGE RATE OF DUNE LINE EROSION
HIGH WATER LINE SHOWS SOME ACCRETION
PROBLEM: ISLAND IS NARROW

0

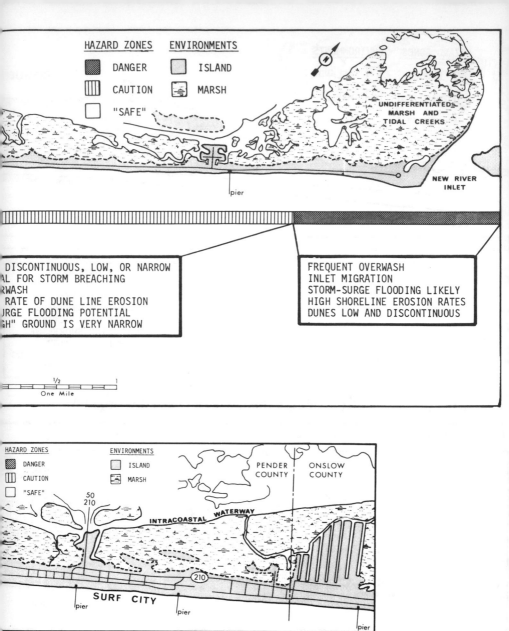

HAZARD ZONES

- ▨ DANGER
- ⊞ CAUTION
- ☐ "SAFE"

ENVIRONMENTS

- ☐ ISLAND
- ⊡ MARSH

UNDIFFERENTIATED
MARSH AND
TIDAL CREEKS

NEW RIVER
INLET

pier

DISCONTINUOUS, LOW, OR NARROW
AL FOR STORM BREACHING
RWASH
RATE OF DUNE LINE EROSION
URGE FLOODING POTENTIAL
GH" GROUND IS VERY NARROW

FREQUENT OVERWASH
INLET MIGRATION
STORM-SURGE FLOODING LIKELY
HIGH SHORELINE EROSION RATES
DUNES LOW AND DISCONTINUOUS

½   1
One Mile

HAZARD ZONES

- ▨ DANGER
- ⊞ CAUTION
- ☐ "SAFE"

ENVIRONMENTS

- ☐ ISLAND
- ⊡ MARSH

50
210

PENDER   ONSLOW
COUNTY   COUNTY

INTRACOASTAL WATERWAY

210

SURF CITY
pier   pier

pier

POLLUTED GROUNDWATER
AREAS OF CROWDED TRAILERS
    SHOULD BE REGARDED AS
    SPECIAL HAZARD TO BE
    AVOIDED

DUNE LINE LOW
DUNE LINE DISCONTINUOUS
HISTORIC OVERWASH
HIGH STORM-SURGE FLOOD POTENTIAL
1954 INLET ARTIFICIALLY FILLED
    (STUMP INLET POSITION)
SIGNIFICANT SHORELINE EROSION RATE
GROUND WATER PROBLEMS

½   1
One Mile

through Labor Day), a passenger ferry, operated by the State, transports visitors to the island from the vicinity of Swansboro. The island is small (3.5 miles of beach), backed by extensive salt marsh, and covered with active dunes. Hammocks Beach is the most accessible island in North Carolina that is close to its natural state. Like Bogue Banks, its northeast-southwest orientation places the beach sand-source perpendicular to southerly wind directions. Overall historic shoreline accretion suggests an ample sand supply. The result is active dune fields with maximum elevations ranging from 30 to 60 feet. Only a few small areas are well vegetated.

As a recreational beach and dune park, this island is put to excellent use; its small size, active dunes, migrating inlets (Bear and Bogue), and local shoreline erosion make it poorly suited for development. Ferries carry passengers only. This prohibits vehicles on the island to protect the natural environment, and controls island population.

Bear (Shacklefoot) Island: Part of a military reservation, the west end of this island has been used for target practice, and large impact crators remain visible surface scars. Access to the island is highly restricted; the only way to get there is by boat. Although smaller in area than Hammocks Beach, Bear Island has about the same length of beach front and a greater area of vegetation. The active dune field has elevations of around 15 feet, though most of the island contains stabilized dunes with elevations up to 30 feet. Historically the shoreline has shown low to moderate erosion. Bear Inlet and Brown's Inlet have histories of active migration. In recent years the island has been subject to erosion on the east end and accretion on the west end; thus it has been growing into Brown's Inlet.

Onslow Beach: Areas of this 11-mile-long island are similar to those of Topsail Island. If the island were publicly owned, it would undoubtedly be developed. Proximity to the mainland and a bridge built by the military connecting the mainland to the island reduce access problems. The northern end of the island, though narrow, has some moderately high elevations—greater than 30 feet—in a fairly continuous dune ridge. Military vehicles, however, threaten dune stability.

On the western portion of the island the dune ridge becomes lower and broken, subjecting the area to overwash. This zone also suffers moderate to high shoreline erosion. In addition, the New River Inlet has a history of migration and associated erosion-deposition problems. The east end of the island is also eroding from inlet migration.

The marine base constructed buildings on the island—some on the beach front, at low elevations, and without the benefit of primary-dune protection. These buildings have suffered overwash and storm damage.

Topsail Island: Figures 45 and 46 summarize the relative safety of the various parts of Topsail Island. With nearly 22 miles of ocean beach front, this is the second largest of North Carolina's southern islands. The island's potential for development is certainly great, and with access via North Carolina Highways 210 and 50, the pressure to develop will likely grow. Currently, the island retains much of its original aesthetic value. The beach is wide and continuous, interrupted only by an occasional fishing pier. Much of the island is forested, protected by foredunes, and at elevations in excess of the one-in-25-year storm-surge level.

Parts of the island, however, are unsuitable for development. Since its earliest residential development in the late 1930s, the classic mistakes in barrier-island development have been made. Sand dunes have been destroyed, protective vegetation stripped, and buildings constructed at low elevations. The price paid was near-total destruction during Hurricane Hazel in 1954. Of 230 buildings, 210 were destroyed and the remainder damaged. The only bridge to the mainland was knocked out, and much of the island was inundated. Hurricane Hazel generated a flood level of 9.5 feet above mean sea-level for Topsail Island; the island's average elevation is 8.9 feet above mean sea-level! In addition, 850,000 cubic yards of sand were lost from the beaches of Topsail and Surf City. Much of this sand was deposited as overwash on the island. In 1955, the beaches were hit hard again by Hurricane Diane. Since Donna in 1960, the island has not been subject to a severe hurricane.

As the memory of Hazel and the hurricanes of the late 1950s faded, earlier mistakes in development were repeated. Marshland was destroyed through dredge-and-fill and finger-canal construction; dunes were leveled by the bulldozer. Today, although the island is subject to the North Carolina Sand Dune Ordinance, there are not adequate personnel to enforce it. Small lots, 25 to 50 feet wide, crowded mobile homes, and occupied areas of filled marsh have all contributed to overloading the natural system with sewage, and polluting ground and shellfish waters.

In consideration of these problems, a summary of the relative safety of various sections of Topsail Island follows.

The New River Inlet to McKee's Pier is generally unsafe for development although there is evidence that development is planned. Potential inlet migration, limited dune protection, sparse vegetation, and historic overwash suggest that construction should be avoided in this zone. Peat layers are exposed on the inlet's shore, and air photos reveal that rapid erosion has occurred in this area. The marsh in back of the island should be left undisturbed. Land area high enough for development forms a very narrow strip, and the road right-of-way occupies much of this strip. Lots in the vicinity of McKee's Pier are advertised as "ocean to sound" tracts; this should suggest to prospective owners that such sites are dangerous. That one can see the beach while standing on the sound side of the road indicates that the island is too narrow to provide a secure location for a cottage in a storm.

McKee's Pier to Northern Access Highway 210 is classified as a caution zone in Figure 45. The generally high potential for overwash and storm-surge flooding, and the fairly rapid rate of shoreline erosion make development here risky. (There are safe sites within this zone, however.) The upland is generally narrow here, and total overwash would occur again in a storm of the magnitude of Hurricane Hazel (1954).

Access Highway 210 to Paradise Fishing Pier is relatively safe for development because of several factors. The rate of dune-line erosion is low, and dune elevations, in excess of 20 feet, are well above the storm-surge flood level. Maritime forest grows in the area, only partly eliminated in a trailer-court development near the pier. The island is backed by a wide area of tidal marshland. Unfortunately, the width of this "safety" zone is narrow, limiting development considerably.

Paradise Fishing Pier to three-quarters of a mile south of the pier is a zone where the upland is so narrow that the current rate of erosion and high potential for breaching of the dunes during a storm may cause future problems. Overwash, flooding, and new inlet formation are likely possibilities. Although there are safe sites today, it will be a short period of time before all of this zone is unsafe.

Northern West Onslow Beach to just south of Ocean City Fishing Pier is an area that appears to be safe. The dune line is nearly continuous and at a moderate elevation. Air photos and past records suggest that the near-shore zone would suffer in a major hurricane. Some of the existing development is at very low elevations and may be subject to flooding during storms. Inlets have occupied this stretch of coast in the past, and the open sound water and limited fringe of marsh offer little protection against inlet formation in the future.

Ocean City Fishing Pier to Pender County Line is fronted by a 10-foot-high dune that offers some protection to the area behind it. Over most of the island the elevation is less than 10 feet, however, and vegetation cover is very limited. The finger canals are poor areas to develop because they are potential sites for new inlets and pollution as well. Groundwater and surface water on the sound side are both polluted. Given the density of development, it is unlikely that the water quality will improve until some sort of regional waste-treatment system is constructed.

PENDER COUNTY

Three islands make up the Pender County coast: the southwest portion of Topsail Island, Lea Island, and No Name Island. All of the islands are privately owned. Topsail is being developed most rapidly in the Pender County section. Lea Island has been subdivided for development; development plans for No Name Island are currently unknown to us.

As noted previously, Topsail Island was dealt a series of heavy blows by Hurricanes Hazel, Diane, Connie, Helene, and Donna; no information on storms has been published for Lea and No Name. Following is a summary of the topography and histories of overwash, erosion, and inlet formation on all three islands.

Topsail Island: The remainder of Topsail Island lies within the boundaries of Surf City and Topsail Beach. A significant portion of this narrow island corridor contains safe sites for development. Heavy development has taken place in unsafe areas, however, and has created new hazards.

Pender County line to the Scotch Bonnet Pier is a continuation of the caution zone that begins in Onslow County. A distinct area to be avoided lies just northeast of the pier. Here dunes are broken and elevations are less than ten feet; the area in back of the dunes is therefore a potential overwash pass. Most of the area lacks adequate vegetation cover. This flat, terrace-like, central strip of island was inundated by Hurricane Hazel.

The Scotch Bonnet Pier to Surf City Pier is labeled as a safe zone in Figure 47. It should be noted, however, that this area is one of overcrowded mobile-home parks. Such crowding creates two potential hazards. First, crowded trailers require the close spacing of septic tanks. The sandy soil, porous and permeable, allows septic

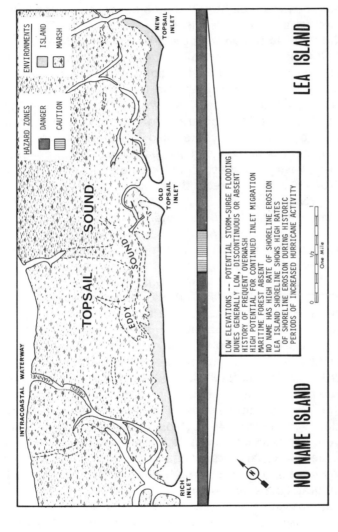

Fig. 47. Site analysis for Lea and "No Name" Islands

107

effluent to seep through it quickly, but cannot filter and purify it. Thus, the sewage either moves down to contaminate groundwater, or rises to the surface of the ground during a heavy rainfall to flow into the marsh. (EPA studies with dye have confirmed the latter.)

Second, the trailers contribute to flying debris during a storm. You may have your trailer well anchored and battened down before the storm, but does your neighbor? Amid a storm, one loose trailer can wreak havoc as a wind-borne missile.

Surf City Pier to the Jolly Roger Pier on Topsail Beach may be considered relatively safe for limited development. The dune line is remarkably continuous and of elevations greater than 15 feet above sea level. The presence of maritime forest or thickets, vegetated back-dunes, and the absence of overwash are signs of stability. Erosion data, though at times contradictory, seem to indicate either a low rate of erosion or minor accretion of the shoreline. The zone safe for development is narrow and fragile. Finger-canal construction, removal or leveling of dunes, and stripping of vegetation should be avoided. Since marsh protects the back side of the island, it, too, should be preserved.

Jolly Roger Pier to Sea Vista Motel includes an area that is partially protected by a continuous frontal dune. Much of the dune line, however, is less than 15 feet above mean sea-level and would not endure a severe hurricane. Most of the island behind the dune is less than 10 feet in elevation and would submerge during a major storm such as Hurricane Hazel. If enough water were pushed into the sound, backflooding could cut a new inlet anywhere from this zone to the end of the island. This area should be approached with caution. If the frontal dune is maintained, a well constructed stilt house on the higher elevations might "weather" most storms.

Sea Vista Motel to New Topsail Inlet is probably the most dangerous part of Topsail Island. A sequence of historic air photos (Reference 39, Appendix C) shows that this end of the island formed as the inlet migrated southwest. (Most of this area was open water in 1938.) Dune formation and vegetation have not been adequate to stabilize the added land; sand has not built up to elevations that would be above storm-surge flood levels. Also, it is likely that the inlet will migrate back to its former position. Yet development of streets, cottages on small lots, and finger canals dredged into the back of the island (Figure 46) has proceeded rapidly. As a result, today's residents are faced with the task of maintaining the ocean-front beach, establishing dunes, and combating sound-side erosion. Water-pollution problems have been created, and any hurricane of measurable severity will damage this area. Moreover, the finger

108

canals may become inlets.

According to an Army Corps of Engineers report, the year-round population of Topsail Beach grew from 41 residents in 1970 to an estimated 1,000 in 1973. The development that accompanied this growth "occurred in an unplanned manner" and generated serious wastewater problems. Development continues today at a rapid rate; the pollution problems persist; and a major hurricane will likely strike the area at some future date.

Lea Island developers are currently offering ocean-front tracts of land for sale. Advertisements for the land contain such key words as "exclusive," "select," "private," and "secluded," to suggest that a fortunate few can own this property, isolated from all others. While you *can* own your own private island, beaches are public domain to the high-tide line. The developers have noted that ocean-front property "still belongs to nature" and claimed that in planning for development of the property, "care has been taken to preserve the quality of the environment."

Most of the island is less than 10 feet in elevation, and much is less than 5 feet above mean sea-level. A continuous foredune is absent over most of the island, and where present, is usually less than 10 feet above mean sea-level. Overwash is common, and the island has undoubtedly been inundated by past hurricanes.

Lea Island has approximately two miles of beach front (Figure 47). New Topsail Inlet, at the northeast end of the island, is migrating into the island as the Topsail spit grows. Though Old Topsail Inlet on the southwest end may also be migrating to the southwest, the sand spit that forms this end of the island is simply too low and unprotected for safe development.

With the exception of the two or three local dunes that exceed 20 feet, the island is poorly suited for development, even of the type seen on Figure Eight Island. The development plan calls for 48 lots ranging in size from over one acre to somewhat under four acres. Developers have the right to subdivide any lot into two lots. It's difficult to imagine 48 safe cottage sites on Lea, and 96 safe ones are inconceivable. The ocean front indeed still belongs to nature!

No Name Island, a 2.5-mile-long barrier backed by wide marsh, is similar in size and shape to Figure Eight Island. Unlike Figure Eight, however, it lacks high elevations and shows numerous overwash passes in the low dunes. A vegetated, 15- to 20-foot-high dune ridge on the back side of the northeast end of the island could provide a few safe building sites, but most of the island is simply too low and unprotected to be safe (Figure 47). High rates of shoreline erosion and inlet migration are also hazardous to development.

109

NEW HANOVER COUNTY

From Rich's Inlet to the vicinity of New Inlet south of Fort Fisher, three barrier islands and a section of mainland coast exhibit 27 miles of beach front. This coastline exemplifies numerous stages of development that range from the highrises of Wrightsville Beach to the natural environments of Masonboro Island, yet unchanged by man. One of North Carolina's more popular resort areas, this region offers attractions that appeal to a variety of tastes. Because of the wide interest in this part of the coast, a field trip guide by Drs. William J. Cleary and Paul Hosier has been included in Appendix D. Following are brief profiles of island safety relative to development.

Figure Eight Island: This beautiful island provides extreme examples of safe and unsafe sites. The island is privately owned, has only one access route via a private bridge and low-elevation causeway, and contains exclusive development. Perhaps the most beautiful homes of the entire North Carolina coast are found on Figure Eight. In addition to their aesthetically pleasing architecture, many of the homes—built on stilts that extend to the roof—appear to have been designed and built to exist in harmony with the natural environment. There is little evidence of dune or forest destruction, though considerable indication of salt-marsh destruction. Most structures are behind the dune line (where one exists) or on high ground in dense maritime forest.

Figure 48 indicates that the safest areas for development are the one-mile stretch of forested dunes on the northeast half of the island, and the one-half-mile area of development behind the dune ridge and away from the finger canals on the southwest half of the island. Areas along the last one-half mile of roadway on the southwest half of the island and at the east end of the causeway are of questionable safety. In these areas the dune ridge is either low and discontinuous, or absent; overwash has occurred here during the 1950s and 1960s. Along the roadway, elevations are generally below storm-surge level. It should be noted here that an area can be overwashed even if it is above storm-surge level; this is illustrated by the unvegetated portion of the mid-island. The absence of shrubs and larger vegetation in this area indicates frequent overwash. Photographs indicate that the shoreline of most of the island is eroding at a significant rate (in excess of 5 feet per year during the late 1960s and early 1970s, although the long-term average has been somewhat less). Structures without natural protection, near the shoreline, or at low elevations may be in jeopardy during storms. This is particularly true for two areas of development located in flood

110

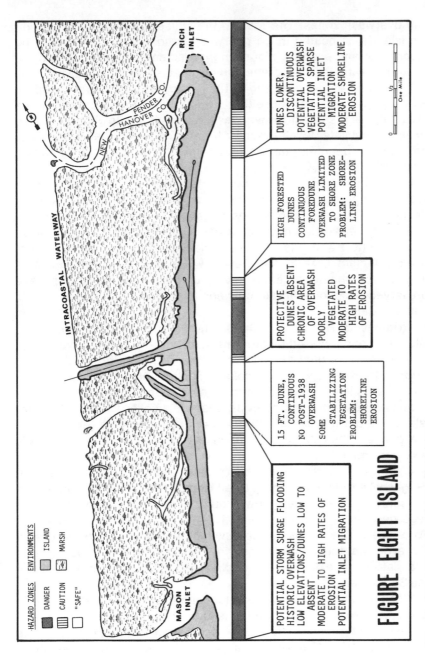

Fig. 48. Site analysis for Figure Eight Island

and overwash zones. The road to the causeway—the only route off the island—is located in an overwash zone and may therefore be blocked during a storm. Figure Eight residents certainly should not delay in leaving the island when an evacuation warning is given.

The extreme northeast end of the island has not been developed. Although some dunes more than 15 feet high do exist, most of the area has been subject to overwash. Its proximity to Rich Inlet also rules against safe development. This section of the island, however, provides a beautiful natural area for the enjoyment of island residents.

Figure Eight is an island of contrasts. Some very well-built homes are on dangerous building sites. In an emergency, even the residents of well constructed homes on safe sites must exit the island on potentially hazardous escape routes. Since most development on Figure Eight Island has occurred relatively recently, there has not been sufficient time to see how it will stand up to the forces of nature. We should note, however, that thus far, residents have preserved spacious areas between cottages; this precaution is commendable.

Wrightsville Beach and Shell Island: Prior to 1965, these two islands were separated by Moore's Inlet, which migrated throughout the 1900s to its final 1965 position before it was artificially filled. Prior to 1965 there was no access to Shell Island other than by boat; this may explain the sharp contrast in development on the two now-joined islands today. Wrightsville Beach is an overdeveloped barrier island without a trace of natural-island environments (except for a few dunes); Shell Island remains in its natural state (though it likely awaits a similar fate).

Figure 49 indicates the lack of safe areas for development on Wrightsville Beach (including Shell Island). The artificially filled inlet, still marked by an area of low ground across the island, should be regarded as a danger zone. Nearly all of the remainder of Wrightsville Beach is safe for development. It should be stressed, however, that these conditions may be transient since this island is in a mature stage of shoreline engineering. (See Chapter 3, Truths of the Shoreline.)

Since the early 1920s, various techniques have been employed to combat shoreline erosion on the island. These ranged from the emplacement of groins in 1923 to the beach-nourishment project of the 1960s and 1970s (Figure 50). Numerous hurricanes have raked the island. Hurricane Hazel destroyed 89 buildings—mainly the row fronting the beach—and damaged several hundred others.

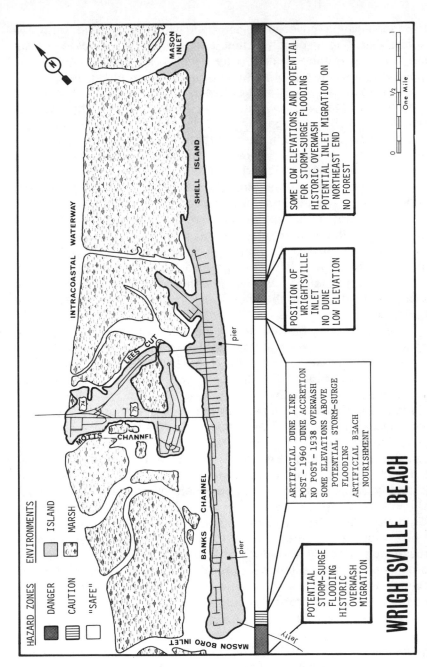

Fig. 49. Site analysis for Wrightsville Beach

HAZARD ZONES

- ▮ DANGER
- ▦ CAUTION
- ☐ "SAFE"

ENVIRONMENTS

- ☐ ISLAND
- ▨ MARSH

ARTIFICIAL DUNE LINE
POST-1960 DUNE ACCRETION
NO POST-1938 OVERWASH
SOME ELEVATIONS ABOVE
POTENTIAL STORM-SURGE
FLOODING
ARTIFICIAL BEACH
NOURISHMENT

POSITION OF
WRIGHTSVILLE
INLET
NO DUNE
LOW ELEVATION

SOME LOW ELEVATIONS AND POTENTIAL
FOR STORM-SURGE FLOODING
HISTORIC OVERWASH
POTENTIAL INLET MIGRATION ON
NORTHEAST END
NO FOREST

POTENTIAL
STORM-SURGE
FLOODING
HISTORIC
OVERWASH
MIGRATION

WRIGHTSVILLE BEACH

0   1/2   1
         One Mile

Hurricane Diane covered streets with water and sand from the beach. Because of beach losses, a nourishment project to rebuild the beach foredune system was initiated in 1965. At this time, 2,993,000 cubic yards of sand were pumped from Banks Channel and placed along 14,000 feet of beach front from north of Mercer's Pier to the Masonboro Inlet jetty. Though renourishment was resumed in 1966 and again in 1970, by 1976 the beach was again scarped by erosion and in need of renourishment. Lacking the non-federal share of funds for renourishment, islanders resorted to bulldozing to smooth the scarp (Figure 18, page 41). By mid-1977 it was apparent that this last effort to stabilize had done nothing but supply more sand for immediate wave attack.

Development at the high-water line does not enhance the safety of the island. Both commercial and domestic buildings have been constructed at the back of the beach in the former location of Moore's Inlet (Figures 49 and 51). Beach erosion and overwash place such structures in jeopardy; it is likely that the Holiday Inn and the beach cottages northeast of the motel will incur severe damage from hurricanes.

Safe development on Wrightsville Beach includes buildings such as the Blockade Runner Motel that have been set back behind the foredune at elevations above the 100-year flood level. Masonboro Inlet has been stabilized by the jetty, so that the potential for inlet migration is limited (Figure 49).

Masonboro Island: The narrow width, low elevation, and resulting widespread overwash make this island highly unsuitable for development (Figure 11, page 24). Although it was originally accessible from Carolina Beach before the Carolina Beach Inlet was cut in 1952, permanent development never took place. This island provides a field model of a near-natural barrier island whose dynamics may be studied in order to better understand what is altering development islands. Presently Masonboro Island is being considered for a state park. Using it for such a purpose would be most reasonable since it would provide 8 miles of public beach and preserve the only extensive natural-island area in New Hanover County. Should the island become such a park, access should be by boat, as the system probably could not support a "permanent" road.

Carolina Beach: The North Carolina coast from Carolina Beach Inlet to Wilmington Beach (Figure 52) illustrates most of the shoreline truths outlined in Chapter 3. Many hurricanes have pounded this coast, but it was not until the 1890s that storm accounts began to make mention of this area. The island was struck by a

Fig. 50. Beach and dune replenishment area, Wrightsville Beach (1977)
Photo by Jim Page

severe storm in 1893. In October 1898, the Navy lookout station was destroyed by heavy storm surf. A year later, numerous resort cottages were washed away or damaged. Carolina Beach, however, continued to grow—as did the dollar-value of the damage resulting from these storms. The most destructive storm of the first half of this century was probably that of August 1, 1944, when Carolina Beach incurred some of the heaviest damage of the entire North Carolina coast. Fortunately, the area was evacuated prior to being hit by 40-foot waves. Two piers were destroyed; trees were blown down; and the water rose high enough to flood second-story levels.

In 1952, the artificial Carolina Beach Inlet was cut to provide a shorter access route to the ocean from waters in back of Carolina Beach and Masonboro Island. Shoreline engineers pointed out that such an inlet would interrupt the natural southerly flow of sand along the beach. Nevertheless, recreational interests triumphed: the inlet was constructed, and the longshore sand-flow was interrupted. Sand was trapped or moved into the inlet, and erosion accelerated on the shoreline.

The major hurricanes of the 1950s would of course have caused shoreline erosion under any set of circumstances; however, the cutoff of sand supply by the inlet left this vulnerable beach without nourishment to maintain its natural protective buffer or to rebuild it-

Fig. 51. Development at high-water line creates hazards: Wrightsville Beach (1977)

Photo by Jim Page

self after storms. For this reason, artificial nourishment was begun in 1955 and has continued to the present.

Hurricane Hazel destroyed over 370 buildings and damaged over 700 others on Carolina Beach. Streets and structures were buried by shifting sand, though high winds and flooding caused most of the damage. Less than a year later, in August 1955, the successive Hurricanes Connie and Diane caused additional damage. In 1959, Hurricane Grace flooded parts of the area. Since then, lesser storms have altered the shoreline.

The behavior and safety of Carolina Beach correlate to two natural divisions in its shoreline. From Carolina Beach Inlet to the vicinity of the Carolina Beach City Hall the coast is that of a barrier island backed by a narrow sound. Most of the shoreline of this area is either unsafe or of questionable safety (Figure 52). The area from Carolina Beach through Wilmington Beach, attached to the mainland without the intervening sound, has partial forest cover and elevations above the 100-year storm-surge flood level, making it a relatively safe zone. However, shoreline development should be avoided because of overwash, erosion, and the need for continuous shoreline stabilization.

Kure Beach: Although the coast from Kure Beach to Fort Fisher is technically part of the mainland, the location of the Cape Fear River

116

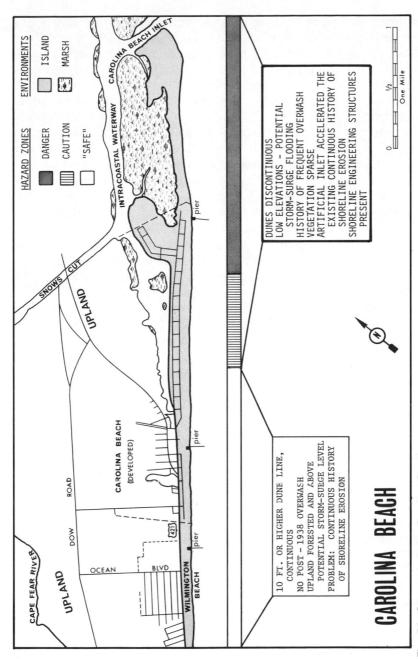

HAZARD ZONES   ENVIRONMENTS

- ▓ DANGER
- ▦ CAUTION   ▦ MARSH
- ☐ "SAFE"
- ▒ ISLAND

CAPE FEAR RIVER

UPLAND

OCEAN

DOW ROAD

BLVD

421

WILMINGTON BEACH

pier

UPLAND

CAROLINA BEACH
(DEVELOPED)

pier

SNOWS CUT

UPLAND

INTRACOASTAL WATERWAY

CAROLINA BEACH INLET

pier

10 FT. OR HIGHER DUNE LINE,
   CONTINUOUS
NO POST-1938 OVERWASH
UPLAND FORESTED AND ABOVE
   POTENTIAL STORM-SURGE LEVEL
PROBLEM: CONTINUOUS HISTORY
   OF SHORELINE EROSION

DUNES DISCONTINUOUS
LOW ELEVATIONS - POTENTIAL
   STORM-SURGE FLOODING
HISTORY OF FREQUENT OVERWASH
VEGETATION SPARSE
ARTIFICIAL INLET ACCELERATED THE
   EXISTING CONTINUOUS HISTORY OF
   SHORELINE EROSION
SHORELINE ENGINEERING STRUCTURES
   PRESENT

N

0   ½
One Mile

CAROLINA BEACH

Fig. 52. Site analysis for Carolina Beach

117

on the back side of the area creates a land form similar to that of a barrier island. Most of the development here is more than 20 feet above mean sea-level, on stable, vegetated areas (Figure 53) and can be considered safe. This safety is indicated by the hurricane record for Kure Beach as compared to that of other beach resorts in the area. Hurricane Hazel, for example, severely damaged or destroyed hundreds of buildings at Carolina and Wrightsville Beaches, but only 80 buildings at Kure Beach. In most of the other 1950s storms, Kure Beach survived with minor damages, and Hurricane Diane (1955) is said to have helped build up the dune line. Even in an area considered safe, shoreline development should be avoided, however. It is not uncommon for sand to be washed into the streets of the first block facing the beach. Some structures, of course, must be placed on the beach (piers, for example); owners of these structures simply must plan for damage and replacement. (Kure Beach fishing pier has been destroyed eleven times.)

The sound side of Kure Beach is a safe area. It will not be developed privately, however, since it is part of the Sunny Point Military Ocean Terminal grounds. Similarly, historic Fort Fisher, a state park, will not be developed. With a high rate of shoreline erosion, the area is put to better use as a park than as construction sites.

The beach extension south of Fort Fisher to the Brunswick County line resumes the barrier-island formation. Figure 53 outlines the reasons this zone would be dangerous to develop.

BRUNSWICK COUNTY

This southernmost shoreline extends from Corncake Inlet, north of Cape Fear, to the South Carolina border. Approximately 40 miles of ocean beach is distributed along six islands of various sizes and at different stages of development. All of the lands are privately owned and extensive development is planned.

With the exception of part of Bald Head Island, this coast has an east-west orientation and is partially protected by Cape Fear. While this orientation protects the coast from the typical northeast winter storms, it places the coast directly across the path of hurricanes that track from southerly directions. This high vulnerability to hurricanes was described in an Army Corps of Engineers report (Reference 43, Appendix C) that recounted the effects of 1954's Hurricane Hazel:

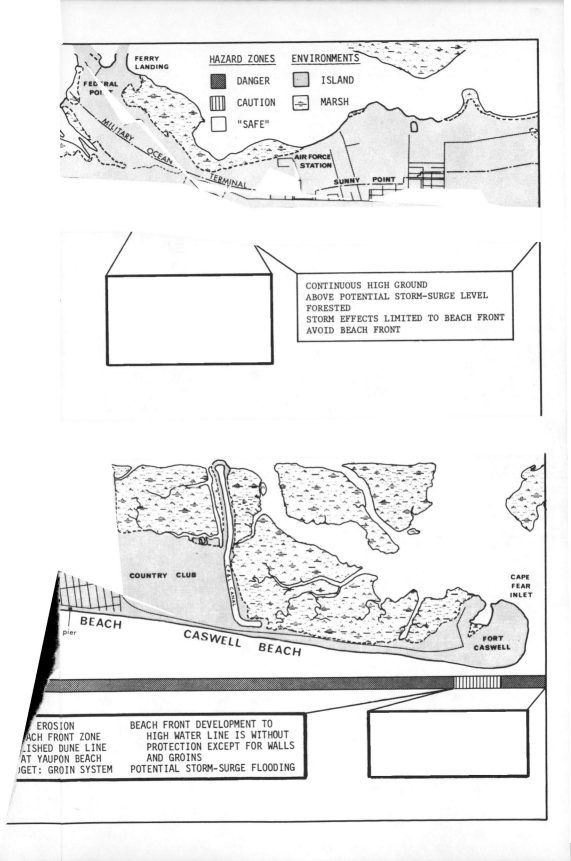

HAZARD ZONES

- DANGER
- CAUTION
- "SAFE"

ENVIRONMENTS

- ISLAND
- MARSH

FERRY LANDING

FEDERAL POINT

MILITARY OCEAN TERMINAL

AIR FORCE STATION

SUNNY POINT

CONTINUOUS HIGH GROUND
ABOVE POTENTIAL STORM-SURGE LEVEL
FORESTED
STORM EFFECTS LIMITED TO BEACH FRONT
AVOID BEACH FRONT

COUNTRY CLUB

C F & L CANAL

CAPE FEAR INLET

BEACH

pier

CASWELL BEACH

FORT CASWELL

EROSION
ACH FRONT ZONE
ISHED DUNE LINE
AT YAUPON BEACH
GET: GROIN SYSTEM

BEACH FRONT DEVELOPMENT TO
HIGH WATER LINE IS WITHOUT
PROTECTION EXCEPT FOR WALLS
AND GROINS
POTENTIAL STORM-SURGE FLOODING

PRE-HAZEL (October 15, 1954)

Fig. 55. Pre-Hazel (1954), Post-Hazel, and Today: Long Beach

Photos courtesy U.S. Corps of Engineers

EDIATELY POST-HAZEL

Fig. 54.

TODAY

> Apart from the loss of life and the property damages suffered by individuals, the most striking aspect of the storm's effects on Brunswick County shores was the absolute totality of the damage and its implications with respect to storm damages under conditions of dense development. In this connection, there was hardly a vestige of human habitation on the Brunswick County shore following the storm. . . . In view of the severity of tides and waves attendant with Hurricane Hazel, it is reasonably certain that, had development been complete in the area, it would also have been totally destroyed.

The danger to life and property on barrier islands cannot be stated more dramatically; however, it appears that today's island residents have either forgotten Hazel or are unaware of the hurricane's impact (Figure 55).

Smith Island (Bald Head Island): Cape Fear is the remains of a series of forested dune and beach ridges separated by low areas, including active marsh. The approximate trend of the wooded ridges is east-west, and they are truncated by the north-south beach of the east side of the island. The island has been the center of a protracted battle between developers and environmentalists, in part because it is the northernmost island in the U. S. that grows certain types of palms and other subtropical plants.

The entire eastern shore from Corncake Inlet to the tip of the Cape is represented as a high-hazard zone in Figure 53. Records indicate that this stretch of shoreline is eroding and frequently overwashed. Only the narrow strips of well-forested high ground inland from the beach can be considered safe for development.

In contrast, the southern flank of the island—especially the southwest sector now being developed—is generally safer. Although this area has been subject to shoreline erosion and partial overwash, most of the development—on the higher-forested areas—has remained intact. This development is somewhat exclusive since Bald Head Island is accessible only by boat; the instability of Corncake Inlet and the related strand of frequent overwash rule out construction of a northern road.

Oak Island: This island (Figure 54), accessible via N. C. Highway 211 to Highway 133, consists of two distinct parts. A heavily forested back area of high ground extends from the Intracoastal Waterway on the landward side to Big Davis Canal along most of the ocean side. Extensive marsh backs this part of the island along its northeast end, and a narrow marsh separates the southwest half of the upland from the island strand facing the ocean. Protected from open wind and water, well forested, and sufficiently elevated above most storm-surge flooding, this upland area is fairly safe for

121

development. The forepart of the island consists of a barrier island approximately 13 miles long; and relatively narrow except in the vicinity of Yaupon Beach, where it is attached to the mainland. Because areas of this frontal island vary, individual beach sections are discussed below.

Caswell Beach makes up the eastern one-third of the island. It is named after old Fort Caswell (1826-1865), the ruins of which are now located inside the grounds of the North Carolina Baptist Assembly. The buildings of this religious retreat are essentially on the sound side of the curved end of the island, away from the inlet shore and protected by a marsh. Accretion has taken place on this end of the island.

The remainder of Caswell Beach, in contrast, shows signs that generally warn against development. Old tree stumps and some black peat layers are exposed on much of the beach between the Coast Guard Lighthouse and the Yaupon Beach line (Figure 56). At the back of the beach is a wave-eroded scarp exposing the roots of shrubs growing on old, stabilized dunes. The red sand exposed on some of these small cliffs suggests forest soil. All these features are natural signs that a forested barrier island (around 1,000 years ago) and a younger salt marsh once occupied the present beach's position. Only a few hundred years ago the beach was well seaward of old *terra firma,* but erosion soon changed the position of what was safe. An Army Corps of Engineers report (Reference 70, Appendix C) states that this section of shoreline is eroding at an average rate of more than 5 feet per year. The thin line of defensive dune between the beach and highway has been breached in several places. From the Carolina Power and Light Company discharge channel to the area of old Fort Caswell the upland area is narrow, and maritime forest vegetation has either not been well established or has been removed. Generally, this entire stretch of island should be regarded as too hazardous for development.

Yaupon Beach is the central community of Oak Island and marks the area where the back-island forest extends to the beach without the intervening marsh. The land slopes evenly down to the beach and dunes are absent. Groins and rubble-fill attest to the severe erosion that is occurring along the entire beach from the end of Highway 133 to Middleton Street (Figure 57). Although portions of the beach front are vegetated, the erosion, low elevation, and overwash render the area unsafe for development. Some lots that are being developed in this zone have unfortunately been stripped of vegetation—the last bit of protection available on the island. In

122

Fig. 56. Stumps on Caswell Beach, a sure sign of erosion (1977)

Photo by Jim Page

contrast, the area along Yaupon Drive is higher, forested, and relatively safe for development.

Long Beach makes up the rest of Oak Island. The back portion of the island between the Intracoastal Waterway and Big Davis Canal is relatively safe from the threats of wave erosion, storm surge and overwash. Only a severe hurricane would pose danger, and the forest cover would act as a buffer to storm damage. The frontal portion of the island from 58th Street to the west end of the island varies in safety. Beach-front buildings on the east end (46th Street to 58th Street and the undeveloped area beyond) lack natural protection (Figure 58). Dunes are absent or scarped, and the beach is eroding, exposing peat and a few stumps at low water. Some cottages have protective wooden walls and groins at the high-tide line. Older air photos show that portions of this part of the island have been overwashed. In a severe storm this frontal row of buildings is likely to be "wiped clean." To the west (beyond 46th Street) the row of frontal dunes is again present; there are some very high dunes through the middle and on the sound side of the island (along 20th to 23rd Streets and 42nd to 54th Streets); and portions of the area are forested. Thus, sites throughout this area must be evaluated individually for safety. A site on or behind a stable (vegetated) dune

123

Fig. 57. A losing battle: Yaupon Beach (1977)

Photo by William J. Neal

would be safe; a beach-front site would not. The area from 54th to 57th Streets marks the former position of an old inlet (open from approximately 1949 to 1956), recognizable by white shells in the sand and the absence of vegetation. This area to the end of the island is either unsafe or potentially unsafe for development. The topographic lows, absence of vegetation, lack of protective marsh on the sound side, and presence of a migrating inlet make any development in the area highly unadvisable.

Holden Beach: This island, which has been undergoing development since the early 1950s, is accessible via N. C. Highway 130. Prior to development, the entire island was subject to overwash; since Hurricane Hazel, however, overwash has been common only on the western portion (Big Beach). Although accretion is occurring, shoreline erosion is occurring at a faster rate. The eastern end of the island is eroding and lacks primary-dune protection. Forested and shrub areas on the inner island provide better protected sites, but much of the island lacks sufficient vegetation or ample elevation to be safe from wind, waves, or storm-surge flooding. Finger canals cause other problems. (See Chapter IV introductory information.)

The extreme western portion of the island (Big Beach) is presently undeveloped. Narrow and sparsely vegetated, the area is subject to

Fig. 58. No protection: Long Beach (1977)

Photo by William J. Neal

126

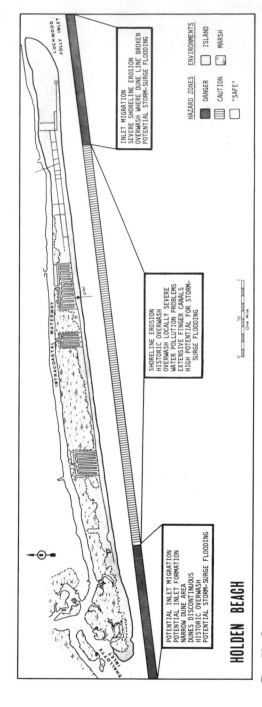

Fig. 59. Site analysis for Holden Beach

erosion. Furthermore, Shallotte Inlet is likely to continue to migrate and affect the configuration of this end of the island.

Ocean Isle Beach (Hales Beach): Development of the central portion of this island has been extensive, especially around a series of long finger canals on the eastern side of N. C. Highway 904. This type of development is extending north around a newer series of fourteen finger canals that join the Intracoastal Waterway through a *single* channel. Circulation and flushing are problems in such canal systems. Furthermore, at least part of this development is on filled marsh. Residents of the area can expect stagnation and related water problems. Shorter finger canals are being constructed on the back side of the western part of the island to provide access to Tubbs Inlet through one of the tidal channels. Development along these finger canals may create a new problem: if inlet migration results in the sand-filling of the tidal-creek mouths, the Army Corps of Engineers may be pressured to spend *public* funds to keep such channels open to transport a relatively few individuals.

Figure 60 summarizes the relative safety of the frontal portions of the island. The areas adjacent to Tubbs and Shallotte Inlets should be regarded as particularly hazardous zones. Portions of the eastern shoreline lack dune protection and are overwashed periodically. Cottage owners have found it necessary to build up an artificial dune line, and this sand row would not offer much protection in a major storm. Many of the beach-front cottage owners should expect damage to their homes, even in an "average" storm. A major hurricane similar to Hurricane Hazel could destroy all of this property.

Sunset Beach and Bird Island: The southern extremity of the North Carolina coast is appropriately marked by the contrasting examples of a developed and an undeveloped island. Sunset Beach, accessible from the mainland by a secondary state road, is developed. The island is a miniature of both "good" and "bad" development seen along the state's coast.

Though hit hard by the hurricanes of the 1950s, Sunset Beach has experienced accretion along the front midsection of the island. The buildup of sand has been so great that it has filled the space under the old fishing pier, requiring the construction of a new pier that extends out over the water. This accretion has resulted in a wide zone of low, irregular topography that is vegetated with grass and shrubs, separating the beach and the older primary dune. This low area would be able to absorb some storm energy and to afford some protection to the houses behind the dune line. However, no struc-

127

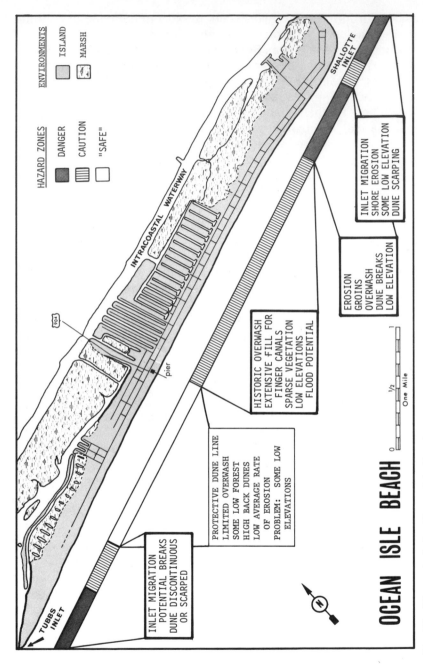

ENVIRONMENTS

☐ ISLAND
▨ MARSH

HAZARD ZONES

■ DANGER
▥ CAUTION
☐ "SAFE"

INTRACOASTAL WATERWAY

SHALLOTTE INLET

TUBBS INLET

pier

INLET MIGRATION
POTENTIAL BREAKS
DUNE DISCONTINUOUS
OR SCARPED

PROTECTIVE DUNE LINE
LIMITED OVERWASH
SOME LOW FOREST
HIGH BACK DUNES
LOW AVERAGE RATE
  OF EROSION
PROBLEM: SOME LOW
  ELEVATIONS

HISTORIC OVERWASH
EXTENSIVE FILL FOR
  FINGER CANALS
SPARSE VEGETATION
LOW ELEVATIONS
FLOOD POTENTIAL

EROSION
GROINS
OVERWASH
DUNE BREAKS
LOW ELEVATION

INLET MIGRATION
SHORE EROSION
SOME LOW ELEVATION
DUNE SCARPING

0   ½   1
One Mile

OCEAN ISLE BEACH

Fig. 60. Site analysis for Ocean Isle Beach

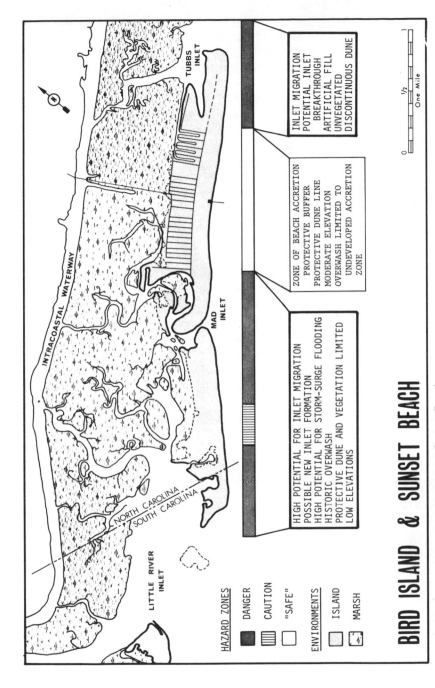

Fig. 61. Site analysis for Bird Island and Sunset Beach

129

tures other than highly expendable ones (such as fishing piers) should be built on the accretion strip.

The eastern extension of the island is unsafe for development (Figure 61). Finger canals have cut through dunes and vegetation. As recently as 1966, Tubbs Inlet was east of the vegetated portion of the island, just beyond the last finger canal. Since then the area has been filled, and the inlet artificially relocated in a position farther east (Figure 62). This artificial position is approximately the same as the natural position of the inlet in the late 1930s. Between the late 1930s and mid-1960s the inlet migrated to the now-filled 1966 position, and there is nothing to suggest that the inlet will not follow this path again. Yet this unstable, artificial-fill zone is being developed! Even the aesthetics cannot support such a risk: the area is quite barren. Property owners in this section should hope that the island continues to accrete and that there is some dune buildup before the next major hurricane.

Mad Inlet, off the western end of the island, has shown a tendency to wander. The tidal creek in back of the western extension has eroded into the island, damaging the developed area. During a storm, a new inlet might cut the island east of Mad Inlet. Although some forested areas remain, there is considerable moving sand on the western back-area of the island. Figure 61 outlines additional reasons that the area should be regarded as a danger zone.

Bird Island, currently undeveloped, is too small to support large-scale development. There are a few sites, at best, that are high enough and have sufficient ground cover to qualify as potentially safe.

SOUTH OF THE BORDER:
A VIEW OF THE FUTURE?

Our traverse has brought us from Currituck County to the vicinity of Calabash—an area that experienced the "eye" of Hurricane Hazel. On a clear day when flying over Bird Island, one can see giant figures on the far southern horizon; it's almost as if the highrise beach-front buildings of North Myrtle Beach were marching north from South Carolina's heavily developed strand. Will these silent sentinels come to dominate the North Carolina coast, or will an acceptable master plan check their current advance?

How do you prefer your beach?

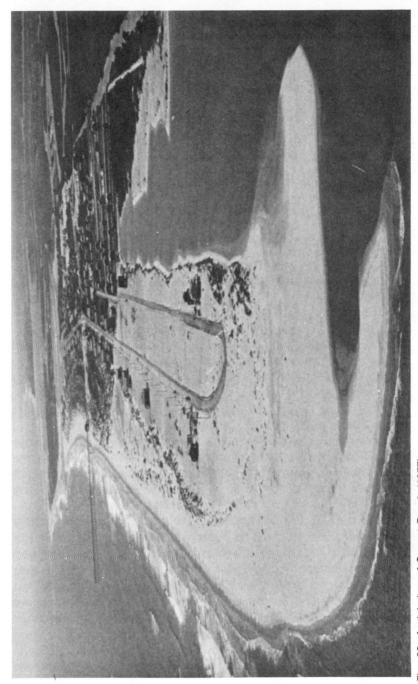

Fig. 62. Aerial view of Sunset Beach (1977)

131

5

The Barrier Island, Land Use, and the Law

INCREASING CONTROLS

From the beginnings of development, the coastal system has been altered and damaged by man. Today, however, an awareness of this problem has arisen, and a turning point has been reached. The maintenance of this system is now recognized as essential to the welfare of both nature and the coastal population. The necessity of planning for wiser use, maintenance, and conservation of the coastal zone is becoming more apparent to an increasingly wider segment of society. The future of the coast now depends on community action.

As noted in previous chapters, barrier islands are dynamic systems. Our philosophy on shoreline development is that land use should be in harmony with the natural processes and environments that constitute these systems. Various segments of society view the coastal zone differently and as a result, hold different philosophies of land use. The extremes range from that of untouched preservationism to that of total unplanned urbanization. Like other decisions affecting the public, decisions on land use are usually made by government. Various special-interest groups create political pressures that often lead to legislation of compromise. In this manner, regulations have been and will continue to be established with the intention of insuring reasonable, multiple land-use of the coastal zone, and of protecting inhabitants as well as the natural environment. Current and prospective owners of barrier-island property should be aware of their responsibilities under current law with respect to development and land use, and of the likelihood of later regulation.

Following is a partial list of current land-use regulations applicable to the North Carolina coast. The explanations we have provided are general; Appendix B lists the agencies that will supply more specific information. The regulations listed range from federal laws protecting all of society to county laws serving the interests of the local population.

THE NORTH CAROLINA COASTAL AREA MANAGEMENT ACT

The Federal Coastal Zone Management Act of 1972 (CZMA) set in motion an effort by all coastal states to manage their shorelines and thereby conserve a vital national resource. Key requirements of CZMA are coastal land-use planning based on land classification, and identification and protection of critical areas.

In 1974, the *North Carolina Coastal Area Management Act* (CAMA) was passed in compliance with the federal CZMA, qualifying North Carolina for federal aid in implementing effective coastal management. CAMA was intended to insure good land-use and resource development, and conservation of resources to protect the quality of life for citizens of the coastal zone. It was prompted by the growing recognition of the barrier-island system as a natural resource, and the increasing realization that the actions of a person on one piece of island property may affect all other property within the system. The CAMA created the Coastal Resources Commission, responsible for the development of a coastal-zone management program. While this program sets statewide goals and objectives, each of the twenty coastal counties prepares additional plans based on its own needs. The Coastal Resources Commission also designates Areas of Environmental Concern (AECs), usually after such areas are recognized by the county. (Environmental conditions in AECs require that special care be exercised by those who alter or develop such areas. High-hazard environments such as inlets or coastal wetlands, for example, are designated AECs.)

The goal of the CAMA is not to stop or prohibit development, but rather to control it. Yet it has met with opposition from coastal residents. It requires planning, which some regard as inconvenient, and a change in attitude or behavior that interferes with the get-rich-quick motives of others.

CAMA is timely in that it fosters the conservation of the barrier islands through required planning and the coordination of existing laws that control development. (See Appendix B, Dredging, Filling, ... Waterways, Dune Alteration, Sanitation.) Though the law is modern, it may encourage citizens of the 1970s to develop the virtues of the old-timers: prudence in building, foresight in responding to island processes, wisdom in planning, and thrifty utilization of the natural resources at hand.

We encourage coastal residents to obtain a copy of *Ecological Determinants of Coast Area Management* (Reference 75, Appendix C), which presents a more thorough treatment of the physical, social, political, and legal questions at issue along the coast.

THE NATIONAL FLOOD INSURANCE PROGRAM

One of the most significant legal pressures applied to encourage land-use planning and management in the coastal zone is the National Flood Insurance Program. The *National Flood Insurance Act of 1968* (Pl 90-448) as amended by the *Flood Disaster Protection Act of 1973* (Pl 92-234) requires that a homeowner meet certain conditions to be eligible to purchase flood insurance. Persons living in flood zones who do not purchase such insurance may not, in the event of a flood, receive any form of federal financial assistance. Such forms of assistance as FHA and VA home-mortgage insurance, aid from the Small Business Administration or U. S. Department of Agriculture, and federal funds for shoreline-engineering, waste-disposal, or water-treatment systems are available only when the individual and community involved comply with the requirements of the law. Communities must adopt certain land-use and control measures in order to make flood insurance available at reasonable rates. Although the law is often associated with river floodplains, it also applies to barrier islands and coastal areas subject to storm-surge flooding. (See Chapter 4.)

The initiative for qualifying for the program rests with the community, which must contact HUD or the National Flood Insurers Association. (See Appendices B and C.) Once the community adopts initial land-use measures and applies for eligibility, HUD designates the community as eligible for subsidized insurance under the Emergency Program. HUD then issues a Flood Hazard Boundary Map that delineates flood-prone areas, and conducts a rate study. Ultimately, HUD provides the community with a Flood Insurance Rate Map and 100-year-flood (flood having a one percent annual probability of occurrence) elevation data. Subsidized insurance is available for all existing and new construction except for those buildings constructed in the flood-hazard area *after* publication of the Flood Insurance Rate Map. Eligibility requirements vary among pole houses, mobile homes, and condominiums.

Before building or buying a home, an individual should ask certain basic questions:

Is the community I'm locating in covered by the program?
If not, why?
Is my building site above the 100-year flood level?
What are the structural requirements for my building?
What are the limits of coverage?

Most lending institutions and building inspectors will be aware of mapped flood-prone areas, but it would be wise to confirm such information with the appropriate insurance representative or program office. (See Appendix B, Insurance.)

Government literature states that the National Flood Insurance Program would not have been necessary "had adequate and assured flood-insurance been available through the private insurance market." The point, in fact, is that private insurance companies operate on sound business principles. They know that property located in high-hazard zones such as floodplains or barrier islands is a great risk—both physically and financially. Any insurance company "worth its salt" either refuses to insure such property, or insures it at a very high rate. For this reason, the National Flood Insurance Program was developed to compensate property owners in high flood-risk areas.

The program undoubtedly has its flaws. Some feel that requirements for insurance eligibility should be more stringent and suggest the possibility of denying flood insurance and federal-disaster assistance to current property owners located in coastal high-hazard areas that do not meet the standards for new construction. Other problems include establishing actuarial rates, funding the necessary coastal studies to define high-hazard areas, and understanding the effects of long-term federal subsidy. Perhaps the greatest obstacle to the success of the program is the uninformed individual who stands the most to gain from it. One study examined public response to flood insurance and found that many people have little awareness of the threat of floods or the cost of insurance, and view insurance as an investment with the expectation of a return rather than a means of sharing the cost of natural disaster.

Purists may debate the merits of taxpayer-subsidized federal programs, but the National Flood Insurance Program's objectives are worthwhile in that pressure is applied to assure wiser management of hazardous flood zones. As taxpayers, we hope that in the long run this program will cost less than the growing expense of. national-disaster relief needs generated by flooding.

WASTE DISPOSAL

Protecting barrier-island water resources is essential to the safeguarding of the many ways in which man uses the island. Fisheries, all forms of water recreation, and the general ecosystem depend on high-quality surface waters. Potable water supply is drawn mainly from groundwater which must also be of high quality. As noted in Chapter 4, water resources are being threatened, and the existing pollution is costly to both local communities and the state. However, with one-fifth of the North Carolina shellfishing areas closed and local residents' health threatened, the loss is more than economic.

Improper land-use relative to waste disposal, and inadequate planning for treatment of the increasing waste necessitate additional regulation at all levels of government.

The *Federal Water Pollution Control Act Amendments of 1972* control any type of land use that generates—or may generate— water pollution. They also regulate dredging and filling of wetlands and water bodies through the Army Corps of Engineers. (See Appendix B, Dredge and Fill, Sanitation, and Water Resources.) The *Marine Protection, Research and Sanctuaries Act of 1972* regulates dumping into ocean water. The *Water Resources Development Act of 1974* also provides for comprehensive coastal-zone planning.

The North Carolina Department of Natural Resources and Community Development and the Department of Human Resources (State Board of Health) share jurisdiction in approving sanitary-disposal systems through a permit system. (See Appendix B, Sanitation, and Septic System Information.) *Laws and Rules for Ground Sewage Disposal Systems* (Chapter 10, Subchapter 10A, Section 1900 of the North Carolina Administrative Code), which governs all disposal systems of 3,000-gallons-or-less-per-day design capacity, took effect on July 1, 1977, and is enforced by the State Board of Health. The new law places greater emphasis on site factors such as soil, topography, and location with respect to water bodies. Systems of greater than 3,000-gallons-per-day design capacity are regulated by the North Carolina Environmental Management Commission.

BUILDING CODES

Most progressive communities require that new construction adhere to the provisions of a recognized building code. If you plan to build in an area that does not follow such a code, you would be wise to insist that your builder do so to meet your requirements. Local building officials in storm areas often adopt national codes that contain building requirements for protection against high wind and water. Compiled by knowledgeable engineers, politicians, and architects, these codes regulate the design and construction of buildings and the quality of building materials. Examples of such codes are the Southern Standard Building Code (Reference 84, Appendix C), used chiefly on the Southeast and Gulf coasts, and the Uniform Building Code (Reference 86, Appendix C), used mainly on the West coast. Both are excellent codes.

It is emphasized that the purpose of these codes is to provide *minimum* standards to safeguard lives, health, and property. These codes protect you from yourself as well as your neighbor.

In North Carolina, builders must adhere to the North Carolina State Building Code. For example, construction in areas subject to winds greater than 75 miles per hour must comply with the code's Appendix D, "Wind Resistive Construction," which specifies means of anchoring structures to resist high winds. Buildings within 150 feet of the high-water mark of the Atlantic Ocean must be supported on piles in accordance with Section 3.0, the Sand Dune Ordinance.

In Hancock County, Mississippi, which suffered greatly from Hurricane Camille in 1969, an ordinance known as the Flood Protection Ordinance of Hancock County has been enacted. Its purpose is to regulate land use in special flood-hazard areas to minimize damage caused by flooding and high winds. Its essential points, noted below, may serve as a guide to other shoreline communities that do not yet have such protective regulations.

> The ordinance applies only to a limited area that includes all land within 1,000 feet of the shoreline, as well as all land below the 15-feet-above-sea-level elevation. This zoning is predicated on a flood level of 13.1 feet above mean sea-level, the highest level of flooding that, on the average, is likely to occur once every 100 years (that is, a flood level that has a one percent chance of occurring each year).

> **Water:** The lowest-floor level of new residential construction must be at least 13.1 feet above mean sea-level. Parts of a non-residential structure and its utility and sanitary facilities con-

structed below this height must be floodproofed up to 13.1 feet above mean sea-level. The floodproofing measures must be certified by a registered professional engineer and include such items as adequate anchorage to resist flotation and lateral movement, installation of watertight doors and bulkheads, and similar measures to improve resistance to flooding. Certain structures such as accessory buildings, sheds, garages, parking lots, and loading areas which normally are not occupied, are exempted from this regulation.

Wind: The wind requirements are based on a wind with a velocity of 120 miles per hour, at a height of 30 feet above the ground, coming from any direction. The force of the wind expressed in pounds per square foot varies with the height and shape of the structure. A table in the code lists the pressures for winds at different heights above the ground, from a low pressure of 22 pounds per square foot for a height of 0 to 5 feet, to a high of 100 pounds per square foot for a height of 1,000 feet and over. These pressures are to be multiplied by the shape factors which are tabulated for various configurations.

Whereas the allowable loads (or stresses) may be increased one third above the normal limit for members and connections subjected to wind or to wind and other loads, such an increase does not apply to foundations, towers, cantilevered projections or metal sheathing. Computations for overturning and uplift are based on at least 150% of the wind overturning moment. The stability (resistance to 150% of the calculated wind uplift) may be provided by dead loads, anchors, attachments, the weight of the earth over footings, the withdrawal resistance of piles, or the resisting moment of vertical members embedded in the ground. All wind forces must be transferred to the ground. In no case shall any roof be designed for less than 30 pounds live load per square foot of horizontal projection.

Unfortunately for Hancock County, Mississippi, this ordinance was written after the bad experience of Hurricane Camille. Had it been in effect long enough prior to that hurricane to effectively control development, a great deal of destruction would have been prevented.

MOBILE-HOME REGULATIONS

Mobile homes differ in construction and anchorage from "permanent" structures. The design, shape, lightweight construction materials, and other characteristics required for mobility—or for staying within axle-weight limits—create a unique set of potential problems for residents of these dwellings. Because of their thinner walls, for example, mobile homes are more vulnerable to wind and wind-borne projectiles than are permanent homes. Thus, North Carolina has a separate building code for mobile homes. Mobile-home dwellers in North Carolina may wish to obtain a copy of the "State of North Carolina Regulations for Mobile Homes" (Reference 101, Appendix C). Recognizing the effects of coastal-zone processes, the code requires that mobile homes manufactured after October 1, 1973, and offered for sale on the North Carolina coast meet the state's hurricane-zone requirements. Most counties and municipalities also have ordinances pertaining to mobile homes (for example, the Carteret County Mobile Home and Trailer Park Ordinance).

Mobile-home anchorage is commonly regulated by local ordinance. Tie-downs should be—and often are—required to make the structure more stable against wind stress. (For recommendations, see Chapter 6 section on mobile homes.) Violations of anchorage or foundation regulations may go undetected unless there are a sufficient number of conscientious inspectors to monitor trailer courts. One poorly anchored mobile home can wreak havoc with adjacent homes whose owners abided by sound construction practice. Some mobile-home-park operators or managers are alert to such problems and see that they are corrected; others simply collect the rent.

The spacing of mobile homes is also regulated by local ordinance. Providing residents with open space between homes, this type of ordinance preserves some aesthetic value for a neighborhood. It also helps to maintain a healthier environment. For example, if mobile-home septic tanks are closely spaced, there is the potential for groundwater or surface-water pollution. Similarly, if mobile homes are built too close to finger canals, canal water may become polluted. (See Chapter 4.)

Some courts and local officials are true to the electorate and see that these ordinances are enforced; many, however, do not. In 1974, the Raleigh *News and Observer* printed an article that traced the history of controversy surrounding mobile-home parks in Surf City:

A 1971 town ordinance required 25 feet of space between trailers, while in fact, they were sometimes separated by as little as 4 feet. A citizens' committee took the town commission to task, and a superior-court judge later ordered the town to "strict compliance" with its 1971 ordinance. Four days later, the town commission passed a new ordinance lowering the required spacing to 15 feet! At the same meeting, moreover, the commission set aside a zone for trailers on the northwest side of the town, an area that state officials regarded as too marshy to safely accommodate septic-tank systems. According to the newspaper article, three of the five commissioners were mobile-home-park owners! While this case may be isolated or extreme, it clearly demonstrates that the mobile-home dweller should not rely on others to see that he is protected. He should see to it himself that his home meets all ordinance regulations, or, better yet, that it is safer than required. (See Chapter 6.)

WIND

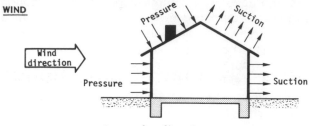

Arrows show direction of forces on house.

DROP IN BAROMETRIC PRESSURE

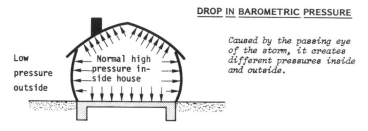

Caused by the passing eye of the storm, it creates different pressures inside and outside.

High pressure inside attempts to burst house open.

WAVES

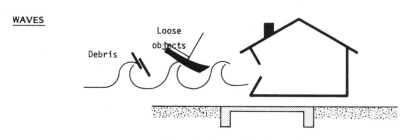

House is damaged by force of waves.

HIGH WATER

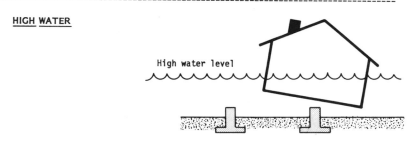

Unanchored house floats off foundations.

Fig. 63. Forces to be reckoned with

6

Hurricane-Resistant Construction

ASSETS AND LIABILITIES:
THE CONCEPT OF BALANCED RISK

Within the constraints of economy and the environment, there generally exists the probability of failure for any structure. The objective in designing a building—whether in the Piedmont of North Carolina or on the Outer Banks—is to create a structure that is both economically feasible and functionally reliable. A person building or buying a home wants a house that he can afford, and one that will last a long time without collapsing. In order to obtain such a house, a balance must be achieved among financial, environmental, and other special conditions.

The individual building or buying a home in an exposed area should fully comprehend the risks involved—the likelihood of harm to his home or family—and weigh them against the benefits he will derive from his residence. Similarly, the developer building a motel should weigh the possibility of destruction and death during a hurricane versus the money or other advantages he may gain from such a building. Then and only then should he proceed with construction. For both the homeowner and the developer, proper construction and location reduce the risks involved.

The concept of balanced risk should take into account the following fundamental considerations:

1. Construction must be economically feasible; therefore,
2. Ultimate and total safety is *not* obtainable for most homeowners on barrier islands.
3. A coastal structure, exposed to high winds, waves, or flooding, should be stronger than a structure built inland.

4. A building with a planned long life, such as a year-round residence, should be stronger than a building with a planned short life, such as a mobile summer home.
5. A building with high occupancy, such as an apartment building, should be safer than a building with low occupancy, such as a single-family dwelling.
6. A building housing elderly or sick people should be safer than a building housing able-bodied people.

The purpose of this chapter is to familiarize the layman with the effects of natural forces on the coastal dwelling, and to guide him in selecting or constructing a safe house or building so that he need not depend entirely on a builder or developer whose profit motive may color his judgment. The subject of construction is treated in considerably more detail in several of the references listed in Appendix C (particularly References 64, 91, and 93). We suggest that the interested reader obtain copies of these references for supplemental study.

FORCES TO BE RECKONED WITH

Hurricanes are large, violent, tropical disturbances with winds rotating counterclockwise (north of the equator) about a low-pressure center. Wind velocities are above 75 miles per hour. The diameter of the storm may vary from 60 to 1,000 miles. Although tornadoes are more violent, they are smaller and of shorter duration. Thus, hurricanes are more destructive—and more feared. One or more tornadoes may strike along with a hurricane, adding to the destruction.

Hurricanes are the greatest menace to the North Carolina coastal dweller. Statistics indicate that these storms have the greatest chances of occurring along the North Carolina-to-Georgia coast in the late summer and early fall months—August, September, and October.

Figures 63, 64A, and 64B illustrate the effects of a hurricane forces on houses and other buildings.

Hurricane Winds

Let us evaluate the speed of a hurricane wind in terms of the pressure it exerts. A 100 m.p.h. wind exerts a pressure or force of

144

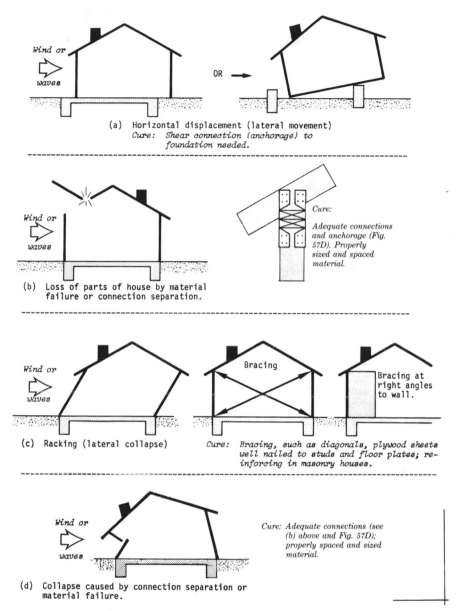

(a) Horizontal displacement (lateral movement)
Cure: Shear connection (anchorage) to foundation needed.

(b) Loss of parts of house by material failure or connection separation.

Cure:

Adequate connections and anchorage (Fig. 57D). Properly sized and spaced material.

(c) Racking (lateral collapse)

Bracing

Bracing at right angles to wall.

Cure: Bracing, such as diagonals, plywood sheets well nailed to studs and floor plates; reinforcing in masonry houses.

(d) Collapse caused by connection separation or material failure.

Cure: Adequate connections (see (b) above and Fig. 57D); properly spaced and sized material.

Fig. 64A. Modes of failure

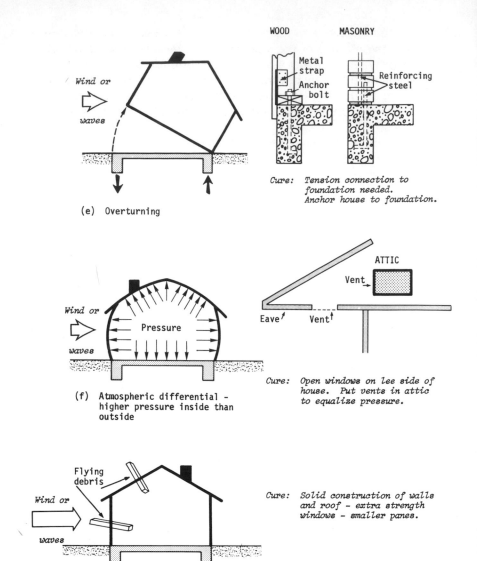

WOOD MASONRY

Metal strap
Anchor bolt

Reinforcing steel

Cure: *Tension connection to foundation needed. Anchor house to foundation.*

(e) Overturning

Wind or waves

Pressure

(f) Atmospheric differential – higher pressure inside than outside

ATTIC

Vent

Eave Vent

Cure: *Open windows on lee side of house. Put vents in attic to equalize pressure.*

Flying debris

Wind or waves

Cure: *Solid construction of walls and roof – extra strength windows – smaller panes.*

(g) Penetration by flying debris

Source: *U. S. Defense Civil Preparedness Agency, publication TR-83*

Fig. 64B. More modes of failure

about 40 pounds per square foot on a flat surface. The pressure varies with the square of the velocity. For example, a wind of 190 m.p.h. velocity would exert a force of 144 pounds per square foot. This force is modified by several factors which must be considered in designing a building. For example, the effect on a round surface such as that of a sphere or cylinder is less than the effect on a flat surface. Also, winds increase with height above ground, so a tall structure is subject to greater pressure than a low structure.

A house or building designed for inland areas is built primarily to resist vertical loads. It is assumed that the foundation and framing must support the load of the walls, floor, and roof, and relatively insignificant wind forces.

A well built house in a hurricane-prone area, however, must be constructed to withstand a variety of strong wind forces that may may come from any direction. While many people think that wind damage is caused by uniform horizontal pressures, most, in fact, is caused by uplift (vertical), suctional, and torsional (twisting) forces. High horizontal pressure on the windward side is accompanied by suction on the leeward side. The roof is subject to downward pressure, and, more importantly, to uplift. Often a roof is sucked up by the uplift drag of the wind; some towers and signboards adequately designed for straightforward winds have fallen from torsional winds. Usually the failure is in the devices that tie the parts of such structures together.

Hurricane Barometric Pressure Changes

As the low-pressure center of a hurricane—and to a greater extent, tornado—suddenly passes by, its effects on structures can be very dramatic. If a house is sealed at a normal barometric pressure of 30 inches of mercury, and the external pressure suddenly drops to 26.61 inches of mercury, the pressure exerted within the house would be 245 pounds per square foot. An ordinary house would explode if it were leakproof. Fortunately, most houses leak, but they must leak fast enough to prevent damage. Hence, wise owners leave windows slightly open during storms. If at all possible, open the windows on the leeward side and close them on the windward. Venting the underside of the roof at the eaves also helps to equalize internal and external pressure (Figure 64B), especially if the entrance hatch from the living floor to the attic is left open.

Hurricane Waves

Waves can cause severe damage not only in forcing water onshore to flood buildings, but also in throwing boats, barges, piers, houses, and other floating debris inland against standing structures. In addition, waves can destroy coastal structures by undermining the sand dunes that lie under them, causing the structures to collapse. It is possible, however, to design buildings for survival in crashing storm surf. Many lighthouses, for example, have survived storm surge. But in the balanced-risk equation, it usually isn't economically feasible to build ordinary cottages to resist such forces.

The force of a wave may be realized when one considers that a cubic yard of water weighs over three-fourths of a ton; hence a breaking wave moving shoreward at a speed of up to 60 miles per hour can be one of the most destructive elements of a hurricane.

Rising Water: Storm Surge

Storm surge is a rise in sea level above the normal water level during a storm. In most hurricanes it is the inundation of the coastal zone by storm surge and the accompanying storm waves which most often causes property damage and loss of life.

Storm surge develops off the coast over deep water, where low pressure in the center of the storm causes the surface of the sea to bulge upward. A second phenomenon occurs simultaneously: the counterclockwise swirl of the hurricane winds induces a similar swirling of the water. This water swirl eventually extends downward to a depth of about 300 feet. The highest wind speeds are to the right of the hurricane's path—to the east if the hurricane is traveling north; hence, the maximum water swirl is also to the right of the storm's path. In a typical storm, the maximum wind speed and water swirl will occur about 15 miles to the right of the track, making this the point in most danger from the storm.

As the hurricane approaches land and the water becomes shallower, the swirling water scrapes bottom and begins to build up in a mound to a height considerably above sea level. At the coastline, storm surge may reach a height of 15 to 20 feet or more above sea level. During Hurricane Camille, the surge rose to 25 feet above mean sea-level in some locations.

Often the pressure of the wind backs water into streams or estuaries already swollen from the exceptional rainfall brought by the hurricane. Water is piled into the sounds by the offshore storm. When the storm moves inland, the sound water suddenly flows back seaward much faster than it flowed into the sound. The result is that a home may be flooded from the sound side of the island. This flooding is particularly dangerous when the wind pressure keeps the intide from running out of tidewater rivers so that the next normal high tide can push the accumulated waters back—and higher still.

People who have cleaned out the mud and contents from a house that was subjected to rising water have vivid memories of the effects of flooding. An unanchored house can float off its foundation and come to rest against another house, severely damaging both. Even if a house itself is left structurally intact, flooding may destroy its contents.

Proper coastal development takes into account the expected level and frequency of storm surge for the area. In general, building standards require that the first habitable level of a dwelling be above the 100-year storm-surge level. (At this level, a building has a one percent probability of being flooded in any given year.)

WHAT TO LOOK FOR IN A HOUSE ALREADY BUILT

If instead of building a new house you are selecting a house already built in an area subject to flooding and high winds, consider the following factors: 1) where the house is located, 2) how well the house is built, and 3) how the house can be improved.

Geographic Location

Chapter 4 outlines the principles for selecting a safe site. Some of the more pertinent suggestions are repeated in the following list for emphasis.

1. Check the elevation above sea level.
2. Check the means of egress for times of emergency.
3. Find out the frequency of high water at the level of the house site and on the exit route. Needless to say, if the house is high enough to eliminate the risk of damage from high water and

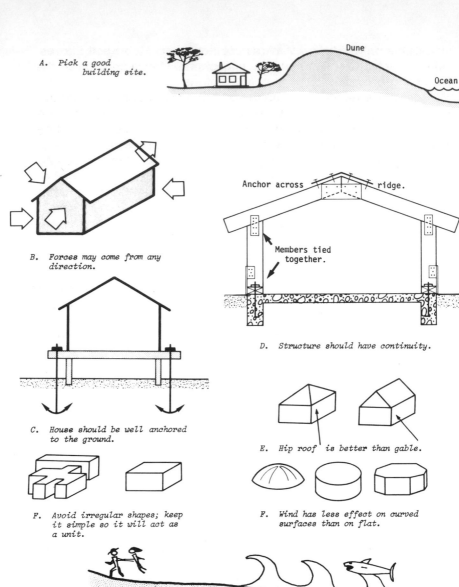

A. Pick a good building site.

Dune

Ocean

B. Forces may come from any direction.

Anchor across ridge.

Members tied together.

C. House should be well anchored to the ground.

D. Structure should have continuity.

E. Hip roof is better than gable.

F. Avoid irregular shapes; keep it simple so it will act as a unit.

F. Wind has less effect on curved surfaces than on flat.

G. PLAN YOUR ESCAPE ROUTE!

Fig. 65. Some rules

vulnerable only to high winds (as are homes on Pine Knoll Shores, Bogue Banks, for example), you can give less consideration to the means of egress.

A low site is vulnerable to flooding from high water and should obviously be avoided. A hilltop location, on the other hand, is more vulnerable to the force of the wind. If the house is surrounded by woods or nearby homes, it is partially protected from the wind. Though damage may be caused by falling trees or limbs, it is usually less than that caused by the full force of unobstructed wind. Two or more rows of trees are better than a single row, and trees 30 feet or more in height afford better protection than smaller ones.

4. Visit prospective property after a hard rain to determine whether the lot drains. In some places the groundwater table is close to the surface of the ground. This factor combined with a flat lot may cause the entire yard to become a pool in a hard rain and to remain one for some time. Also consider street drainage at this time. Some coastal areas are so flat that rainwater floods the street and does not drain off for a day or two.

You can modify the house after you have bought it but cannot change its location. At this point, then, stop and consider: Do the pleasures and benefits of this location balance the risks and disadvantages? If not, look elsewhere for a home; if so, then study the house itself.

How well built is the house?

In general, the principles used to evaluate an existing house are the same as those used in building a new one. (See References 84 to 92, Appendix C.)

Before you thoroughly inspect the house in which you are interested, look closely at the adjacent homes. If poorly built they may float over against your house and damage it in a flood. You may even want to consider the type of people you will have as neighbors: will they "clear the decks" in preparation for a storm or leave items in the yard to become wind-borne missiles?

1. *The house should be well anchored to the ground.* If it is simply resting on blocks, rising water may cause it to float off its foundation and come to rest against your neighbor's house or out in the middle of the street. If well built and well braced internally, it may be possible to move the house back to its proper location, but chances are great that the house will be too racked to be habitable (Figure 64A).

151

If the house is on piles, posts, or poles, check to see if the floor beams are adequately bolted to them. If it rests on piers, crawl under the house—if space permits—to see if the floor beams are securely connected the to the foundation. If the floor system rests unanchored on piers, do not buy the house.

It is difficult to discern whether a house built on a concrete slab is properly bolted to the slab because the inside and outside walls hide the bolts. If you can locate the builder, ask him if such bolting was done. Better yet, if you can get assurance that construction of the house complied with the provisions of a building code serving the needs of that particular region, you can be reasonably sure that all parts of the house are well anchored—the foundation to the ground, the floor to the foundation, the walls to the floor, and the roof to the walls.

Be aware that many builders, carpenters, and building inspectors—particularly the older ones—who are accustomed to traditional construction, are apt to regard metal connectors, collar beams, and other such devices as newfangled and unnecessary. If consulted, they may assure you that a house is as solid as a rock when in fact, it is far from it. Nevertheless, it is wise to consult the builder or knowledgeable neighbors when possible.

2. *The roof should be well anchored to the walls* to prevent uplifting and separation from the walls. Visit the attic to see if such anchoring exists. Simple toe-nailing (nailing at an angle) is not adequate; metal fasteners are needed. Depending on the type of construction and the amount of insulation laid on the floor of the attic, these may or may not be easy to see. If a roof truss or braced rafters were used, it should be easy to see whether the various members—such as the diagonals—are well fastened together. Again, simple toe-nailing will not suffice. Some builders, unfortunately, nail together the parts of a roof truss just enough to hold it together to get it in place. A collar beam or gusset at the peak of the roof (Figure 66) provides some assurance of good construction.

3. *Quality roofing material should be well anchored to the sheathing.* A poor roof covering will be destroyed by hurricane-force winds, allowing rain to enter the house and damage ceilings, walls, and house contents. Galvanized nails—two per shingle—should be used to connect wood shingles and shakes to wood sheathing, and should be long enough to penetrate through the sheathing (Figure 66). Threaded nails should be used for plywood sheathing. For roof slopes that rise 1 foot for every 3 feet or more of horizontal distance, exposure of the shingle should be about one-fourth of its length (4

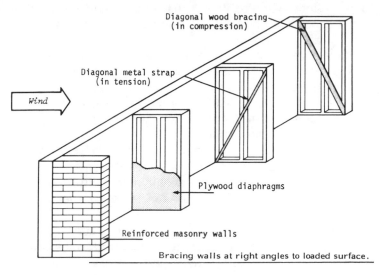

Diagonal wood bracing (in compression)

Diagonal metal strap (in tension)

Wind

Plywood diaphragms

Reinforced masonry walls

Bracing walls at right angles to loaded surface.

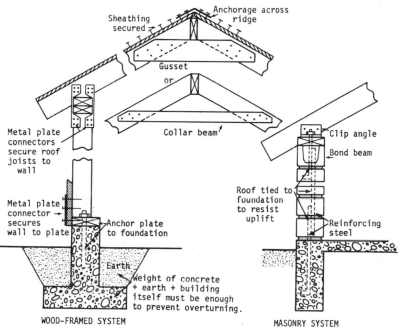

Anchorage across ridge

Sheathing secured

Gusset

or

Metal plate connectors secure roof joists to wall

Collar beam

Clip angle

Bond beam

Roof tied to foundation to resist uplift

Metal plate connector secures wall to plate

Anchor plate to foundation

Reinforcing steel

Earth

Weight of concrete + earth + building itself must be enough to prevent overturning.

WOOD-FRAMED SYSTEM

MASONRY SYSTEM

(Source: U. S. Defense Civil Preparedness Agency, Publication TR-83)

Fig. 66. Where to strengthen a house

153

inches for a 16-inch shingle). If shakes (thicker and longer than shingles) are used, less than one-third of their length should be exposed.

In hurricane areas, asphalt shingles should be exposed somewhat less than usual. A mastic or seal-tab type or an interlocking shingle of heavy grade should be used. Roof underlay of asphalt-saturated felt and galvanized roofing nails, or approved staples—six for each three-tab strip—should be used.

Corrugated iron sheets are sufficient if held down properly so that they can't detach from the sheathing to become missiles. New construction in Darwin utilizes battens or strips on top of the roof sheets to aid in holding them down. If the sheets are aluminum, the nails or screws should not be iron; the two materials are not compatible, and combining them results in corrosion.

The fundamental rule to remember in framing is that all structural elements should be fastened together and anchored to the ground in such a manner as to resist all forces, regardless of which direction these forces may come from. This prevents overturning, floating off, racking or disintegration.

4. *The shape of the house is important.* A hip roof, which slopes in four directions, is better able to resist high winds than a gable roof, which slopes in two directions (Figure 65). This was found to be true in Hurricane Camille, and later, in Cyclone Tracy, which devastated Darwin, Australia, in December 1974. The reason is twofold: the hip roof offers a smaller shape for the wind to blow against, and its structure is such that it is better braced in all directions.

Note also the horizontal cross-section of the house (the shape of the house as viewed from above). The pressure exerted by a wind on a round or elliptical shape is about 60% of that exerted on the common square or rectangular shape; the pressure exerted on a hexagonal or octagonal cross-section is about 80% of that exerted on a square or rectangular cross-section (Figure 65).

The design of a house or building in a coastal area should minimize structural discontinuities and irregularities. A house should have a minimum of nooks and crannies and offsets on the exterior, as damage to a structure tends to concentrate at these points. When irregularities are absent, the house reacts to storm winds as a complete unit (Figure 65).

5. *Brick, concrete-block, and masonry-wall houses should be adequately reinforced.* (This reinforcing is hidden from view.) Building codes applicable to high-wind areas specify the type of

mortar, reinforcing, and anchoring to be used in construction. If you can get assurance that the house was built in compliance with a building code, consider buying it.

A poured concrete bond-beam at the top of the wall just under the roof is one indication that the house is well built. However, most bond beams are formed by putting in reinforcing and pouring concrete in U-shaped concrete blocks. From the outside, however, you can't distinguish these U-shaped blocks from ordinary ones, and therefore can't be certain that a bond beam exists; the vertical reinforcing should penetrate the bond beam.

Some architects and builders use a stacked bond—one block directly above another—rather than overlapped or staggered blocks, because they believe it affords a better appearance. The stacked bond is definitely weaker than the latter. Unless you have proof that the walls were adequately reinforced to overcome this lack of strength, you should avoid this type of construction.

In Hurricane Camille, the brick veneer of many homes separated from the wood frame, even when the houses remained standing. Asbestos-type outer wall panels used on many houses in Darwin, Australia, were found to be brittle, and broke up under the impact of wind-borne debris in Cyclone Tracy. Both types of construction should be avoided along the coast.

Consult a good architect or structural engineer for advice if you are in doubt about any aspects of the house. A few dollars spent for wise counsel may save you from later financial grief.

What can be done to improve an existing house?

If you presently own a house or are contemplating buying one in a hurricane-prone area, you will want to know how to improve occupant protection in the house. If so, you should obtain the excellent publication, *Wind Resistant Design Concepts for Residences,* by Delbart B. Ward (Reference 91, Appendix C). Of particular interest are the sections on building within a residence a shelter module in which to take refuge during a tornado. Several other pertinent references are listed in Appendix C.

Suppose your house is resting on blocks but not fastened to them, and is thus not adequately anchored to the ground. Can anything be done? One solution is to treat the house like a mobile home, screwing ground anchors into the ground to a depth of 4 feet or more and fastening them to the underside of the floor systems.

155

(See Reference 64, Appendix C, *How to Live with an Island,* Figures 23-26, for illustrations of a type of ground anchor that can be used.) Calculations to determine the needed number of ground anchors will differ between a house and a mobile home, since one is affected differently from the other by the forces of wind and water. Note that recent practice is to put these commercial steel-rod anchors in at an angle so as to better align them with the direction of the pull. If a vertical anchor is used, the top 18 inches or so should be incased in a concrete cylinder about 12 inches in diameter. This prevents the top of the anchor rod from bending or slicing through the wet soil from the horizontal component of the pull.

Diagonal struts—either timber or pipe—may also be used to anchor a house that rests on blocks. This is done by fastening the upper ends of the struts to the floor system, and the lower ends to individual concrete footings substantially below the surface of the ground. These struts must be able to take both uplift when on the windward side and compression when on the leeward side, and should be tied into the concrete footing with anchoring devices such as straps or spikes.

If the house has a porch with exposed columns or posts, it should be possible to install tie-down anchors on the tops and bottoms of them. Steel straps should suffice in most cases.

When accessible, roof rafters and trusses should be anchored to the wall system. Usually the roof trusses or braced rafters are sufficiently exposed to make it possible to strengthen joints (where two or more members meet)—particularly at the peak of the roof—with collar beams or gussets (Figure 66).

A competent carpenter, architect, or structural engineer can review the house with you and help you decide what modifications are most practical and effective. Do not be misled by someone who is resistant to new ideas. One builder told a homeowner, "You don't want all those newfangled straps and anchoring devices. If you use them the whole house will blow away, but if you build in the usual manner (with members lightly connected) you may lose only part of it."

In fact, of course, the very purpose of the straps is to prevent any or all of the house from blowing away. The Southern Standard Building Code (Reference 84, Appendix C) says, "Lateral support securely anchored to all walls provides the best and only sound structural stability against horizontal thrusts, such as winds of exceptional velocity." And the cost of connecting all elements securely adds very little to the cost of the of frame of the dwelling—under

156

10%—and a very much smaller percentage to the total cost of the house.

If the house has an overhanging eave and there are no openings on the underside of it, it may be quite feasible to cut openings and screen them. These openings keep the attic cooler (a plus in the summer) and help to equalize the pressure inside and outside of the house during a storm with a low-pressure center.

Examine the house and select the best room to stay in during a storm. (This is *not* an alternative to evacuation prior to a hurricane.) A small windowless room such as a bathroom, utility room, den, or storage space, is usually stronger than one with windows. A sturdy inner room—with more than one wall between it and the outside—is safest. The fewer doors, the better; an adjoining wall or baffle wall shielding the door adds to the protection.

Consider bracing or strengthening the interior walls. Such reinforcement may require removing the surface covering and installing plywood sheathing or strap bracing. Where wall studs are exposed, bracing straps offer a simple way to achieve needed reinforcement against the wind. These straps are commercially produced and are made of 16-gauge galvanized metal with pre-punched holes for nailing. These should be secured to studs and wall plates as nail holes permit. Bear in mind that they are good only for tension. A 10d (10 penny) nail is 3 inches long. Where compression forces are to be resisted, use 1″ x 6″ lumber with three 10d nails per stud and wall plate. If plywood is used it should be 4′ x 8′ x ½″ thick for the full wall height. Secure plywood at the edges with 10d nails at 4″ centers and at inner studs with 10d nails at 8″ centers (Figure 66).

If after reading this, you agree that something should be done to your house, do it now. Do not put it off until the next hurricane or tornado hits you. Do not be like the man (described by the French philosopher Montaigne) who, in his travels, came upon a river and stood on the bank, waiting for the river to flow past so he could cross with dry feet.

KEEPING DRY: POLE OR "STILT" HOUSES

In coastal regions subject to flooding by waves or storm surge, one method of minimizing damage is to raise the lowest floor of a residence above the expected water level. This is done by building on a mound of compacted soil or by constructing on an elevated foundation anchored in the subsoil. The first method is not suited to

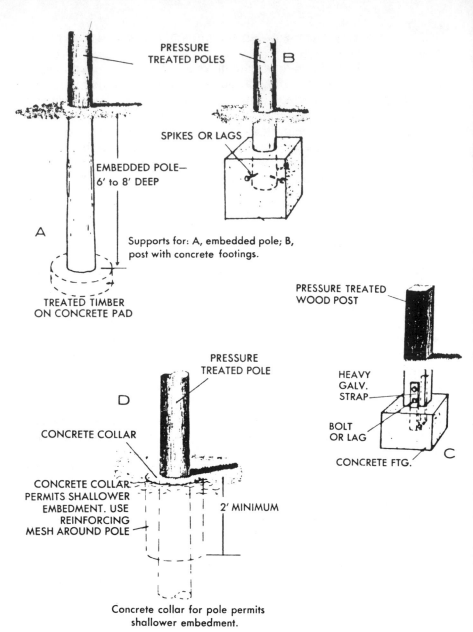

PRESSURE TREATED POLES

B

SPIKES OR LAGS

EMBEDDED POLE—
6' to 8' DEEP

A

Supports for: A, embedded pole; B, post with concrete footings.

TREATED TIMBER
ON CONCRETE PAD

PRESSURE TREATED
WOOD POST

PRESSURE
TREATED POLE

D

CONCRETE COLLAR

HEAVY
GALV.
STRAP

CONCRETE COLLAR
PERMITS SHALLOWER
EMBEDMENT. USE
REINFORCING
MESH AROUND POLE

2' MINIMUM

BOLT
OR LAG

CONCRETE FTG.

C

Concrete collar for pole permits
shallower embedment.

Fig. 67. Shallow and deep supports for poles and posts

Source: Southern Pine Association

158

the coastal zone because mounded soil erodes easily during flooding and overwash. In contrast, elevated foundations (on piles, posts, piers, or walls) are not as liable to fail in erosion from floods.

In order to obtain flood insurance, certain requirements must be met. An important one is that the first habitable floor of a home be above the 100-year storm-surge level. This will require many future coastal-zone residences to be on elevated foundations such as poles or "stilts." Persons interested in the National Flood Insurance Program and current building-design criteria for pole-house construction should obtain a copy of *Elevated Residential Structures* (Reference 99, Appendix C). Regardless of insurance, it is wise to use pole-type construction with deep embedment of the poles where foundation material can be eroded by waves or wind.

Materials used in pole construction vary:

Piles are long, slender columns of wood, steel, or concrete driven into the earth to a sufficient depth to support the vertical load of the house and the horizontal forces of flowing water, wind, and waterborne debris (Figure 67). Pile construction is especially suitable in areas where scouring—soil "washing out" from under the foundation of a house—is a problem.

Posts are usually of wood; if of steel they are called columns. Unlike piles they are not driven into the ground, but rather are placed in a pre-dug hole at the bottom of which may be a concrete pad (Figure 67). They may be held in place by backfilling and tamping earth into the hole after the post is in place, or by pouring concrete in the annular space. Posts are more readily aligned than driven piles and are therefore better to use if poles must extend to the roof. In general, treated wood is the cheapest and most common material for both posts and piles.

Piers are vertical supports, thicker than piles or posts, usually made of reinforced concrete or reinforced masonry (concrete blocks or bricks). They are set on footings and extend to the underside of the floor frame.

Foundation walls can be used to raise the first habitable floor of the residence to the desired level. It is important that these walls be located parallel to the flow of the floodwaters and that they provide unobstructed space through which the water may flow.

Pole construction can be of two types. The poles may be cut off at the first-floor level to support the platform that serves as the dwelling floor. (In this case, piles, posts, or piers can be used.) Or they may be extended to the roof and rigidly tied into both the floor and the roof. In this way, they become major framing members for the

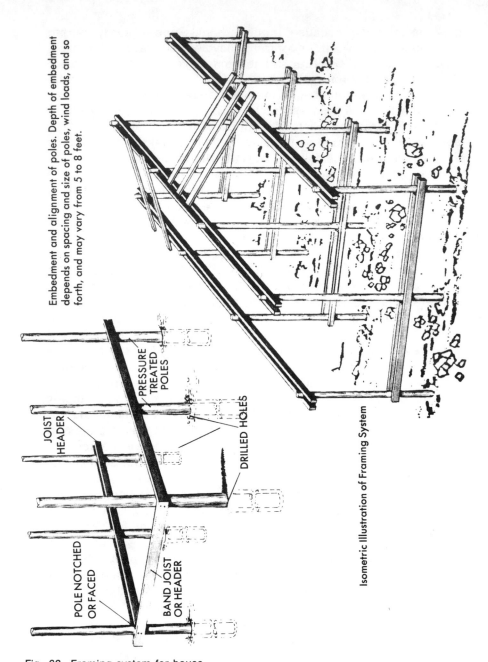

Embedment and alignment of poles. Depth of embedment depends on spacing and size of poles, wind loads, and so forth, and may vary from 5 to 8 feet.

Isometric Illustration of Framing System

JOIST HEADER

PRESSURE TREATED POLES

DRILLED HOLES

POLE NOTCHED OR FACED

BAND JOIST OR HEADER

Fig. 68. Framing system for house

Source: Southern Pine Association

160

structure and provide better anchorage to the house as a whole (Figures 68, 69, and 70). A combination of full- and floor-height poles is used in some cases, with the shorter poles restricted to supporting the floor inside the house.

Where the foundation material can be eroded by waves or winds, the poles should be deeply embedded and solidly anchored either by driving, or by drilling deep holes with a concrete pad at the bottom. Where the embedment is shallow, a concrete collar around the poles improves anchorage (Figure 67). The choice depends on the soil conditions. Piles are more difficult to align to match the house frame than are posts, which can be positioned in the holes before backfilling.

When holes are dug rather than driven, the posts should extend 6 to 8 feet into the ground to provide anchorage. The lower end of the post should rest on a concrete pad, spreading the load to the soil over a greater area to prevent settlement. Where the soil is sandy or the embedment less than, say, 6 feet, it is best to tie the post down to the footing with straps or other anchoring devices. It is also wise to drill slightly oversize holes for the posts to allow for alignment when the major framing members—the floor and the roof—are installed. It is only after these members are installed and squared that the holes should be backfilled and tamped, or a concrete collar poured. Driven piles should extend to a depth of 8 feet or more.

The floor and the roof should be securely connected to the poles with bolts or other fasteners. When the floor rests on poles that do not extend to the roof, attachment is even more critical. A system of metal straps is often used. Unfortunately, it is very common for builders to simply attach the floor joists to a notched pole by one or two bolts. Hurricanes have proven this method insufficient. During the next hurricane on the North Carolina coast, many houses will be destroyed because of inadequate attachment.

Section 3.0 of the North Carolina State Building Code, the Sand Dune Ordinance, requires that buildings erected within 150 feet of the Atlantic Ocean be constructed on pile-type foundations, and that the piles be driven no less than 8 feet below the natural grade of the lot. It also contains helpful details on the size, quality, and spacing of the piles, ties, and bracing, and the methods of fastening the structure to them. The ordinance assumes that the piles will be sawed off smoothly along a horizontal plane, resulting in a platform-type construction. Building inspectors, however, are usually amenable to other designs that are equally or more effective, so builders need not avoid pole-type construction, in which poles extend to the roof.

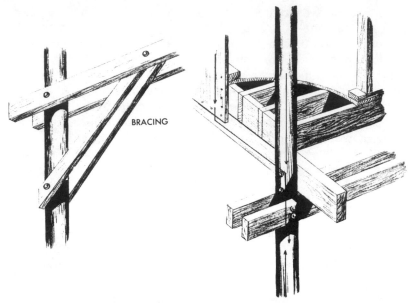

BRACING

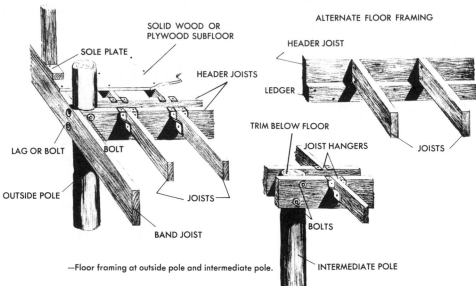

SOLID WOOD OR
PLYWOOD SUBFLOOR

SOLE PLATE

HEADER JOISTS

LAG OR BOLT   BOLT

OUTSIDE POLE

JOISTS

BAND JOIST

ALTERNATE FLOOR FRAMING

HEADER JOIST

LEDGER

JOISTS

TRIM BELOW FLOOR

JOIST HANGERS

BOLTS

INTERMEDIATE POLE

—Floor framing at outside pole and intermediate pole.

Fig. 69. Tying floors to poles

Source: Southern Pine Association

162

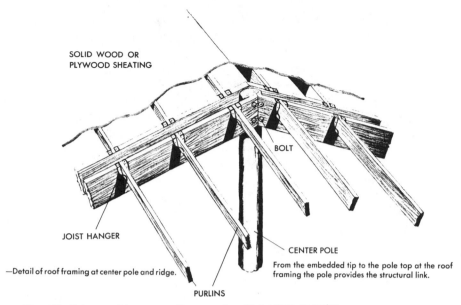

SOLID WOOD OR
PLYWOOD SHEATING

JOIST HANGER

BOLT

CENTER POLE

—Detail of roof framing at center pole and ridge.

From the embedded tip to the pole top at the roof framing the pole provides the structural link.

PURLINS

Fig. 70. Tying roof trusses, rafters, and ceiling joints to poles

Source: Southern Pine Association

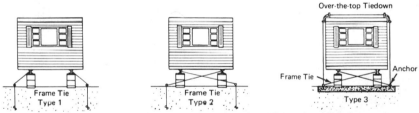

Over-the-top Tiedown

Anchor

Frame Tie

Frame Tie
Type 1

Frame Tie
Type 2

Type 3

These sketches illustrate various methods for connecting frame ties to the mobile home frame. Type 2 system can resist greater horizontal forces than Type 1. Type 3 system involves placement of mobile home on concrete slab. Anchors embedded in concrete slab are connected to ties.

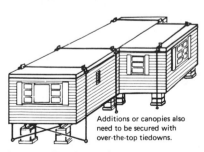

Additions or canopies also need to be secured with over-the-top tiedowns.

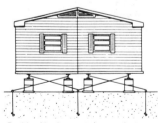

Double wides do not require over-the-top tiedowns but are subject to the same frame tie requirements presented on page 8.

Fig. 71. Tie-downs for mobile homes

Source: U.S. Defense Civil Preparedness Agency, Publication TR-75

163

The space under an elevated house, whether pole-type or otherwise, must be kept free of obstructions in order to minimize the impact of waves and floating debris. If the space is enclosed, the enclosing walls should be designed so that they can break away or fail under flood loads, but remain attached to the house or be heavy enough to sink; thus, the walls cannot float away and add to the water-borne debris problem. Alternative ways of avoiding this problem are designing walls that can be swung up out of the path of the floodwaters, or building them with louvers that allow the water to pass through. The louvered wall should be used only where no floating debris is expected.

MOBILE HOMES

Because of their light weight and flat sides, mobile homes are vulnerable to the high winds of hurricanes, tornadoes, and severe storms. Such winds can toss and overturn unanchored mobile homes to destruction, or smash them into neighboring homes and property. Nearly six million Americans live in mobile homes today. High winds damage or destroy nearly five thousand of these homes every year, and the number will surely rise unless protective measures are taken.

There are several lessons to be learned from past experiences in storms. One is that mobile homes should be located properly. After Hurricane Camille, it was observed that where mobile-home parks were surrounded by woods and homes were close together, damage to the homes was minimized, caused mainly by falling trees. In unprotected areas, however, many mobile homes were overturned and often destroyed from the force of the wind. The protection afforded by trees is greater than the possible damage from falling limbs. Two or more rows of trees are better than a single row, and trees 30 feet or more in height afford better protection than shorter ones. If possible, position the mobile home so that the narrow side faces the prevailing winds.

Locating your mobile home in a hilltop park will greatly increase your vulnerability to the wind. A lower location screened by trees and above storm-surge flood levels is safer from the wind. A location that is too low, obviously, increases the likelihood of flooding. There are fewer safe locations for mobile homes than for stilt houses.

Another lesson taught by past experience is that the mobile home must be tied down or anchored to the ground so that it will not over-

Anchors

NOTE: *Auger-type anchors using steel rods should be put in at an angle so they are in line with the direction of the pole. If both anchor rods are in place vertically, a concrete cylinder sleeve 10"-12" in diameter and 18" deep should be poured at the top of the anchor to prevent it from slicing through wet soil when loaded with horizontal forces.*

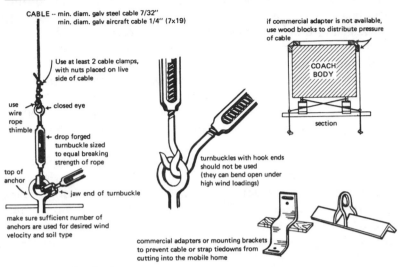

CABLE -- min. diam. galv steel cable 7/32"
min. diam. galv aircraft cable 1/4" (7x19)

Use at least 2 cable clamps, with nuts placed on live side of cable

use wire rope thimble

closed eye

drop forged turnbuckle sized to equal breaking strength of rope

top of anchor

jaw end of turnbuckle

make sure sufficient number of anchors are used for desired wind velocity and soil type

turnbuckles with hook ends should not be used (they can bend open under high wind loadings)

commercial adapters or mounting brackets to prevent cable or strap tiedowns from cutting into the mobile home

if commercial adapter is not available, use wood blocks to distribute pressure of cable

COACH BODY

section

Fig. 72. Anchors for tie-downs

Source: *U.S. Defense Civil Preparedness Agency, Publication TR-75*

turn in high winds (Figures 71 and 72). Simple prudence dictates the use of tie-downs, and in many communities, ordinances require it. Many insurance companies, moreover, will not insure mobile homes unless they are adequately anchored with tie-downs.

A mobile home may be tied down with cable or rope, or rigidly attached to the ground by connecting it to a simple wood-post foundation system. An alert mobile-home-park owner can provide permanent concrete anchors or piers to which hold-down ties could be fastened. In general, the entire tie-down system will not cost more than $150.

Mobile-home owners should be sure to obtain a copy of the booklet *Protecting Mobile Homes from High Winds* (Reference 100, Appendix C), which treats the subject in more detail than do we. This booklet lists specific steps that one should take on receiving a hurricane warning and suggests a type of mobile-home-park community shelter. It also includes a map of the United States with lines that indicate areas subject to the strongest sustained winds.

HIGHRISE BUILDINGS ON THE BEACH

A highrise building on the beach is generally designed by an architect and a structural engineer who are presumably well qualified and aware of the requirements for building on the shoreline. However, tenants of such a building should not assume that it is therefore invulnerable. Many people living in apartment buildings of two or three stories were killed when the buildings were destroyed by Hurricane Camille.

Despite the assurances that come with an engineered structure, life in a highrise building holds definite drawbacks which prospective tenants should take into consideration. The negative conditions that must be evaluated stem from high wind, high water, and poor foundations.

Pressure from the wind is greater near the shore than it is inland, and greater the higher we get from the ground. A highrise building near the shore is subject to the combined effects of both. The Uniform Building Code specifies that an inland structure up to 30 feet (two or three stories) in height should withstand 15 pounds of wind pressure per square foot, whereas the same structure on the shore should withstand 40 pounds per square foot (2½ times more). The pressure specified increases with height: at 100 feet (10 stories) it is only 30 pounds per square foot inland, but 75 pounds per square foot on the shore—again 2½ times more. Moreover, if you are living inland in a two-story house and move to the eleventh floor of a highrise on the shore, you should expect five times more wind pressure than you are accustomed to. This can be a great—and possibly devastating—surprise.

The high wind-pressure can cause unpleasant motion of the building. It is worthwhile to check with current residents of a highrise to find out if it has undesirable motion characteristics; some have claimed that the swaying is great enough to cause motion sickness. More seriously, high winds can break windows, harming property and people, or, worse yet, severely damage the building so that the tenants have to relocate until repairs are made.

Those who are interested in researching the subject further—even the knowledgeable engineer or architect who is engaged to design a structure near the shore—should obtain a copy of *Structural Failures: Modes, Causes, Responsibilities* (Reference 88, Appendix C). Of particular importance is the chapter entitled "Failure of Structures Due to Extreme Winds." This chapter analyzes wind damage to engineered highrise buildings from the storms at Lubbock and Corpus Christi, Texas, in 1970.

APPENDIX A

Hurricane Checklist

HURRICANE CHECKLIST

**When A Hurricane Threatens, Keep This Checklist Handy
For Protection Of Family And Property**

WHEN HURRICANE THREATENS:

—Listen for official weather reports.
—Read your newspaper and listen to radio and television for official announcements.
—Note the address of the nearest Emergency Shelter.
—Pregnant women, the ill and infirm should call a physician for advice.
—Be prepared to turn off gas, water, and electricity where it enters your home.
—Fill tubs and containers with water (one quart per person per day).
—Make sure your car's gas tank is full.
—Secure your boat. Use long lines to allow for rising water.
—Secure moveable objects on your property:
   -Doors
   -Shutters
   -Outdoor Furniture
   -Garden Tools
   -Hoses
   -Gates
   -Garbage Cans
   -Other
—Board up or tape windows and glassed areas. Remove furniture in their vicinity.
—Stock adequate supplies:
   -Transistor radio
   -Flashlights
   -Fresh batteries
   -Candles

-Canned heat
-Matches
-Hammer
-Nails
-Boards
-Screwdriver
-Pliers
-Axe*
-Hunting Knife
-Rope
-Tape
-Plastic drop cloths, waterproof bags, ties
-First-aid kit
-Prescribed medicines
-Containers for water
-Water purification tablets
-Disinfectant
-Insect repellent
-Canned food, juices, soft drinks
-Gum, candy
-Life jackets
-Hard-top head gear
-Charcoal bucket and charcoal
-Fire extinguisher
-Buckets of sand
-Can opener and utensils

*Take axe (to cut an emergency escape opening) if you go to the upper floors or attic of your home. Take rope for escape to ground when water subsides.

IF EVACUATION IS ADVISED:

—Leave as soon as you can. Follow official instructions only.
—Take these supplies
   -Change of clothes
   -Disposable diapers
   -Baby formula
   -Special medicine
   -Identification tags: Include name, address, and next of kin (wear them.)
   -Blankets and pillows in waterproof casings
   -Radio
   -Flashlight
   -Fresh batteries
   -Food, water, gum, candy

-Purse, wallet, valuables
-Rope, hunting knife
-Life jackets
-Waterproof bags and ties
-Games and amusements for children
-Can opener and utensils
—Disconnect all electric applicances except refrigerator and freezer. Their controls should be turned to the coldest setting and the doors kept closed.
—Leave food and water for pets. Seeing-eye dogs are the only animals allowed in the shelters.
—Shut off water at the main valve (where it enters your home).

169

AFTER THE HURRICANE HAS PASSED:

—Listen for official word of danger having passed.
—Eat nothing and drink nothing that has been touched by flood waters.
—Place spoiled food in plastic bags and tie securely.
—Dispose of all mattresses, pillows and cushions which have been in flood waters.
—Contact relatives as soon as possible.

NOTE: If you are stranded, signal for help by waving a flashlight at night or white cloth during the day.

DURING THE HURRICANE:

Follow these instructions:
—Stay indoors and away from windows and glassed areas.
—If you are advised to evacuate, DO SO AT ONCE.
—Listen for continuing weather bulletins and official reports.
  —Use your telephone only in an emergency.
—Follow official instructions only. Ignore rumors.
—Keep OPEN a window or door on the side of the house opposite the storm winds.
—Beware the "EYE OF THE HURRICANE." A lull in the winds is not an indication that the storm has passed. Remain indoors unless emergency repairs are necessary. Exercise caution. Winds may resume suddenly, in the opposite direction and with greater force than before. Remember, if wind direction does change, the open window or door must be changed accordingly.
—Be alert for rising water.
—If electric service is interrupted, note the time.
    -Turn off major appliances, especially air conditioners.
    -Do not disconnect refrigerators or freezers. Their controls should be turned to the coldest setting and doors closed to preserve food as long as possible.
    -Keep away from fallen wires. Report location of such wires to the utility company.

—If you detect GAS:
    -Do not light matches or electrical equipment.
    -Extinguish all flames.
    -Shut off gas supply at the meter.*
    -Report gas service interruptions to the gas company.

*NOTE: Gas should be turned back on only by a gas serviceman or licensed plumber.

—WATER:
    -The only SAFE water is the water you stored before it had a chance to come in contact with flood waters.
    -Should you require an additional supply, be sure to boil water for thirty (30) minutes before use.
    -If you are unable to boil water, treat water you will need with water purification tablets.

NOTE: An official announcement will proclaim tap water "safe." Treat all water except stored water until you hear the announcement.

A Guide to Federal, State, and Local Agencies Involved in Coastal Development

A GUIDE TO FEDERAL, STATE, AND LOCAL AGENCIES INVOLVED IN COASTAL DEVELOPMENT

Numerous agencies at all levels of government are engaged in planning, regulating, or studying coastal development in North Carolina. These agencies issue permits for various phases of construction and provide information on development to the homeowner, developer, or planner. Following is an alphabetical list of topics related to coastal development; under each topic are the names of agencies to consult for information on that topic.

Much of the information contained in this appendix was taken from *Information for Buyers and Owners of Coastal Property in North Carolina* (Reference 49, Appendix C). Persons needing a complete list of federal and state agencies involved in coastal development should obtain a copy of Reference 42, Appendix C.

Aerial Photography, Orthophoto Maps, and Remote-Sensing Imagery

Persons interested in aerial photography, remote-sensing techniques, or agencies that supply aerial photographs or images should obtain a copy of:

Aerial Photography for Planning and Development in Eastern North Carolina: A Handbook and Directory, by Simon Baker, 1976. North Carolina residents may obtain a copy from UNC Sea Grant College Program, 1235 Burlington Laboratories, North Carolina State University, Raleigh, NC 27607.

Beach Erosion

Information on beach erosion, inlet migration, floods, and high winds is available from:

Center for Marine and Coastal Studies
1204 Burlington Laboratories
North Carolina State University
Raleigh, NC 27607
Phone: (919) 737-3326

173

District Engineer
U. S. Army Corps of Engineers
P. O. Box 1890
Wilmington, NC 28401
Phone: (919) 763-9971

Water Planning and Development Division
N. C. Department of Natural Resources
and Community Development
P. O. Box 27687
Raleigh, NC 27611
Phone: 919-733-2594

Bridges and Causeways

The U. S. Coast Guard has jurisdiction over the issuing of permits to build bridges or causeways that will affect navigable waters. Information is available from:

Commander, 7th Coast Guard District
1018 Federal Building
51 First Avenue, S.W.
Miami, FL 33130
Phone: (305) 350-4108

Building Codes and Zoning

The North Carolina State Building Code contains special provisions for building in hurricane-prone areas. Check to be sure that the property in which you are interested is zoned for your intended use, and that adjacent property zones do not conflict with your plans. For information, contact the city or county building inspector or:

Mr. John R. Valentine
Building Code Consultant
Engineering Division
N. C. Department of Insurance
P. O. Box 38
Marshallberg, NC 28553
Phone: (919) 729-4196

Mr. Kern Church
Deputy Commissioner
N. C. Department of Insurance
430 N. Salisbury Street
Raleigh, NC 27611

Civil Preparedness (Region 3) (see also Disaster Assistance)

Mr. Claude B. Thompson
Thomasville, GA 31792
Phone: (912) 226-1761

Coastal Area Management Act, North Carolina (CAMA)

The 1974 CAMA calls for local land-use planning in coastal counties to be carried out under guidelines established by the Coastal Resources Commission. The Commission designates areas of environmental concern (AEC's) where special environmental, historical, or scientific factors must be considered in developing an area. Permits from the State for major developments or from local government (if it chooses to act as a permit-letting agency) for minor development are required for the development of these areas. Learn where areas of environmental concern are in relation to your property. For further information, write or call:

Office of Marine Affairs
417 N. Blount Street
Raleigh, NC 27605
Phone: (919) 733-2290

Mr. Dave Adams, Assistant Secretary
N. C. Department of Natural Resources
and Community Development
P. O. Box 27687
Raleigh, NC 27611
Phone: (919) 733-4006

Coastal Resources Commission
512 N. Salisbury Street
Raleigh, NC 27611
Phone: (919) 733-2293

or

Coastal Resources Commission
P. O. Box 650
Morehead City, NC 28557

Office of Coastal Zone Management
National Oceanic and Atmospheric Administration
3300 Whitehaven Street, N.W.
Washington, DC 20235
Phone: (202) 634-6791
(provides publications to aid planners and managers)

Disaster Assistance

For information, call or write:

N. C. Division of Civil Preparedness
Administration Building
116 West Jones Street
Raleigh, NC 27603
Phone: (919) 733-3867
or

Housing (see **Subdivisions**)

Hurricane Information

The National Oceanic and Atmospheric Administration is the best agency from which to request information on hurricanes. NOAA Storm-Evacuation Maps are prepared for vulnerable areas and cost $2.00 each. To find out whether a map for your area is available, call or write:

> Distribution Division (C-44)
> National Ocean Survey
> National Oceanic and Atmospheric Administration
> Riverdale, MD 20840
> Phone: (301) 436-6990

Insurance

In coastal areas special building requirements must often be met in order to obtain flood or windstorm insurance. To find out the requirements for your area, check with your insurance agent or the Kemper Insurance Company, which services the National Flood Program in North Carolina. Further information is available from:

> Kemper Insurance Company
> 1229 Greenwood Cliff
> Charlotte, NC 28204
> Phone: (704) 372-7150

> Federal Insurance Administration
> National Flood Insurance Program
> Department of Housing and Urban Development
> 451 Seventh Street, S.W.
> Washington, DC 20410
> Phone, Asst. Administrator for Flood Insurance:
> (202) 755-5581

> State Coordinating Agency for Flood Insurance
> Division of Community Assistance
> N. C. Department of Natural Resources
> and Community Development
> P. O. Box 27687
> Raleigh, NC 27611

Information on the state building code, regulations governing mobile homes, and related areas is available from:

> N. C. Department of Insurance
> P. O. Box 26387
> Raleigh, NC 27611
> Phone: (919) 733-3901

Land Acquisition

When acquiring property or a condominium—whether in a sub-division or not—consider the following: (1) Owners of property next to dredged canals should make sure that the canals are designed for adequate flushing to keep the canals from becoming stagnant. Requests for federal permits to connect extensive canal systems to navigable water are frequently denied! (2) Description and survey of land in coastal areas are very complicated. Old titles granting fee-simple rights to property below the high-tide line may not be upheld in court; titles should be reviewed by a competent attorney before they are transferred. A boundary described as the high-water mark may be impossible to determine. (3) Ask about the provision of sewage disposal and utilities including water, electricity, gas, and telephone. (4) Be sure any promises of future improvements, access, utilities, additions, common property rights, etc., are in writing. (5) Be sure to visit the property and inspect it carefully before buying it. (See the following sections on **Planning** and **Subdivisions**.)

Maps

A wide variety of maps are useful to planners and managers and may be of interest to individual property owners. Topographic, geologic, and land-use maps and orthophoto quadrangles are available from:

Distribution Section
U. S. Geological Survey
1200 South Eads Street
Arlington, VA 22202

A free index to the type of map desired (for example, the "Index to Topographic Maps of North Carolina") should be requested and then used for ordering specific maps.

N. C. Department of Natural Resources
and Community Development
Division of Earth Resources
P. O. Box 27687
Raleigh, NC 27611

Flood-zone maps: See **Insurance**.
Planning maps: Call or write your local county commission.
Soil maps and septic suitability: See **Soil**.
Nautical charts in several scales contain navigation information on North Carolina's coastal waters. A nautical-chart index map is available from:

Federal Disaster Assistance Administration
Region 4 Office
Suite 750
1375 Peachtree Street, N.E.
Atlanta, GA 30309

American National Red Cross
Disaster Services
Washington, DC 20006
Phone: (202) 857-3722

Dredging, Filling, and Construction in Coastal Waterways

North Carolina law requires that all those who wish to dredge, fill, or otherwise alter marshlands, estuarine bottoms, or tidelands apply for a permit from the North Carolina Division of Commercial and Sports Fisheries. For information, write or call:

Permit Section
N. C. Division of Marine Fisheries
P. O. Box 27687
Raleigh, NC 27611
Phone: (919) 733-3767

or

P. O. Box 769
Morehead City, NC 28557
Phone: (919) 726-7021

Federal law requires that any person who wishes to dredge, fill, or place any structure in navigable water (almost any body of water) apply for a permit from the U. S. Army Corps of Engineers. Information is available from:

Permits and Statistics Branch
U. S. Army Corps of Engineers
P. O. Box 1890
Wilmington, NC 28401
Phone: (919) 763-9971

Dune Alteration

North Carolina law prohibits the destruction, damaging, or removal of any sand dune or dune vegetation. Individual counties as well may have ordinances pertaining to dune alteration. Permits for certain types of alteration may be obtained from the local dune-protection officer. For information, call or write to him at the local county courthouse.

Geologic Information

Branch of Distribution
U. S. Geological Survey
1200 South Eads Street
Arlington, VA 22202
(Request *Geologic and Water-Supply Reports and Maps, North Carolina,* free index.)

U. S. Geological Survey District Office
P. O. Box 2857
Raleigh, NC 27602

N. C. Department of Natural Resources
and Community Development
P. O. Box 27687
Raleigh, NC 27611
Phone: (919) 733-3833

Hazards (see also Beach Erosion and Insurance)

Literature describing natural hazards on barrier islands is available from:

UNC Sea Grant College Program
1235 Burlington Laboratories
North Carolina State University
Raleigh, NC 27607
(Request list of publications)

or

Office of Coastal Zone Management
National Oceanic and Atmospheric Administration
3300 Whitehaven Street, N.W.
Washington, DC 20235

Health (see also Sanitation and Septic-System Information)

The local Department of Health is in charge of issuing home septic-tank permits. Questions may be directed to the officer of the local agency or to:

N. C. Department of Human Resources
Division of Health Services
Sanitary Engineering Section
P. O. Box 2091
Raleigh, NC 27602

History/Archaeology

N. C. Department of Archives and History
109 East Jones Street
Raleigh, NC 27602

National Ocean Survey
Distribution Division (C-44)
National Oceanic and Atmospheric Administration
Riverdale, MD 20840
Phone: (301) 436-6990

County-highway base maps are available for $0.15 each from:

N.C. Department of Transportation
Division of Highways
P. O. Box 25021
Raleigh, NC 27611

The Division of Highways is also a source of air photographs. (An index photograph of your part of the coast is available for $6.24 from the above address.)

North Carolina in Maps (1966), a book containing historic maps and descriptive text of North Carolina, is available for $10.00 from:

N. C. Department of Archives and History
109 East Jones Street
Raleigh, NC 27611

Marine and Coastal-Zone Information

North Carolina has three multipurpose Marine Resources Centers. Located conveniently along the coast, the centers are designed as learning laboratories and serve a variety of functions. Exhibits, aquaria, and various displays are open year-round, and admission is free. In addition, lectures, seminars, and film series are held. Each center has a professional staff available to answer questions, and many Sea Grant publications which are free or low in cost. Centers are located at the following addresses:

Marine Resources Center
Roanoke Island
Manteo, NC 27954
Phone: (919) 473-3493

Marine Resources Center
Bogue Banks
Morehead City, NC 28557
Phone: (919) 726-0121

Marine Resources Center
Fort Fisher
Kure Beach, NC 28449
Phone: (919) 458-8257

Other sources of information include:

UNC Sea Grant College Program
1235 Burlington Laboratories
Raleigh, NC 27607
Phone: (919) 737-2454
(distributes free monthly newsletter and other publications)

and

Center for Marine and Coastal Studies
1204 Burlington Laboratories
North Carolina State University
Raleigh, NC 27607
Phone: (919) 737-3326

Coastal Plains Center for Marine Development Services
1518 Harbour Drive
Wilmington, NC 28401
Phone: (919) 791-6432
(distributes newsletter and other publications)

Duke University Marine Laboratory
Beaufort, NC 28516
Phone: (919) 728-2111

Movies

The following films are available on loan or for sale from:

UNC Sea Grant College Program
1235 Burlington Laboratories
North Carolina State University
Raleigh, NC 27607

Waterbound: Our Changing Outer Banks. Color film produced after a 1973 storm in the area between Kitty Hawk and Buxton. Documents the impact of a relatively minor storm in an area of dune-diking that dates back to the 1930s. Suitable for a wide audience.

An Act to Protect. Traces the history of the Coastal Area Management Act from the problems prompting the legislation, through its legislative history, to its specific applications. Problems treated include erosion, and water quality, supply, and contamination. A member of the Coastal Resources Commission discusses coastal management. Provides good introduction to land-use planning.

The Currituck Film. Addresses the land-use issue for all of Currituck County, but includes a specific section on the coast. Good footage of storm action and dune movement. Recommended for its treatment of the land-use issue relative to a countywide political unit.

Parks and Recreation

N. C. Division of Parks and Recreation
512 N. Salisbury Street
Raleigh, NC 27601
Phone: (919) 733-4181

Cape Hatteras National Seashore Headquarters
Manteo, NC 27954

Cape Lookout National Seashore Headquarters
Beaufort, NC 28516
Phone: (919) 728-2121

Bureau of Outdoor Recreation
U. S. Department of the Interior
Southeast Regional Office
148 Cain Street
Atlanta, GA 30303
Phone: (404) 526-4405

Planning and Land Use (see also Coastal Area Management Act)

Division of Coastal Management
N. C. Department of Natural Resources
and Community Development
P. O. Box 27687
Raleigh, NC 27611
Phone: (919) 733-2293

Center for Urban and Regional Studies
University of North Carolina
108 Battle Lane
Chapel Hill, NC 27514
(Ask for publication list on development and planning.)

Division of Land Management
N. C. Department of Natural Resources
and Community Development
P. O. Box 27687
Raleigh, NC 27611
Phone: (919) 733-3833

For specific information on your area, check with your local town or county commission. Many local governments have planning boards which answer to the commission and have available copies of existing or proposed land-use plans.

Roads and Property Access

The N. C. Department of Transportation is not required to furnish access to all property owners. Before buying property, make sure that access rights and roads will be provided.

Permits to connect driveways from commercial developments to State-maintained roads must be obtained from the district engineer of the Division of Highways.

Subdivision roads—privately built roads including those serving seasonal residences—must meet specific standards in order to be eligible for addition to the State highway system. Information on these requirements may be obtained from the district engineer or the secondary roads officer of the local Division of Highways. Further information is available from:

Secondary Roads Officer
Division of Highways
N. C. Department of Transportation
P. O. Box 25201
Raleigh, NC 27611
Phone: (919) 733-3250

Sanitation

Before construction permits will be issued, improvement permits for septic tanks must be obtained from the local Department of Health. Improvement permits are based on soil suitability for septic-tank systems and apply to conventional homes and mobile homes outside of mobile-home parks, in areas that are not served by public or community sewage systems and that generate less than 3,000 gallons of effluent per day.

A permit must be obtained from the North Carolina Division of Environmental Management for any discharge into surface water and for wastewater-treatment systems of design capacities that exceed 3,000 gallons per day. Septic-tank systems will not be approved in high-density areas (those producing more than 1,200 gallons of wastewater per acre per day, or containing more than three residential units per acre).

More information may be obtained from the county health department or

Division of Environmental Management
Northeastern Field Office
1502 Market Street
Washington, NC 27889
Phone: (919) 946-6481

Division of Environmental Management
Southeastern Field Office
3143 Wrightsville Avenue
Wilmington, NC 28401
Phone: (919) 762-3394

Office of Water and Air Resources
Water Quality Division, Eastern Region
209 Cotanche Street
Greenville, NC 27834
Phone: (919) 758-0642

A permit for the construction of a sewage disposal or any other structure in navigable waters must be obtained from the U. S. Army Corps of Engineers. More information is available from:

Permits and Statistics Branch
U. S. Army Corps of Engineers
P. O. Box 1890
Wilmington, NC 28401
Phone: (919) 763-0071

A permit for any discharge into navigable waters must be obtained from the U. S. Environmental Protection Agency. Recent judicial interpretation of the Federal Water Pollution Control Amendments of 1972 extends above the mean high-water mark federal jurisdiction for protection of wetland. Federal permits may now be required for the development of land that occasionally is flooded by water draining indirectly into a navigable waterway. Information may be obtained from:

Enforcement Division
Environmental Protection Agency
Region IV
1421 Peachtree Street, N.E.
Atlanta, GA 30309

or

Division of Marine Fisheries
N. C. Department of Natural Resources
and Community Development
P. O. Box 769
Morehead City, NC 28557
Phone: (919) 726-7021

Septic-System Information and Permits (see also Sanitation)

General information may be obtained from:

UNC Sea Grant College Program
1235 Burlington Laboratories
North Carolina State University
Raleigh, NC 27607
Phone: (919) 737-2454

or

Department of Soil Science
North Carolina State University
Raleigh, NC 27607

On-site soil information is available from the local conservation district office, the county extension office, or a private consultant. Home-system permits may be obtained from the local Department of Health. Business- or industrial-system permits may be obtained from the regional office of the Department of Natural Resources and Community Development.

Soils (see also **Septic-System Information** and **Vegetation**)

Soil type is important in terms of (1) the type of vegetation it can support, (2) the type of construction technique it can withstand, (3) its drainage characteristics, and (4) its ability to accommodate septic systems. An extensive soil survey of the Outer Banks was in progress at the time this book was being written. Ultimately, soil reports including maps and ratings of soil types will be available for most of the North Carolina coast. The following agencies cooperate to produce a variety of reports that are useful to property owners:

U. S. Department of Agriculture
Soil Conservation Service
P. O. Box 27307
Raleigh, NC 27611
Phone: (919) 755-4210
(published maps and reports; supplies information to Soil and Water Conservation district offices; operates annual "beach clinics" in conjunction with the soil- and water-conservation districts)

N. C. Department of Natural Resources
and Community Development
Division of Earth Resources
P. O. Box 27687
Raleigh, NC 27611
(cooperates in publication of soil reports and maps)

Department of Soil Science
North Carolina State University
Raleigh, NC 27607

Persons seeking information on soil should check first with the Soil and Water Conservation district office.

Subdivisions

Subdivisions containing more than 50 lots and offered in interstate commerce must be registered with the Office of Interstate Land Sales Registration (as specified by the Interstate Land Sales Full Disclosure Act). Prospective buyers must be provided with a property report. This office also produces a booklet entitled *Get the Facts . . . Before Buying Land* for people who wish to invest in land. Information on subdivision property and land investment is available from:

Office of Interstate Land Sales Registration
U. S. Department of Housing and Urban Development
Washington, DC 20410

or

Office of Interstate Land Sales Registration
Atlanta Regional Office
U. S. Department of Housing and Urban Development
230 Peachtree Street, N.W.
Atlanta, GA 30303
Phone: (404) 526-4364

Vegetation

Information on vegetation may be obtained from the local Soil and Water Conservation district office. For information on the use of grass and other plantings for stabilization or aesthetics, consult the publications listed in Appendix C under **Vegetation.** *Seacoast Plants of the Carolinas for Conservation and Beautification* is particularly useful.

Water Resources (see also Dredge and Fill and Sanitation)

A variety of agencies are concerned with water quality and availability. The following ones will answer questions on this subject:

N. C. Department of Natural Resources
and Community Development
Office of Water and Air Research
P. O. Box 9392
512 N. Salisbury Street
Raleigh, NC 27603
Phone, Water Pollution Control Division: (919) 733-3006
Phone, Groundwater Division, Chief: (919) 733-3004

Water Resources Research Institute of UNC
124 Riddick Building
North Carolina State University
Raleigh, NC 27607
Phone: (919) 737-2815 or 737-2816

U. S. Geological Survey
Water Resources Division
Room 440, Century Station
Raleigh, NC 27602
Phone: (919) 755-4510

Weather

General information may be obtained from:

National Weather Service, Eastern Region
585 Stewart Avenue
Garden City, NY 11530
Phone: (516) 248-2101

Hurricane information is available from:

National Oceanic and Atmospheric Administration
Office of Coastal Zone Management
3300 Whitehaven Street, N.W.
Washington, DC 20235
Phone: (202) 634-6791

For current weather information, listen to your local radio and television stations.

APPENDIX C

101 Useful References

101 USEFUL REFERENCES

The following publications are listed by subject; subjects are arranged in the approximate order that they appear in the preceding chapters. A brief description of each reference is provided, and sources are included for those readers who would like to obtain more information on a particular subject. Most of the references listed are either low in cost or free; we encourage the reader to take advantage of these informative publications.

History

1. *The Outer Banks of North Carolina, 1584-1958,* by David Stick, 1958. A popular book tracing the history of the Outer Banks. Recommended to all coastal residents of North Carolina, particularly those of Carteret, Hyde, and Currituck Counties. Contains storm history, accounts of the origins of most points of interest, and examples of early development. Enjoyable narrative style. Published by the University of North Carolina Press, Chapel Hill, NC 27514. Available in most North Carolina bookstores for around $7.00.

Hurricanes

2. *Early American Hurricanes, 1492-1870,* by D. M. Ludlum, 1963. Informative and entertaining descriptions of storms affecting the Atlantic and Gulf coasts. Storm accounts in chronological order provide insight into the frequency, intensity, and destructive potential of hurricanes. Published by the American Meteorological Society, Boston, MA. Available in public and university libraries.

3. *North Carolina Hurricanes,* by C. B. Carney and A. V. Hardy, 1967. Brief descriptions of all known tropical storms that have struck the North Carolina coast since 1586. Emphasizes the destructive history of hurricanes in the state. Excellent reading. Published as an ESSA Technical Report, U. S. Department of Commerce, Washington, DC 20230. Available in public and college libraries.

4. *Atlantic Hurricanes,* by G. E. Dunn and B. I. Miller, 1960. Discusses at length hurricanes and associated phenomena such as storm surge, wind, and sea action. Includes a detailed account of Hurricane Hazel, 1954, and suggestions for pre- and post-hurricane procedures. An appendix includes a list of hurricanes for the Carolinas. Published by the Louisiana State University Press, Baton Rouge, LA. Available in public and college libraries.

5. *Hurricane Information and Atlantic Tracking Chart,* by The National Oceanic and Atmospheric Administration, 1974. A brochure which describes hurricanes, defines terms, and lists hurricane safety rules. Out-

lines method of tracing hurricanes and provides a tracking map. Available from the Superintendent of Documents, U. S. Government Printing Office, Washington, DC 20402. Price $0.30.

6. *Bibliography on Hurricanes and Severe Storms of the Coastal Plains Region and Supplement,* by the Coastal Plains Center for Marine Development Services, 1970 and 1972. A list of references which provides a good starting point for persons seeking detailed information on hurricanes and hurricane research. Available from the Coastal Plains Center for Marine Development Services, P. O. Box 3643, Wilmington, NC 28401.

Geology and Oceanography

7. *Reconnaissance Geology of the Submerged and Emerged Coastal Plain Province, Cape Lookout Area, North Carolina,* by R. B. Mixon and O. H. Pilkey, 1976. A technical report which describes the geology of the coastal plain and continental shelf in the areas of Beaufort and Morehead City. Includes a geologic map of the area. Available as U. S. Geological Survey Professional Paper No. 859 from the Superintendent of Documents, U. S. Government Printing Office, Washington, DC 20402. Price $1.35.

8. *Geological Bibliography of North Carolina's Coastal Plain, Coastal Zone, and Continental Shelf,* by S. R. Riggs and M. P. O'Connor, 1975. List of references aimed at those involved in various aspects of coastal-zone management. Valuable to any student of geology who wishes to read literature on specific geologic subjects. Citations complete from the 1800s through November 1974. Available as Bulletin No. 83 from the Mineral Resources Section, North Carolina Department of Natural Resources and Community Development, P. O. Box 27687, Raleigh, NC 27611.

9. *The Oceanographic Atlas of North Carolina,* by John Newton, Orrin Pilkey, and Jack Blanton, 1972. A summary of the physical and geological oceanography of North Carolina's coastal waters. Includes topographical maps and shipwreck lists. Available from the Director, North Carolina Science and Technology Research Center, P. O. Box 12235, Research Triangle Park, NC 27709. Price $4.64, including postage.

10. *Relict Sediment Deposits in a Major Transgressive Coastal System,* by S. R. Riggs and M. P. O'Connor, 1974. Technical study of sediment in the barrier-island coastal system around Roanoke and Bodie Islands. Available from UNC Sea Grant, 1235 Burlington Laboratories, North Carolina State University, Raleigh, NC 27607.

Barrier Islands

11. *Barrier Islands and Beaches,* 1976. Proceedings of the May 1976 barrier-islands workshop. A collection of technical papers prepared by scientists studying islands. Provides an up-to-date, readable overview of barrier islands. Comprehensive coverage—from aesthetics to flood insurance—by the experts. Topics include island ecosystems, ecology, geology, politics, and planning. Good bibliographic source for those studying barrier islands. Available from the Publications Department, Conservation Foundation, 1717 Massachusetts Avenue N.W., Washington, DC 20036. Price $4.00. (Request the Foundation's free list of publications.)

12. *Barrier Island Formation,* by J. H. Hoyt, 1967. A technical paper in which Hoyt develops his theory of barrier-island formation. Published in the *Bulletin* of the Geological Society of America, v. 78, pp. 1125-1136. Available only in the larger university libraries.

13. *Coastal Geomorphology,* edited by D. R. Coates, 1973. Another collection of technical papers including R. Dolan's "Barrier Islands: Natural and Controlled," and P. J. Godfrey and M. M. Godfrey's "Comparison of Ecological and Geomorphic Interaction between Altered and Unaltered Barrier Island Systems in North Carolina." Interesting reading for anyone willing to overlook the jargon of coastal scientists. Published by the State University of New York, Binghamton, NY 13901. Available only in the larger university libraries.

14. *Effects of Hurricane Ginger on the Barrier Islands of North Carolina,* by R. Dolan and P. J. Godfrey, 1973. A technical account of one storm's effects. Published in the *Bulletin* of the Geological Society of America, v. 84, pp. 1329-1334. Available only in the larger university libraries.

Barrier Island Environments

15. *Know Your Mud, Sand, and Water: A Practical Guide to Coastal Development,* by K. M. Jurgensen, 1976. A pamphlet describing the various island environments relative to development. Clearly and simply written. Recommended to island dwellers. Available from UNC Sea Grant, 1235 Burlington Laboratories, North Carolina State University, Raleigh, NC 27607.

16. *Barrier Beaches of the East Coast,* by P. J. Godfrey, 1976. A clearly written paper describing beaches and associated barrier-island environments as related through the island processes. Published in *Oceanus,* v. 19, no. 5, pp. 27-40. This issue was devoted entirely to estuaries.

17. *Barrier Island Ecosystems of Cape Lookout National Seashore and Vicinity, North Carolina,* by P. J. Godfrey and M. M. Godfrey, 1977. The Godfreys have studied Core Banks for several years, particularly the processes of overwash, plant response, and dune and marsh development. Valuable to persons interested in the ecosystems of the Cape Lookout area. Available as Scientific Monograph Series 13 from the National Park Service, Washington, DC 20240.

Beaches

18. *Waves and Beaches,* by Willard Bascom, 1964. A discussion of beaches and coastal processes. Published by Anchor Books, Doubleday and Co., Garden City, NY 11530. Available in paperback from local bookstores.

19. *Beaches and Coasts,* 2nd edition, by C. A. M. King, 1972. Classic treatment of beach and coastal processes. Published by St. Martin's Press, Inc., 175 Fifth Avenue, New York, NY 10010.

20. *Beach Processes and Sedimentation,* by Paul Komar, 1976. The most up-to-date technical explanations of beaches and beach processes.

Recommended only to serious students of the beach. Published by Prentice Hall, Englewood Cliffs, NJ 07632.

21. *Land Against the Sea,* by the U. S. Army Corps of Engineers, 1964. Readable introduction to coastal geology and shoreline processes. However, authors' belief in the value of certain engineering methods is either outdated or unsubstantiated. Available as Miscellaneous Paper No. 4-64 from the U. S. Army Corps of Engineers, Coastal Engineering Research Center, Kingman Building, Ft. Belvoir, VA 22060.

22. *Atlantic Beaches,* by J. N. Leonard, 1972. The aesthetics of the beach in words and pictures. Published as part of the American Wilderness Series by Time-Life Books, Rockefeller Center, New York, NY 10020.

Recreation

23. *Recreation in the Coastal Zone,* 1975. A collection of papers presented at a symposium sponsored by the U. S. Department of the Interior, Bureau of Outdoor Recreation, Southeast Region. Outlines different views of recreation in the coastal zone and the approaches taken by some states to recreation-related problems. The symposium was co-sponsored by the Office of Coastal Zone Management. Available from that office, National Oceanic and Atmospheric Administration, 3300 Whitehaven Street N.W., Washington, DC 20235.

24. *Seashells Common to North Carolina,* by Hugh Porter and Jim Tyler, 1971. An excellent handbook describing and illustrating the state's seashells. Written for the layman. An essential reference for the shell collector. Available from UNC Sea Grant, 1235 Burlington Laboratories, North Carolina State University, Raleigh, NC 27607.

25. *Marine Fishes Common to North Carolina Waters,* by Frank Schwartz and Jim Tyler, 1970. Descriptions and illustrations of various marine fish. Written for the layman. Available from UNC Sea Grant (address under previous reference).

26. *A Checklist of the Marine Animals of Beaufort,* by Dr. William Kirby-Smith. Periodically updated list of all known marine animals of the Beaufort area. Includes technical names. Probably of more interest to the serious collector. Available from Dr. William Kirby-Smith, Duke Marine Laboratory, Beaufort, NC 28516. Price $1.00.

27. *Coastal Fishing and Vacation Guide,* 1977. Magazine containing information on fishing, accommodations, services, recreational facilities, ferry services, and discount coupons. A "must" for fishermen and highly recommended for vacationers on the North Carolina coast. Published annually by the Graphic Press, Inc., 418 Dawson Street, Raleigh, NC 27611. Price $3.00.

Shoreline Engineering

28. *Shore Protection Guildelines,* by the U. S. Army Corps of Engineers, 1971. Summary of the effects of waves, tides, and winds on beaches and engineering structures used for beach stabilization. Available free from the Department of the Army, Corps of Engineers, Washington, DC 20318.

29. *Shore Protection Manual,* by the U. S. Army Corps of Engineers, 1973. The "bible" of shoreline engineering. Published in three volumes. Request publication 08-0-22-00077 from the Superintendent of Documents, U. S. Government Printing Office, Washington, DC 20402. Price $14.25.

30. *Help Yourself,* by the U. S. Army Corps of Engineers. Brochure addressing the erosion problems in the Great Lakes region. May be of interest to barrier-island residents as it outlines shoreline processes and illustrates a variety of shoreline-engineering devices used to combat erosion. Free from the U. S. Army Corps of Engineers, North Central Division, 219 South Dearborn Street, Chicago, IL 60604.

31. *Coastal Hydraulics,* by A. M. Muir Wood, 1969. A shoreline-engineering textbook suitable for engineering students. Published by Gordon and Breach Science Publishers, Inc., 150 Fifth Avenue, New York, NY 10011.

32. *Publications List, Coastal Engineering Research Center (CERC) and Beach Erosion Board (BEB),* by the U. S. Army Corps of Engineers, 1976. A list of published research by the U. S. Army Corps of Engineers. Free from the U. S. Army Corps of Engineers, Coastal Engineering Research Center, Kingman Building, Ft. Belvoir, VA 22060.

33. *Where Beaches Have Been Going: Into the Ocean,* by Gary Soucie, 1973. Mr. Soucie, a former Outer Banks newsman, writes candidly about structural engineering devices, referring to their use in shoreline stabilization as an "utter failure." Published in *Smithsonian* magazine, v. 4, no. 3, pp. 54-61.

Hazards

34. *A Survey of North Carolina Beach Erosion by Air Photo Methods,* by H. E. Wahls, 1973. A summary of historic shoreline-erosion rates along the North Carolina coast, determined from the study of air photographs dating back to 1938. Bar graphs present data on the high-water line and "toe" of the dune for various portions of the coast. Long- and short-term erosion averages provided for each segment of the coast. North Carolina residents may request one free copy from the Center for Marine and Coastal Studies, North Carolina State University, Raleigh, NC 27607.

35. *Aerial Photographic Study of Shoreline Erosion and Deposition, Pamlico Sound, North Carolina,* by G. L. Stirewalt and R. L. Ingram, 1974. A study reporting examples of erosion on the sound sides of barrier islands including Bodie Island north of Oregon Inlet; Hatteras Island in the vicinities of Salvo, Avon, and Buxton; and Ocracoke village on Ocracoke Island. Islands within sounds and mainland-coast areas are also discussed. A Sea Grant publication available from the Center for Marine and Coastal Studies (address under previous reference).

36. *A Preliminary Study of Storm Induced Erosion for North Carolina,* by C. E. Knowles, J. Langfelder, and R. McDonald, 1973. A study of beach profiles at most fishing piers within the state. Provides a data base for predicting storm-induced beach recession. Tables on predicted storm-surge levels and breaking depths of waves for one-in-25-, -50-, and -100-

year storm frequencies; data for each pier (dune height, toe-of-dune height and distance from mean high-water position, recession from toe of dune for three storms of above-noted return frequencies); range of recession lines for various parts of the coast. Free to North Carolina residents from the Center for Marine and Coastal Studies (address under reference 34).

37. *Shoreline Waves, Another Energy Crisis,* by Victor Goldsmith, 1975. Shelf bathymetry is shown to be a controlling factor in wave refraction which, in turn, controls wave-height distribution along the beach. Suggests that wave-energy distribution may be controlled by modifying bathymetry. Free from Sea Grant College Program, Virginia Institute of Marine Science, Gloucester Point, VA 23062. Request VIMS Contribution No. 734.

38. *The Citizen's Guide to North Carolina's Shifting Inlets,* by Simon Baker, 1977. A guide to recent inlet history. Contains excellent air photographs of each inlet in the state. Two historic shoreline positions marked in red on each photograph. Allows reader to compare historic and present inlet-shoreline positions and illustrates their instability. Brief explanatory text accompanying the photographs raises questions that should concern all coastal residents and taxpayers. Available from UNC Sea Grant, 1235 Burlington Laboratories, North Carolina State University, Raleigh, NC 27607.

39. *A Historical Review of Some of North Carolina's Coastal Inlets,* by Jay Langfelder and others, 1974. Describes past and potential migration trends of North Carolina's active inlets. Discusses inlet widening and shoreline erosion. Contains air photographs from 1938 to 1972 which illustrate the changes in size and position for each inlet. A useful companion reference to reference 38. Available from UNC Sea Grant (address under previous reference).

40. *A Flow Study of Drum Inlet, North Carolina,* by P. R. Blankinship, 1976. A more technical reference on an artificial inlet and its history of change. Contains a list of additional references on the state's inlets. Available from UNC Sea Grant (address under reference 38).

41. *Hydrology and Circulation Patterns in the Vicinity of Oregon Inlet and Roanoke Island, North Carolina,* by J. J. Singer and C. E. Knowles, 1975. A technical report on currents in the sounds and ebb- and flood-tide flow in the inlet. Available from UNC Sea Grant (address under reference 38).

42. *Natural Hazard Management in Coastal Areas,* by G. F. White and others, 1976. The most recent summary of coastal hazards along the entire U. S. coast. Discusses adjustments to such hazards and hazard-related federal policy and programs. Summarizes hazard-management and coastal-land-planning programs in each state. Appendices include a directory of agencies, an annotated bibliography, and information on hurricanes. An invaluable reference, recommended to developers, planners, and managers. Available from the Office of Coastal Zone Management, National Oceanic and Atmospheric Administration, 3300 Whitehaven Street N.W., Washington, DC 20235.

43. *Guidelines for Identifying Coastal High Hazard Zones,* by the U. S. Army Corps of Engineers, 1975. Report outlining such zones with emphasis

on "coastal special flood-hazard areas" (coastal floodplains subject to inundation by hurricane surge with a one percent chance of occurring in any given year). Provides technical guidelines for conducting uniform flood-insurance studies and outlines methods of obtaining 100-year-storm-surge elevations. Recommended to island planners. Available from the Galveston District, U. S. Army Corps of Engineers, Galveston, TX 77553.

Vegetation

44. *Vegetation and Ecological Processes on Shackleford Bank, North Carolina,* by S. F. Au, 1974. Informative study of an undeveloped island. Lists plant-community makeup and relates vegetative changes to geologic and historic factors, particularly to damage from grazing animals. Publication No. NPS 113 from the U. S. Government Printing Office, Washington, DC 20402. Currently out of print, but may be available in public or university libraries.

45. *Seacoast Plants of the Carolinas for Conservation and Beautification,* by K. E. Braetz, 1973. An excellent discussion of beach and dune environments relative to natural plants. Suggestions for plantings to stabilize and protect dunes and to landscape the beach. Evaluations of perennial beach plants. Descriptions and illustrations of various natural and ornamental plants. Available from coastal offices of the District Conservationists or from UNC Sea Grant, 1235 Burlington Laboratories, North Carolina State University, Raleigh, NC 27607. Price $2.00.

46. *The Dune Book: How to Plant Grasses for Dune Stabilization,* by Johanna Seltz, 1976. Brochure outlining the importance of sand dunes and means of stabilizing them through grass plantings. Available from UNC Sea Grant (address under previous reference).

47. *Vegetative Dune Stabilization in North Carolina,* by Carl T. Blake and others, 1973. A one-page agronomy-information leaflet which outlines the types of plants to use for dune stabilization. Includes instructions on transplanting. Available from Agricultural Information, North Carolina State University, Raleigh, NC 27607.

Site Analysis

48. *Handbook: Building in the Coastal Environment,* by R. T Segrest and Associates, 1975. A well illustrated, clearly and simply written book on Georgia coastal-zone planning, construction, and selling problems. Topics include vegetation, soil, drainage, setback requirements, access, climate, and building orientation. Includes a list of addresses for agencies and other sources of information. Much of the information applies to North Carolina. Available from the Graphics Department, Coastal Area Planning and Development Commission, P. O. Box 1316, Brunswick, GA 31520. Price $2.00.

49. *Information for Buyers and Owners of Coastal Property in North Carolina,* prepared by the Center for Marine and Coastal Studies. An excellent pamphlet outlining hazards and environmental factors of importance to coastal property owners. Includes information on permits, codes, in-

197

surance, and land-use planning. Free from the Center for Marine and Coastal Studies, North Carolina State University, Raleigh, NC 27607.

50. *Handbook for Coastal Property Owners,* by Neale Bird, 1976. A four-page pamphlet which may interest Carolinians "south of the border." Subject matter similar to that of two preceding references. Free as Marine Advisory Bulletin 10 from the South Carolina Sea Grant Office, South Carolina Marine Resources Center, P. O. Box 21559, Charleston, SC 29407.

Water Problems

51. *Your Home Septic System, Success or Failure.* Brochure providing answers to commonly asked questions on home septic-systems. Lists agencies that supply information on septic-tank installation and operation. Available from UNC Sea Grant, 1235 Burlington Laboratories, North Carolina State University, Raleigh, NC 27607.

52. *Rules and Regulations Governing the Disposal of Sewage from any Residence, Place of Business, or Place of Public Assembly in North Carolina.* Provides details of the laws that govern liquid-waste disposal. Available from the State Board of Health, Cooper Memorial Building, Raleigh, NC 27606.

53. *Report of Investigation of the Environmental Effects of Private Waterfront Lands,* by W. Barada and W. M. Partington, 1972. An enlightening reference which treats the effects of finger canals on water quality. Available from the Environmental Information Center, the Florida Conservation Foundation, Inc., 935 Orange Avenue, Winter Park, FL 32789.

Individual Islands

54. *The Status of the Barrier Islands of the Southeastern Coast,* by Langdon Warner, 1976. General information on island environments, development pressures, government stiumulants to private development, and property assessments. Tables summarize the status of development on barrier islands in each southeastern coastal state. A readable, useful reference. Persons seeking more detailed information on the development status, property assessments, and local land-use regulations on individual islands may wish to obtain *Barrier Island Inventory,* price $15.00. Both references available from the Open Space Institute, 36 West 44th Street, Room 1018, New York, NY 10036.

55. *The Currituck Plan,* prepared for the three-man Executive Committee for Programming and Funding, Currituck County Planning Commission, 1972. A four-phase planning study on the development of North Carolina's northernmost coastal county. Examines the constraints and pressures on development and a variety of alternatives for access and development. Persons interested in the development of Currituck Bank should inquire about the status of the plan and study it. Write the Currituck Plan, P. O. Box 8, Currituck, NC 27929.

56. *Fare-Thee-Well, Currituck Banks,* by Gary Soucie, 1976. Published in *Audobon* magazine, v. 78, no. 1, pp. 22-35.

57. *Cape Hatteras Shoreline Erosion Policy Statement,* prepared by the Denver Service Center, National Park Service, 1974. Describes the natural environments of the Cape Hatteras National Seashore islands and traces the history and economy of the Outer Banks. Outlines alternative management proposals for various zones along the islands and reviews five alternative land-use plans. Distributed through the National Park Service, Southeast Region, 1895 Phoenix Boulevard, Atlanta, GA 30349.

58. *Cape Lookout National Seashore, Statement for Management,* prepared by the National Park Service, 1976. Management outline that includes a variety of environmental data for Core and Shackleford Banks. Similar to previous reference. Available from the National Park Service (address under previous reference).

59. *Man's Impact on the Outer Banks of North Carolina,* by Robert Dolan, 1972. A brief summary of the effects of dune-diking on the Outer Banks. Several photographs illustrate the effects of the 1962 Ash Wednesday Storm on the Buxton area. (One shows the inlet cut on the northern edge of the town; it was later filled at a cost of $1.5 million.) Outlines man's responses to such storms. Available as Dune Stabilization Study, Natural Resource Report No. 3, National Park Service, Office of Natural Science, Washington, DC 20240.

60. *Dune Stabilization and Beach Erosion,* by Robert Linn and Robert Dolan, 1972. Brief review of the erosion problem on the Outer Banks. Discusses the effects of the Ash Wednesday Storm and outlines the drawbacks of engineering techniques used to combat erosion. Stresses the need for a man-*and*-nature rather than a man-*over*-nature strategy. Notes the high cost of attempts to "draw a line" of defense against the sea. Available from the National Park Service (address under previous reference).

61. *1973 Buxton Beach Nourishment Project, An Annotated Photographic Atlas, Cape Hatteras National Seashore, North Carolina,* by Robert Dolan and others, 1974. Study designed to provide a baseline against which to compare the long-term history of the 1973 beach fill. Readable, photographically illustrated documentation of the results of shoreline engineering. Also illustrates shoreline erosion, overwash, and damage wrought to the project by the February 1973 Lincoln's Birthday Storm. Available from Coastal Research Associates, the University of Virginia, Charlottesville, VA 22903.

62. *Termination II: How the National Park Service Annulled its "Commitment" to a Beach Erosion Control Policy at the Cape Hatteras National Seashore,* by R. D. Behn and M. A. Clark, 1976. A lesson in modern history about a very significant change in the policy of the National Park Service. The study traces the agency's initial commitment to shoreline engineering on the Outer Banks, the futile spending of millions of dollars on "protective" projects, and the gradual abandonment of the commitment in the mid-1970s. Interesting reading. Available from the Center for Policy Analysis, Institute of Policy Sciences and Public Affairs, Duke University, Durham, NC 27706.

63. *Ocracoke Inlet to Beaufort Inlet, North Carolina: Combined Hurricane Survey Interim Report and Beach Erosion Report,* by the U. S. Army Corps of Engineers, 1964. A hurricane survey for Portsmouth Island, Core and Shackleford Banks. Published by the U. S. Army Corps of Engineers, Wilmington District, Wilmington, NC 28401.

64. *How to Live with an Island,* by O. H. Pilkey, Jr., O. H. Pilkey, Sr., and R. Turner, 1975. A guide to living and building on Bogue Banks, North Carolina. Predecessor of *From Currituck to Calabash.* Outlines good construction practice for homes on or near the beach in greater detail than does the later book. Available from the Director, North Carolina Science and Technology Research Center, P. O. Box 12235, Research Triangle Park, NC 27709. Price $3.00.

65. *Effect of Development on Barrier Island Evolution, Bogue Banks, North Carolina,* by D. T. Stanczuk, 1975. An unpublished master's thesis on shoreline erosion and the effects of engineering structures on Bogue Banks. Available through interlibrary loan from Duke University, Durham, NC 27706.

66. *The Land Use Plan for Pine Knoll Shores, North Carolina,* 1976. An excellent example of a community plan designed in compliance with county and state plans. Available through the Pine Knoll Shores Town Board of Commissioners or Planning Board.

67. *Interim Survey Report of Hurricane Protection, Beaufort Inlet to Bogue Inlet, North Carolina,* by the U. S. Army Corps of Engineers, 1965. A somewhat dated report that may still be of interest to persons living on Bogue Banks and nearby islands. Available from the U. S. Army Corps of Engineers, Wilmington District, P. O. Box 1890, Wilmington, NC 28401.

68. *Investigation of Erosion, Carolina Beach, North Carolina,* (District Report) by the U. S. Army Corps of Engineers, Wilmington District, 1970. An eye-opening study on beach-nourishment projects and the effects of artificially opening an inlet. When the Carolina Beach Inlet was artificially opened in 1952, severe erosion was prompted on over 7,000 feet of shoreline south of the inlet, and the overall shoreline-erosion rate increased from 0.6 to 2.8 feet per year. The study is a post-1965 follow-up on hurricane-protection and beach-erosion-control construction. Available from the U. S. Army Corps of Engineers (address under previous reference).

69. *Recent History of Erosion at Carolina Beach, North Carolina,* by Limberios Vallianos, 1970. A technical paper that summarizes the above study. Published in the *Proceedings of the 12th Conference on Coastal Engineering,* American Society of Civil Engineers, v. 11, pp. 1223-1242. Available from the U. S. Army Corps of Engineers (address under reference 67).

70. *General Design Memorandum, Phase I: Hurricane-Wave Protection, Beach-Erosion Control, Brunswick County, North Carolina, Beach Projects, Yaupon Beach and Long Beach Segments,* by the U. S. Army Corps of Engineers, 1973. A detailed study of Oak Island. Includes information on

storm history, shoreline-erosion rates, and proposed structures for protection. Also contains maps, air photographs, and designs of proposed protective devices. Shows how detailed pre-project preparation must be and provides an information resource for future studies of Oak Island. (This proposed project was never initiated.) Available for inspection at the office of the U. S. Army Corps of Engineers, Wilmington District, Wilmington, NC 28401.

Conservation and Planning

71. *The Water's Edge: Critical Problems of the Coastal Zone,* edited by B. H. Ketchum, 1972. The best available scientific summary of coastal-zone problems. Published by the M.I.T. Press, Cambridge, MA 02139.

72. *Design with Nature,* by Ian McHarg, 1969. A now-classic text on the environment. Stresses that when man interacts with nature, he must recognize its processes and governing laws, and realize that it both presents opportunities for and requires limitations on human use. Published by Doubleday and Company, Inc., Garden City, NY 11530.

73. *Coastal Ecosystems, Ecological Considerations for Management of the Coastal Zone,* by John Clark, 1974. A clearly written, well illustrated book on the applications of the principles of ecology to the major coastal-zone environments. Available from the Publications Department, The Conservation Foundation, 1717 Massachusetts Avenue N.W., Washington, DC 20036.

74. *Who's Minding the Shore,* by the Natural Resources Defense Council, Inc., 1976. A guide to public participation in the coastal-zone management process. Defines coastal ecosystems and outlines the Coastal Zone Management Act, coastal-development issues, and means of citizen participation in the coastal-zone management process. Lists sources of additional information. Available from the Office of Coastal Zone Management, National Oceanic and Atmospheric Administration, 3300 Whitehaven Street N.W., Washington, DC 20235.

75. *Ecological Determinants of Coastal Area Management* (two volumes), by Francis Parker, David Brower, and others, 1976. Volume 1 defines the barrier-island and related lagoon-estuary systems and the natural processes that operate within them. Outlines man's disturbing influences on island environments and suggests management tools and techniques. Volume 2 is a set of appendices that includes information on coastal-ecological systems, man's impact on barrier islands, and tools and techniques for coastal-area management. Also contains a good barrier-island bibliography. Available from the Center for Urban and Regional Studies, University North Carolina, 108 Battle Lane, Chapel Hill, NC 27514. Price $1.00 for both volumes.

76. *Coastal Development and Areas of Environmental Concern,* edited by Simon Baker, 1975. Proceedings of a symposium held at East Carolina University in March 1975. The collection of papers outlines sensitive environments, types of sites to be preserved, and implementations of CAMA. Interesting papers on sand dunes, salt marshes, archaeological sites, and

historic sites. Especially recommended is the paper entitled "Scenery for Sale" (pp. 28-41), by A. Conrad Neumann, which summarizes the natural, economic, and social pressures exerted on barrier islands. Available from UNC Sea Grant, 1235 Burlington Laboratories, North Carolina State University, Raleigh, NC 27607.

77. *Carrying Capacity: A Basis for Coastal Planning,* by three faculty members and 14 students of the University of North Carolina at Chapel Hill, 1974. An excellent summary of the environmental, economic, sociological and legal factors affecting development in Carteret County, particularly Bogue Banks. Available from the Center for Urban and Regional Studies (address under reference 75). Price $3.50.

78. *Citizen Participation in North Carolina's Coastal Area Mananement Program,* by Steve Tilley, 1974. Study which suggests ways to increase communication between the coastal community and government. Examines such topics as public hearings, citizen suits, homeowners' associations, and various forms of citizen participation in coastal management. Recommended reading for coastal citizens to increase their sensitivity to coastal problems. One copy free to North Carolina residents from the Center for Marine and Coastal Studies, Sea Grant Program, North Carolina State University, Raleigh, NC 27607.

79. *Proceedings of a Conference on Coastal Management, May 1974,.* A series of papers delivered at a conference sponsored by the Center for Marine and Coastal Studies, North Carolina State University. Reviews various group interests in the Coastal Area Management Act. Groups include state government, local government, developers and consultants, planners, business, and the public. Interesting reading. Available from the Center for Marine and Coastal Studies (address under previous reference).

80. *The Fiscal Impact of Residential and Commercial Development. A Case Study,* by T. Muller and G. Dawson, 1972. A classic study which demonstrates that development may ultimately increase, rather than decrease community taxes. Available from the Publications Office, the Urban Institute, 2100 M Street N.W., Washington, DC 20037. Price $3.00. Refer to URI-22000 when ordering.

81. *Report of the Conference on Marine Resources of the Coastal Plains States,* 1974. Collection of papers presented at a meeting in Wilmington. Topics include seabed mineral resources, sport fishing, recreation and tourism, and coastal-zone planning. Of special interest is a paper entitled "Responsible Development and Reasonable Conservation," by David Stick. Sponsored and published by the Coastal Plains Center for Marine Development Services, 1518 Harbour Drive, Wilmington, NC 28401.

82. *Coastal Planning—The Designation and Management of Areas of Critical Environmental Concern,* by T. J. Schoenbaum and K. G. Sillman, 1976. Most recent in the series of Sea Grant publications on coastal planning. A good supplement to references 75 and 76. Available from UNC Sea Grant, 1235 Burlington Laboratories, North Carolina State University, Raleigh, NC 27607.

83. *Legal Measures Concerning Marine Pollution,* edited by S. W. Wurfel, 1975. A set of papers written in 1974 by law students at the University of North Carolina at Chapel Hill. Summarizes marine pollution problems, and regulatory laws and their enforcement. *The Continental Shelf Lands of the United States: Mineral Resources and the Laws Affecting their Development, Exploitation, and Investment Potential,* by Elliott Dahles, Jr., 1975, may also be of interest, as offshore development will have a significant impact on barrier islands. Persons interested in this reference may also want to obtain *State and Federal Jurisdictional Conflicts in the Regulation of United States Coastal Waters,* by T. Suher and K. Hennessee, 1974. All three references available from UNC Sea Grant, 1235 Burlington Laboratories, North Carolina State University, Raleigh, NC 27607.

Building a New Home

Both current and prospective owners and builders of homes in hurricane-prone areas should supplement the information and advice provided in *From Currituck to Calabash* with that offered in references dealing specifically with safe construction. These excellent references contain sound, useful information that should help the residents of such areas to minimize the losses caused by extreme wind or rising water. Many of these publications are free. Some, government publications, are paid for by your taxes, so why not use them? The following references are recommended to those readers who wish to investigate further the subject of hurricane-resistant construction. (See also references 42, 48, 49, and 64.)

Building a Home (general)

84. *Southern Standard Building Code.* Available from Southern Building Code Congress, 1116 Brown Marx Building, Birmingham, AL 35203; or Southern Building Code Publishing Company, 3617 8th Avenue South, Birmingham, AL 35222.

85. *Dwelling House Construction Pamphlet of Southern Standard Building Code.* Conforms to the Southern Standard Building Code and applies only to dwellings of wood-stud or masonry-wall construction. Available from Southern Building Code Congress or Southern Building Code Publishing Company (addresses under previous reference). Price $1.45.

86. *The Uniform Building Code.* Available from International Conference of Building Officials, 5360 South Workman Mill Road, Whittier, CA 90601.

87. *Hurricane Exposes Structure Flaws,* by Herbert S. Saffir. In *Civil Engineering Magazine,* February 1971, pp. 54-55.

88. *Structural Failures: Modes, Causes, Responsibilities,* 1973. See especially the chapter entitled "Failure of Structures due to Extreme Winds," pp. 49-77. Available from the Research Council on Performance of Structures, American Society of Civil Engineers, 345 East 47th Street, New York, NY 10017. Price $4.00.

89. *North Carolina Uniform Residential Building Code,* prepared by the North Carolina Building Inspectors' Association, 1968 edition with amendments for 1969-1976. For coastal regions, two sections are particularly appropriate: (1) Appendix D, "Windstorm Resistive Construction," specifies the type of anchoring required in areas subject to winds greater than 75 m.p.h. Included are details on framing, masonry, walls, roof structures, and roof coverings. (2) Section 3.0 of Appendix D, "Piles Required" (the Sand Dune Ordinance), specifies that all buildings erected within 150 feet of the high-water mark of the Atlantic Ocean must be constructed on pile-type foundations. Included are details on the piles and the methods of fastening the structure to them. Published by the North Carolina Building Code Council. Available from the North Carolina Department of Insurance, Engineering Division, P. O. Box 26387, Raleigh, NC 27611. Price $0.50.

90. *Building Code Laws of North Carolina,* by the North Carolina Building Code Council, 1971 edition. Compilation of general statutes pertaining to the enforcement of the code. Available from the North Carolina Department of Insurance (address under previous reference). Price $0.50.

91. *Wind Resistant Design Concepts for Residences,* by D. B. Ward. Displays with vivid sketches and illustrations construction problems and methods of tying structures down to the ground. Considerable text and excellent illustrations devoted to methods of strengthening residences. Offers recommendations for relatively inexpensive modifications that will increase the safety of residences subject to severe winds. Chapter 8, "How to Calculate Wind Forces and Design Wind-Resistant Structures," should be of particular interest to the designer. Available as TR-83 from the Defense Civil Preparedness Agency, Department of Defense, The Pentagon, Washington, DC 20301; or the Defense Civil Preparedness Agency, 2800 Eastern Boulevard, Baltimore, MD 21220.

92. *Hurricane-Resistant Construction for Homes,* by T. L. Walton, Jr., 1976. An excellent booklet produced for residents of Florida, but equally as useful to those of the North Carolina coast. A good summary of hurricanes, storm surge, damage assessment, and guidelines for hurricane-resistant construction. Technical concepts on probability and its implications on home design in hazard areas. A brief summary of federal and local guidelines. Available from Florida Sea Grant Publications, Florida Cooperative Extension Service, Marine Advisory Program, Coastal Engineering Laboratory, University of Florida, Gainesville, FL 32611.

Wood Structures

93. *Houses Can Resist Hurricanes,* by the U. S. Forest Service, 1965. An excellent paper with numerous details on construction in general. Polehouse construction is treated in particular detail (pp. 28-45). Available as Research Paper FPL 33 from Forest Products Laboratory, Forest Service, U. S. Department of Agriculture, P. O. Box 5130, Madison, WI 53705.

94. *Wood Structures Survive Hurricane Camille's Winds.* Available as Research Paper FPL 123, October 1969, from Forest Products Laboratory (address under previous reference).

95. *Wood Structures Can Resist Hurricanes,* by Gerald E. Sherward, 1972. See *Civil Engineering Magazine,* September 1972, pp. 91-94.

Masonry Construction

96. *Standard Details for One-Story Concrete Block Residences,* by the Masonry Institute of America. Contains nine fold-out drawings which illustrate the details of constructing a concrete-block house. Principles of reinforcement and good connections aimed at design for seismic zones, but apply to design in hurricane zones as well. Written for both layman and designer. Available as Publication 701 from Masonry Institute of America, 2550 Beverly Boulevard, Los Angeles, CA 90057. Price $3.00.

97. *Masonry Design Manual,* by the Masonry Institute of America. An 8.5- by 11-inch, 384-page manual which covers all types of masonry including brick, concrete block, glazed structural units, stone, and veneer. Very comprehensive and well presented. Probably of more interest to the designer than to the layman. Available as Publication 601 from the Masonry Institute of America (address under previous reference). Price $14.00.

Pole-House Construction

98. *Pole House Construction.* Available from the American Wood Preservers Institute, 1651 Old Meadows Road, McLean, VA 22101.

99. *Elevated Residential Structures, Reducing Flood Damage through Building Design: A Guide Manual,* prepared by the Federal Insurance Administration, 1976. An excellent publication outlining the threat of floods and the necessity for proper planning and construction. Illustrates construction techniques. Includes a glossary, worksheets for estimating building costs, and a list of additional references. Available from the U. S. Federal Insurance Administration, Department of Housing and Urban Development, 451 7th Street S.W., Washington, DC 20410; or order publication 0-222-193 from the Superintendent of Documents, U. S. Government Printing Office, Washington, DC 20402.

Mobile Homes

100. *Protecting Mobile Homes from High Winds,* TR-75, prepared by the Defense Civil Preparedness Agency, 1974. An excellent 16-page booklet which outlines methods of tying down mobile homes and means of protection such as positioning and wind-breaks. Publication 1974-0-537-785, available free from the Superintendent of Documents, U. S. Government Printing Office, Washington, DC 20402; or from the U. S. Army, AG Publications Center, Civil Defense Branch, 2800 Eastern Boulevard (Middle River), Baltimore, MD 21220.

101. *State of North Carolina Regulations for Mobile Homes,* published by the North Carolina Department of Insurance, 1972 edition. A compilation of state regulations pertaining to mobile homes. Contains special requirements governing homes in hurricane areas. Available from the North Carolina Department of Insurance, Box 26837, Raleigh, NC 27611. Price $1.00.

APPENDIX D

Field Trip Guides

APPENDIX D1
FIELD TRIP GUIDE

THE NORTHERN OUTER BANKS OF NORTH CAROLINA

by

Stanley R. Riggs
and
Stephen B. Benton

Geology Department
Title I Environmental Education Program
East Carolina University
Greenville, North Carolina
27834

This is a shortened version of a field trip guide by the same authors, to be published during the summer of 1978 by UNC Sea Grant, 1235 Burlington Laboratories, North Carolina State University, Raleigh, NC 27607. UNC/SG Publication 78-03.

Fig. D1　Looking east along the causeway across Roanoke Sound during a recent small storm. The wind tide from the Albemarle Sound has flooded the barrier, almost closing one of the two access routes.

0.0　**START. HWY. 64-264 ON ROANOKE ISLAND SIDE OF WASHINGTON BAUM BRIDGE.** Go east and cross Roanoke Sound.

This section of the causeway, east of the bridge, is the first portion of the road to be flooded during storms. Thus, one of the only two escape routes from the Outer Banks is completely cut off when most needed (Figures D1 and D2).

The islands you are traveling over and the extensive salt-marsh islands to the north and south are remnants of the Roanoke Inlet tidal delta (Figure D3). Even after the inlet closed (around 1817), salt-marsh buildup on the delta continued to widen the island. (See Chapter 2 for explanation of island widening.)

2.5　Whalebone junction. Turn south (right) on Hwy. 12.

7.9　Turn east (left) toward the National Park Service Park Ranger Office on Coquina Beach Road.

8.1　**STOP 1.　COQUINA BEACH PARKING LOT.** Notice that the National Park Service has designed this new facility to be compatible with the environment. The sunshades offer

Fig. D2 The same view during a storm, probably in the 1930s. Escape has not always been easy. *Source: National Park Service*

minimal resistance to the frequent high-velocity storm winds and have been built on skids so they can be moved easily. The bathhouse is constructed of massive materials, raised on stilts, and set well behind the dune line. Most important, the pilings extend through the roof, tying the entire unit together.

Until two or three years ago, Coquina Beach was one of the most rapidly eroding stretches of beach in the National Seashore; 15 feet of beach retreated per year between 1960 and 1970. In 1973, the ocean breached the dunes here, destroying the old bathhouse and the "permanent" sunshades that were located approximately where the picnic tables are now (Figure D4).

10.7 Turn west (right) into the Oregon Inlet marina and fishing center. Bear left; drive to the left of the boat docks and to the south end of the parking lot.

11.2 **STOP 2. OREGON INLET MARINA PARKING LOT.** This inlet, which formed during a hurricane in 1846, might better be called an *out*let since its primary function is to allow freshwater flow from the land and water piled up in the

Fig. D3   Aerial view looking west at the old Roanoke Inlet flood tidal delta shoals and marsh in Roanoke Sound. Notice the Washington Baum Bridge at the upper right, which connects the shoals to Roanoke Island in the background.

sound during storms to escape past the barrier island into the sea. Inlets are natural, self-adjusting safety valves. During storms or floods they open up by flushing sand out. Between storms they close down by shoaling to minimal-sized channels. Sometimes during storms new inlets will open where needed to relieve the "pressure." When the storm or flood has passed, these temporary inlets may close up naturally. Without inlets the barrier islands would act as dams, and storm damage due to flooding would increase.

You are looking out over a vast accumulation of submerged sand shoals (sandbars) which extend as far as the eye can see. This extensive shoal system is better known as a *tidal delta.* There is a popular belief that inlets rob and trap in their tidal deltas much sand that belongs on the beach. This is a very nearsighted and dangerous outlook on our barrier-island system. The tidal delta is a major, much needed, sediment storage-bin for the entire coastal system. High-energy storms and floods flush out the inlet and move the sand laterally to adjacent beach areas, where it is used to absorb the storm energy. Furthermore, the tidal delta

Fig. D4 The old sunshade-bathhouse at Coquina Beach just after the February storm in 1973. Subsequent storms during March destroyed the structure.

provides the "platform" or base by which the island widens and migrates. (See Chapter 2.)

Walk to the bridge. During the early phases of bridge construction in 1962, most of this area was underwater. However, by the time the bridge was completed and the fishing catwalks were being added on, the catwalks were already over dry land. Within a year after the bridge was completed, the Oregon Inlet shoal system in front of you had grown approximately to its present size. This constricted the main inlet channel, which responded by scouring itself deeper; thus the center pilings of the bridge were in serious danger from undermining. (They were subsequently protected with blankets of rip-rap.) Though there has been considerable minor fluctuation in the size of the shoals since the bridge was built, there has not been a *major* storm in this area since the 1962 Ash Wednesday Storm. What will happen to the bridge when the next storm "blows out" the inlet-shoal safety valve?

Walk south across the tide flats. Besides numerous tracks of worms, snails, crabs, and birds, you will see those of a relative newcomer—the off-road vehicle (ORV). Because of the explosive increase in ORV's and their severe impact upon the marsh and dune systems, the National Park Service has restricted ORV usage to a 100-foot-wide zone along the ocean and inlet-channel shorelines, and designated the remainder of the shoal system a salt-marsh management area. It has been estimated that as much as 80 to 90 per cent of the ocean-fish species that are important to man are directly or indirectly dependent on the salt marsh.

Return to your car and head over the spectacular 2.5-mile-long Oregon Inlet Bridge.

12.5 On the bridge. The islands to the west along the main channel are dredge-spoil islands and covered with shrub vegetation. It has only recently been discovered that these islands are important nesting sites for many seabirds that cannot co-exist with man's activities, particularly his ORV's.

14.6 South end of bridge. Continue south 0.4 miles on Hwy. 12. Turn sharply back left (north) on county road 1257 toward the Coast Guard Station; drive 0.8 miles to the abrupt turn in the road, and park.

16.2 **STOP 3. OREGON INLET.** The southward migration of Oregon Inlet is obvious from here. Since opening in 1846, the southern shore of the inlet has migrated two miles, taking with it the sites of both of the original lighthouses, built in 1814 and 1859, and the original lifesaving station. In 1976, the dredge dock and a portion of the road were removed by a small storm. The rubble you see here will prevent further erosion until the next storm.

The U.S. Army Corps of Engineers has proposed to stabilize this exceedingly dynamic inlet by emplacing an 8,100-foot jetty on the south side and a 10,000-foot jetty on the north side. The estimated cost is $48 million plus annual maintenance costs in excess of $5.5 million. The project is justified on the basis of aid to local economy, increased development potential, and safety of the fishing fleet. North Carolina coastal geologists and oceanographers, however, are skeptical of the long-range benefits of stabilizing inlets. It is known from past experience that the long-range effect of jetty construction is frequently adverse and cannot be accurately predicted by pre-construction studies. Many questions must be answered prior to jetty construction.

Fig. D5   Bulldozed berms, sand fencing, and grass plantings are used to repair an overwash section of the barrier dune breached by a storm.

Source: National Park Service

17.0   Return to Hwy. 12 and proceed south (left).

19.0   **STOP 4.   GOING-TO-THE-SEA HIGHWAY.** Park along the remnant of the road that might now be called the "going-to-the-sea" highway. The main road was relocated about 1967 because of the migration of the island; the results of this migration process are dramatically underscored when a "permanent" structure such as this road is considered.

21.6   Along this stretch, notice that the barrier dune ridge has suffered various stages of destruction. There are numerous steep, straight, knife-edged sections between the irregular and higher ridges. These knife-edged portions occur in areas where the dunes have been breached by overwash and subsequently rebuilt with bulldozers, sand fencing, and grasses (Figure D5). Driving along this section, you can get a feel for the major cost of building and maintaining a barrier dune ridge along the entire length of Cape Hatteras National Seashore. This system cost about $3 million to build in the 1930s. Between 1957 and 1971, approximately $5.5 million was spent for general repair and fertilization. This figure does *not* include the money spent on beach maintenance, beach protection, road replacement, structural repair after storms, etc.; these costs amounted to an added expenditure of approximately $10 million between 1957 and 1972. The dune was built under the mistaken impression that the natural-island system needed protection. (See Chapter 2 for discussion of dune dikes.)

23.9 **STOP 5. NEW INLET.** Turn west (right) onto a short dirt road that runs to the sound. You are parked on the site of a series of relatively unstable inlets that first appeared on the maps in 1738. Apparently they were relatively small, ephemeral, and little used during the colonial period since the larger, longer-lived Roanoke Inlet was open until the early 1800s. After the closing of Roanoke Inlet, a series of major inlets opened in the vicinity of the present Oregon Inlet and provided the primary flowage through the barrier islands. By the time the present Oregon Inlet opened in 1846, New Inlet was almost closed, and it finally closed completely in 1922. An unsuccessful attempt was made in 1925 to open the inlet artificially. New Inlet reopened in 1933 as a result of hurricanes and remained open until 1945. The wooden bridges that you see were built during this period and stand as monuments to the dynamic nature of the inlets and the impermanence of man's structures. What are the chances that this is the destiny of the great Oregon Inlet Bridge?

28.4 To the west is a well developed, broad and low-sloping overwash fan which formed during the 1962 Ash Wednesday Storm (Figure D6). Active erosion will continue here from both the ocean and sound sides until the island breaches and an inlet forms. This portion of the barrier island *needs* an inlet to build up the back side of the island.

30.5 **STOP 6. FISHING PIER.** Turn east (left) at the J.J. Drive-in and proceed to the Hatteras Island Fishing Pier. A small northeaster during the fall of 1970 caused the shoreline to recede 92 feet at the pier. A similar storm in 1973 destroyed the pier. The anomalously wide and very reasonable set-back distance for the houses to the south and north exists solely because the National Park Service boundary extends that far inland at this point. Notice the abundant ORV tracks along the beach here (Figure D7). What is the impact of

Fig. D6   Large overwash fans breach the Cape Hatteras barrier dune during a
storm. Notice the size of the overwash fan in the foreground.

Source: National Park Service

Fig. D7   A typical beach scene during the fishing seasons. What is the impact of
these ORV's upon the beach system, the abundant population of burrow-
ing organisms of the beach, and sunbathers?

217

spinning tires and sediment compaction upon the multitude of organisms that live and burrow in the loose beach sands?

31.2 Return to Hwy. 12 and proceed south (left).

32.4 Notice that the old part of the town of Waves is nestled in the trees on the sound side.

34.0 Where is the old part of Salvo located?

46.5 Avon is a very old Outer Bank community developing at a rapid rate. The growth of this area has already exceeded the land's natural carrying-capacity with respect to water supply and sewage disposal. This has been underscored recently with the controversy over the construction of a water pipeline from Frisco. The surface aquifer, or groundwater table, is simply a shallow lens of fresh water derived from rainfall that floats on top of the denser, underlying salt water. The aquifer here is limited and extremely vulnerable. The water is contaminated by salt water during storm overwash or flooding and may take several weeks to months of flushing by rainfall to render the water potable again; this is one important reason that water tanks and cisterns were integral parts of early Outer Banks homes. Also, the aquifer on the back side of the island is generally of less desirable quality due to a sulfur taste resulting from the salt marshes. Of even greater importance today, however, is that everyone is dependent upon septic tanks for sewage treatment and that these tanks contaminate the same limited aquifer as well as the near-shore marshes and shellfish beds. Presently the continued development in Avon is limited. With an improved water supply, growth and development can continue at least for a while. The proposed pipeline will be built along the side of the highway that, as we have already seen, "goes to the sea." To what extent, then, are we forced to increase our effort to protect yet another "vital and permanent" structure along an extremely vulnerable section of barrier island?

53.1 **STOP 7. BUXTON OVERWASH AREA, NORTH SIDE.** Park to the east (left) on the remnants of the most recent going-to-the-sea highway (Figure D8). There is one very important benefit in losing sections of the highway to the sea: they make excellent parking and beach-access areas.
　　From the dune crest you will see the following:

218

Fig. D8   Aerial view of North Carolina's "Million Dollar Coast". Sand is being pumped from Cape Point in the far distance, to the Buxton overwash area where the beach sticks out into the ocean. This is an attempt to stabilize a high hazard area where storm erosion is severe. Notice the relocated highway behind the "renourished" section of the beach.

Source: National Park Service

1. To the south, the highway that went to sea in February 1973 (Figure D8). The barrier dune upon which you stand was also destroyed at that time. The pavement from the old road has been bulldozed into a small barrier ridge adjacent to the new road.

2. To the west, numerous sand shoals and salt-marsh islands which extend out into Pamlico Sound (Figure D8). These flood-tide delta shoals formed when inlets existed at this site.

3. To the east, the remnant of a $2-million-per-mile beach built in 1973. This is North Carolina's GOLD COAST (Figure D8).

With a very high rate of shoreline recession, common overwash, and the occasional formation of an inlet, this site has been considered a critical area for a long time. This narrow portion of the barrier, known as The Haulover, was the site of one or more historic inlets known as Cape Inlet

Fig. D9   Aerial view of the same general area as Figure D8 during the 1962 Ash Wednesday storm. Notice the newly cut "Buxton Inlet" in the foreground.

Source: National Park Service

and Chacandepeco Inlet, which existed from at least 1585 to the mid-to-late 1600s. It was at this site that the Ash Wednesday Storm of 1962 opened up Buxton Inlet (Figures D9 and D10), later filled with sand pumped from the flood-tide delta, and that a new dune system and road were rebuilt at a cost of $1.5 million. However, the shoreline continued to recede at the rate of 10 to 20 feet per year on the ocean side, and 3 feet per year on the sound side. In February 1969 and 1970, several major northeast storms overwashed this area. Extensive sandbagging was done after each of these storms; then, in February 1973, the ocean again washed over the road and into the sound (Figure D11). Every high tide for the next month continued to wash up to 4 feet of sand over the road with the North Carolina Department of Transportation bulldozers pushing the sand back onto the beach every low tide. One-half mile of the road was relocated to its present site. This was followed by a $4.3-million project to pump 1.3 million cubic yards of sand from Cape Point to replenish less than 2 miles of beach—from

Fig. D10   Ground view of the "Buxton Inlet" shortly after the 1962 storm.

Source: National Park Service

Fig. D11   View north of the Buxton washover during the 1973 storm from Cape Hatteras Lighthouse. The washover is at the break in the barrier dune line in front of the cottages and motels in the upper left of the photo. Notice pipeline for the beach nourishment project in front of the dune.

Fig. D12   The outer portion of the Hatteras Court Motel at Buxton following the February, 1973 storm. Notice the extensive peat bed, nylon sandbags, and the water pipes that supplied the cottages above them.

this point south to the groin field at the U.S. Naval facility.

You are looking at the north end of this project. At the time of this writing, there had been at least one more period of active overwash and less than half of the reconstructed beach width remained. How much longer will it be before this area is washed over again, or another inlet opens from the sound side? Remember that the Avon water pipeline must cross this high-hazard area! The continued growth and development of Avon increases its dependence upon this extremely vulnerable water pipeline; future destruction during a major storm can only increase the impact of such a disaster.

53.7   **STOP 8.   BUXTON OVERWASH AREA, SOUTH SIDE.** Stop and park on the south end of this section of the going-to-the-sea highway, about 50 yards north of the Hatteras Court Motel.

To the south are a series of motels that were in the surf zone most of the 1973 winter and were severely damaged in the February 1973 storm (Figure D12). Notice the extensive sand-fencing around the Hatteras Court Motel. In 1973

222

before it was destroyed, the motel extended seaward to about the outer sand ridge. Figure D12 shows the remains of the motel after the storm; the water pipes to the outer cabins are below the outer sand dune. The picture also shows the extensive peatbed below you. Notice what was left of the nylon sandbagging. Also notice that the Hatteras Court Motel has built a new motel on pilings on the west side of the highway, a logical and intelligent response to the long-term changes. The next motel to the south, however, which also was seriously damaged in 1973, will be rebuilt on the same site and will continue to fight the ocean's receding shoreline.

54.2   Turn south on the National Park Service Road to Cape Hatteras National Seashore Visitors' Center. The next 0.8 mile you will be driving through the unique maritime forest known as Buxton Woods.

55.1   Turn east (left) at the junction toward the Visitors' Center and Hatteras Lighthouse.

55.2   **STOP 9. CAPE HATTERAS LIGHTHOUSE.** Park in the Cape Hatteras National Seashore parking lot and walk to the lighthouse. Built in 1870, this lighthouse, which rises 208 feet from its base, is the tallest lighthouse in the United States.

    1. To the south is Cape Point, with its large pond that was dug as a source of beach-replenishment sand in 1971 and 1973. Extending seaward from the Cape are the infamous Diamond Shoals, outlined by the tortuous interaction of various currents and waves across the shallow sand shoals.

    2. To the east and below you are three groins built in 1969 to protect the U.S. Naval facility and the Cape Hatteras Lighthouse (Figure D13). Notice how the groin field has effectively trapped sand and built a significant beach. Also notice, however, the severely eroded updrift (north) (Figure D11) and downdrift (south) beaches.

    3. To the north you see the U.S. Naval facility; the motel area that was severely damaged in the 1973 storms (Figure D11); the very narrow portion of the barrier where Buxton Inlet was formed; the salt-marsh islands from the inlet flood-tide delta; Pamlico

Fig. D13   Jetty protecting the beach in front of the Cape Hatteras lighthouse in Buxton. Notice the break about midway out in the structure.

Sound; and the remnants of the new multi-million-dollar beach built in 1973, which extends from the groins to the north, to the far side of the Buxton Inlet overwash area (Figure D8).

4. To the west you see the very wide, east/west-oriented Hatteras Island. Note the extensive ridge and swale topography that characterizes the entire island (Figure D14). Many of the swales have marshes and freshwater ponds in them; this is part of the more extensive groundwater system that Avon is hoping to share.

When the lighthouse was built in 1870, it was over 1,500 feet from the shoreline. By 1935, erosion had progressed to the point where the lighthouse, awash in the surf zone, was abandoned and replaced by a steel tower one mile to the northwest. However, extensive sand-fencing and grass-planting by the Civilian Conservation Corps and the National Park Service in the late 1930s formed an extensive series of barrier dune ridges; by 1950 the lighthouse was declared safe and the light was returned. The development of the

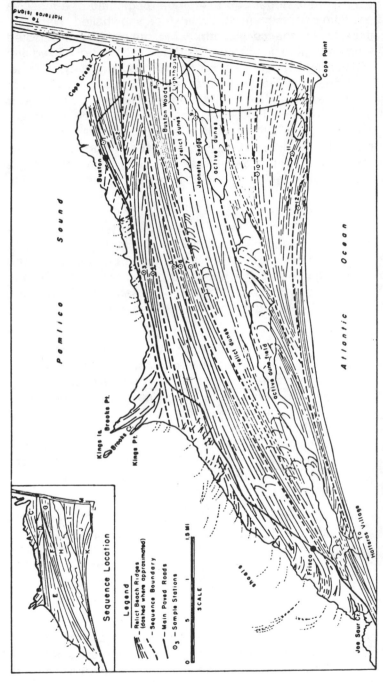

Fig. D14   Relict beach ridges on Hatteras Island which contain the maritime forest of Buxton Woods. Sequence A is the oldest set of ridges while L is the youngest. (From Fisher, J. J., 1967, *Development Pattern of Relict Beach Ridges, Outer Banks Barrier Chain, North Carolina*, Ph.D Dissertation, UNC Chapel Hill, 250p.)

225

barrier dune ridges represents the beginning of a massive economic investment that has since snowballed. With continued maintenance and rebuilding, the barrier dunes lasted long enough to encourage rapid development of a fixed line of "permanent" structures: the U.S. Naval facility, houses, and motels. However, by the early 1960s, large portions of the barrier dunes had been breached. Overwash was becoming the dominant process; the surf was once more approaching the lighthouse and other structures. Something had to be done! Following is a brief list of the projects undertaken in attempts to reverse the long-term, continuous process of shoreline recession in response to a slowly rising sea level:

1. In 1966, the National Park Service contracted to have 312,000 cubic yards of sand extracted from the tidal-delta sand shoals of Buxton Inlet in Pamlico Sound to replenish the beaches in the vicinity of the lighthouse. The $300,000 project was a failure due largely to the fact that the inlet sand-shoals were too fine-grained for such a high-energy beach.

2. In 1969, the U. S. Navy contracted to have three groins constructed within the problem area. These three 500-foot groins were considered experimental and were expected to fail; they did, even before construction was complete (Figure D13). They have since been repaired and modified. Total cost: about $1.2 million. Though they have trapped sand and been partially effective, the adjacent shorelines north (Figure D11) and south of the groin field have continued to erode, possibly at an even faster rate in response to the groins.

3. The National Park Service continued to try to hold the line utilizing 4' by 8' nylon sandbags (Figure D12) at a cost greater than $300,000 by late 1970. However, in response to a single storm in October 1970, the National Park Service estimated an additional $240,000 cost for sandbagging to repair the dunes in this area alone.

4. In 1971, the National Park Service contracted to have another 200,000 cubic yards of sand extracted from Cape Point, this time to replenish the north side of

the groin field. This $500,000 project was somewhat more successful since the sand was of the proper grain size; however, the quantity of sediment was not sufficient to have a very significant impact upon the beach system.

5. Erosion continued; consequently, bulldozing and sandbagging continued.

6. In 1973, the National Park Service contracted to have 1.3 million cubic yards of sand pumped from the Cape Point spit to replenish 9,000 feet of beach north of the groin field at a cost of $4.3 million.

7. Since the 1973 project, the National Park Service has been involved in a very controversial re-evaluation of its shoreline-erosion policy in an effort to address the entire natural and social environment of the seashore. The ultimate result will be a comprehensive, barrier-island, environmental-management policy.

55.4   Return to junction and continue straight ahead (west).

55.7   Turn west (right) into the Cape Hatteras National Seashore parking lot for the Buxton Nature Trail.

STOP 10. BUXTON WOODS NATURE TRAIL. This beautiful trail winds across one of the east-west beach ridges that makes up the bulk of Hatteras Island (Figure D14) and takes you through one of the largest maritime forests on the Outer Banks. The swale contains an extensive freshwater marsh (locally, called sedge) with an abundance of wildlife. Go slowly and absorb the beauty of this unique natural system.

SOUTHEASTERN NORTH CAROLINA SHORELINES: WRIGHTSVILLE BEACH TO FORT FISHER

by

William J. Cleary
and
Paul E. Hosler

Program in Marine Sciences
University of North Carolina
Wilmington, North Carolina
28401

This is a shortened version of a field trip guide by the same authors, entitled "New Hanover Banks, Then and Now: A Guide to the New Hanover County Beaches." Available as UNC-SG Publication No. 77-14 from UNC Sea Grant, 1235 Burlington Laboratories, North Carolina State University, Raleigh, NC 27607.

0.0 **START. U.S. 76 BRIDGE OVER ATLANTIC INTRA-COASTAL WATERWAY.**

0.3 Bear left following U.S. 74. Saline Water Plant on right.

0.4 The Channel Walk development, located left (north) of the road, represents an area of once-flourishing marsh that was bulkheaded and infilled with dredged material from nearby channels in 1966.

1.5 Stoplight. Turn left; follow U.S. 74. Moore's (also called Barren or Wrightsville) Inlet flowed through this area from 1905 to 1915. You are now riding on the old tidal delta of the former inlet.

1.8 Surf Club on right. Sewage treatment plant on left. Local residents recently sued the beach community because the capacity of the plant had been exceeded on numerous occasions, leading to the closure of shellfishing areas in the vicinity.

2.0 **STOP 1. HOLIDAY INN/ISLANDER/SHELL ISLAND DE-VELOPMENT.** Park cars wherever possible, and walk out onto the beach in front of the Holiday Inn. This section of Wrightsville Beach was once Moore's Inlet. Moore's Inlet has had a complex history of migration and was located in the early 1950s 0.5 km (.3 miles) south of your location. The inlet was closed in 1965 by the Corps of Engineers as part of the hurricane-protection project for Wrightsville Beach. Notice the blackened shell material; this represents lagoonal deposits used as fill. Usually when an inlet closes and dunes develop, that section of the island becomes one of the most stable sections due to the development of vegetated sand flats to the rear of the former inlet.

In this case, dune flattening and dredging behind the island have altered the natural system, rendering a potentially stable section of the island less stable. Water piling into the deep sound behind Shell Island during a hurricane approach will likely be released as the hurricane passes, forcing water over the lowest section of the beach. This places the development in a highly vulnerable position during inlet formation.

Compare the vegetation of the Shell Island development with that on the undeveloped section of the island to the north. Note that the vegetation that has colonized the fill material is much sparser than the natural vegetation. Dunes and vegetation generally grow in concert; the vegetation acts as a brake in causing sand to accumulate, while the the sand, in turn, stimulates the growth of plants. The coarse-sandy, shelly fill material is not nearly as conducive to the establishment and growth of sea oats and other beach plants as is natural, windblown sand. The lack of vegetation in these areas further compounds the effects of beach erosion. Under natural conditions, a dense vegetation mantle retards erosion of the dune system. Here, vegetation is lush only where sand has moved up from the beach by natural means.

Walk north along the berm beyond the developed section. This section of Shell Island as well as the remaining 5 km (3 miles) to the north is characterized by multiple dune rows. Walk over to the back side of the island to the area where the grasslands border a shallow tidal creek. This location is approximately 650 m (2,000 feet) north of the Holiday Inn. As you cross the dunes, look south from the high dune ridge. Note that the imaginary line formed by the rear dune cuts through the center of the Holiday Inn, placing it and several dwellings between you and the hotel in extremely vulnerable positions.

Return to your vehicles and proceed to the stoplight (N. Lumina and U.S. 74). Along the way you will notice landscaped areas containing a variety of vegetation including the Palmetto *(Sabal palmetto)*. Man has extended the northern limit of the Palmetto from Bald Head Island, 40 km (25 miles) to the south.

2.3   **STOP 2. MERCER'S PIER.** Stoplight. Turn left if parking spots are available, or park along one of the side streets. Parking meters and the median are located where the throat of Moore's Inlet existed in 1920. Mercer's Pier was built in the early 1940s, after the inlet migrated to the north, and has been rebuilt several times. From atop the pier at low tide you can see at regular intervals along the beach some of the groins that were emplaced (as early as 1923) to impound the eroding sand. The sloping section of the upper beach immediately in front of the lifeguard stand represents the results of the 1976 grading of the artificial dune and berm. Note that the pilings emplaced in the fill material directly in front of the steps of Mercer's Pier are being undermined, as evidenced by the exposure of the supports and the abundant blackened oyster shells strewn about the toe of the dune. Note again the relatively sparse vegetation on the berm and foredune.

Return to cars and proceed south along N. Lumina Blvd.

3.3 **STATION ONE.** The condominium is located behind the berm constructed in 1965 and is relatively safe from mild hurricane surge — for a while. Note, however, the condition of the artificial berm. Plans are now being formulated to renourish it once again.

3.5 **STOP 3. BLOCKADE RUNNER HOTEL** (optional stop). This hotel opened in 1964 and occupies the former location of several earlier, famous structures. One of the first structures built on Wrightsville Beach was a bathhouse constructed in 1888. In 1898 the Seashore Hotel was constructed; a steel pier built later, surviving a fire and several storms, was destroyed by a northeaster in January 1921. During this period the dune line retreated over 15.25 m (50 feet). Subsequent hotels were built on this site, the most recent one after the destruction of the Ocean Terrace by Hurricane Hazel in 1954. The roadbed and foundation of State Station No. 3 of the Wilmington and Sea Coast Railroad underlie the parking lot. The Blockade Runner provides an example of good beach development; a large volume of sand has been maintained between it and the sea. Note, however, that the newer section has been built closer to the beach than was the original; people apparently were beginning to forget Hurricane Hazel when this section was added.

Another feature of the Blockade Runner Hotel that represents good development is the location nearest the ocean of expendable structures such as the patio and the swimming pool. If a storm removes part of the beach, the motel structure is likely to remain intact with only a minimal loss of property. The location of these structures is aesthetically pleasing as well.

Return to cars and proceed south on Waynick Blvd.

As you travel south from the Blockade Runner, note the narrowness of the island. Banks Channel was the source of some of the sand used in the construction of the berm. The channel has been deepened considerably and its sides have been steepened. Erosion is occurring along this section of the channel because of the constant waves generated by boat wakes. No stabilizing marsh grass is present along the banks; the waves would unearth it.

4.4   Stop sign. Turn right onto S. Lumina Blvd.

5.0   **STOP 4. MASONBORO INLET JETTY AND THE AR-TIFICIAL BERM.** Turn around at the end of the island and find a spot to park. Several new houses are being construct-ed in this vicinity. Normally, building this close to the inlet is not a good investment, but the proximity of the jetty should minimize the chances of significant loss. Notice the sand fencing and the relatively large amount of sand that has collected in the past several years.

Major hurricanes of the 1950s devastated Wrightsville Beach, destroying many homes and causing massive ero-sion along the beach front. As a result, the remaining strand line possessed no frontal dunes as protection from hurricanes, and structures were exposed to storm surge.

In 1965 a cooperative federal, state, and local hurricane-protection project was completed on Wrightsville Beach. This project entailed the construction of an artificial berm along the entire length of the island from just south of Moore's Inlet to Masonboro Inlet, a distance of 4.3 km (2.7 miles). The berm, 50 feet wide and 12 feet high, was backed by a 15-foot-high, 25-foot-wide artificial dune. Constructed by the U.S. Army Corps of Engineers, the project was designed to protect the beach from destructive storms.

As previously stated, the dredge spoil used to construct the berm was primarily from Banks Channel. The material contained large quantities of very coarse materials (shells and sand) which appear blackened as a result of the reduc-ing conditions present in the channel environment. Though unpleasant to walk on, the material serves to protect struc-tures along the beach.

During the initial construction of the berm nearly 3,000,000 cu. yd. (2,295,000 m^3) of fill material was pumped onto the beach. The beach was renourished in 1966 when 360,000 cu. yd. (275,400 m^3) of material was added. Again in 1970, nearly 1,500,000 cu. yd. (1,147,500 m^3) of fill was used to renourish the beach. Today the artificial berm is severely scarped along nearly the entire length of the island. In time, a new beach-nourishment program will have to be instituted.

Masonboro Inlet, separating Wrightsville Beach from Masonboro Island, has been fickle during the past 40 years: on occasion it has been extremely wide and shallow, and at other times, narrow and deep. In the process of widening and narrowing, it has migrated back and forth across a 2.4 km (1.5 miles) stretch from just north of its present location to approximately 1.6 km (1 mile) south of Masonboro Island.

Note the jetty construction. The portion of the jetty nearest the shore is low and narrow; it was constructed in this manner to act as a weir. Sediments moving along the shore were to be carried across the jetty into a previously dredged depositional basin on the Masonboro Island side of the jetty. From here the trapped sand would be pumped periodically to Masonboro Beach to nourish the downdrift side of the jetty.

This unique system has not worked. The inlet gorge has shifted northward (jettyward) from its original position to a point where it now threatens to undermine both the sheet-metal weir and the outer rock jetty. The Corps of Engineers has armored the bottom of the channel with large stones, but a major storm would likely remove part of this armor and undermine the jetty. In addition, boats must now pass close to the jetty in order to navigate the inlet. The numerous temporary buoys in the vicinity of the inlet attest to the rapid and unpredictable shoaling of its inner portions.

A positive effect of the system, however, is that the southern end of Wrightsville Beach has been building seaward as sand in the littoral drift has been trapped by the jetty.

A jetty has also been planned for the south side of Masonboro Inlet. A model of the inlet has been constructed and data are being analyzed in order to assess the potential impact of a second jetty on the dynamics of the inlet.

Leave parking area and return to Hwy. 76 bridge across the Intracoastal Waterway where tour began.

7.4   Atlantic Intracoastal Waterway.

7.5   Babies Hospital. During Hurricane Hazel in 1954, water stood in the parking lot of the hospital.

7.8   Follow U.S. 76 West; bear left, inside lane.

9.5   Stoplight. Turn left onto Greenville Loop Road.

12.4   Fish Camp Restaurant. Turn left onto Masonboro Loop Road.

13.2   Hewlett's Creek. Bear right following Masonboro Loop Road.

14.5   Whiskey Creek. It is not too difficult to ascertain the occupation of the early inhabitants of this area. Bear left; stay on Masonboro Loop Road.

21.1   Junction Masonboro Loop Road and U.S. 421. Proceed across median and turn left onto U.S. 421 South. Proceed to Carolina Beach.

23.5   Snow's Cut.

25.0   Turn left at first traffic light onto King St. (City Hall is on right.)

25.1   Turn left and proceed north on Canal Drive.

26.7   **STOP 5. CAROLINA BEACH PIER.** Stop and park your car. The ramp to the pier provides an excellent view of an area that has been undergoing severe erosion. To the north is Carolina Beach Inlet; to the south, the town of Carolina Beach.

     Prior to 1952, the section of Carolina Beach facing north was part of Masonboro Island. In January 1952, a public hearing was held in order to act on a permit request to open a tidal inlet 2,285 m (7,500 feet) north of Carolina Beach. Although the Beach Erosion Board advised that erosion to the south might occur, support for the inlet project was overwhelming, and the Corps of Engineers granted the permit. In September, the inlet was created and the trouble began.

     Erosion on the Carolina Beach section of the coast before the opening of the inlet was approximately 18.3 cm (0.6 feet) per year. Following the opening of the inlet, erosion increased dramatically to 4.0 m (13 feet) per year between 1952 and 1955. The hurricanes of 1954 and 1955 devastated the Carolina Beach extension portion of the area. Since 1952, the overall erosion rate along the northern portion of Carolina Beach has averaged 12.2 m (40.2 feet) per year. The greatest measured erosion rate has occurred along the segment closest to the inlet—one of the inlet's negative effects. The sediment trapped by the inlet has caused the northerly beaches to become feeder beaches for the southern section of Carolina Beach.

Thus, a dilemma exists. Carolina Beach Inlet is largely responsible for the erosion suffered by the town of Carolina Beach; however, the people who are asking for erosion-control measures on the beach are against the closure of the inlet, now a well established fishing outlet in the area.

South of the inlet, beach erosion has carved into the shoreline a re-entrant which terminates against the north end of a rip-rap seawall. Remnants of an earlier wall and a groin portray the history of several attempts to stabilize the shoreline. The engineering was carried out to save beach property, protecting the interests of a very few, and at a long-term cost that ultimately will exceed the value of the protected property.

Proceed south along Canal Drive, retracing your path toward City Hall.

28.4 Stoplight. Turn right onto King St. and then left onto Lake Park Blvd. This section is typical of the highly commercialized section of the beach. Very little planning has gone into the development of the area. The area through which you are now passing is not a barrier island; it is a mainland beach. Note the lack of sound-side marsh in this environment on the right.

The mainland beach area of Carolina Beach and Kure Beach has a long, interesting, and expensive record of beach-stabilization attempts. This beach has long been adversely influenced by hurricanes and northeasters. Its history is one of extensive loss of property and beach due to severe storms. From 1857 to 1934, Carolina Beach experienced an average recession rate of 70 cm (2.3 feet) per year. During this time erosion and accretion both occurred; however, erosion was predominant. Between 1940 and 1955 the average recession rate along the beach was 4.5 m (14.7 feet) per year.

The Corps of Engineers report on erosion at Carolina Beach relates the damage due to hurricanes:

Cottages nearest the ocean were smashed to pieces or lifted intact from their foundations and hurled against nearby cottages. The ocean face only was ripped from many cottages, while others had both front and rear ripped off, leaving only the shell. Boardwalks and piers were torn apart, with piles being twisted off. Sand, washed inland, was deposited 3 and 4 feet deep in the streets.

28.5   Bear left at fork in road. This section of U.S. 241 has frequently been closed because of water ponding in this natural depression. The lake to the right may represent a drowned creek valley now dammed by the beach. Hurricane Hazel destroyed the first hotel — named the Breakers—built on the shoreline in 1924. It was located at the corner of Ocean Blvd. and South Carolina Ave. The debris and piles of rubble from the Breakers hotel were hauled to Fort Fisher to help curb the erosion in that area.

29.5   Wilmington Beach.

31.0   Kure Beach corporate limits.

31.4   **STOP 6.   KURE BEACH.** Stoplight, turn left (east). Kure Beach is a mainland beach. Note that the average elevation of the town is much higher than that of Wrightsville Beach.

The pier directly in front of you, built in 1927, is the second-oldest fishing pier on the east coast. One of its claims to fame is the fact that it has been destroyed and rebuilt twelve times, rebuilt most recently after Hurricane Hazel in 1954. To the left (north) of the pier the town has recently constructed 15.2 m (50 feet) of a bulkhead in addition to the already existing one. Notice the concrete strewn about in front of the new section; this rubble represents earlier seawalls, a common scene on the American beach. Mr. Robertson, the present pier owner, has a realistic philosophy on living by the shore: If the sea wants something, it is going to take it; there is nothing we can do about it. This statement was particularly true of Hurricane Hazel, for it cut away the first two streets of Kure Beach. Prior to 1954, the present beach road was the third street west of the high-tide line.

32.3   Entrance to Fort Fisher.

33.8   **STOP 7.   FORT FISHER HISTORICAL SITE.** A coquina (highly fossiliferous limestone) rock outcrop is present just north of the picnic area. Note the extensive erosion of the beach near the picnic area. Historic records show that erosion at this point has been approximately 366 m (1,200 feet) since 1862. A portion of the fort has been removed by erosion. Early excavation of the coquina for road construction by Kure and the New Hanover counties undoubtedly disturbed the area. The live oak trees standing in the picnic area have been opened up to the force of salt-laden air. Even these resistant trees are gradually dying because of the lack of dunes to protect their leaves from salt spray.

A worthwhile side trip is a visit to the museum (closed on Mondays).

Take a short trail to the large mounds along the Cape Fear River. This location provides a spectacular view of the river and the extensive marshes that border it.

34.8   Return to U.S. 421 South. Make a loop around the Fort Fisher Monument. To the south is the area of historic inlets that the fort was designed to protect. Farther south is Bald Head Island. This large, wooded island is being developed; at present, however, the island may be reached only by boat.

40.5   **STOP 8. N.C. MARINE RESOURCES CENTER** (optional stop). Park in lot. Return to U.S. 421 and drive south to end of road past ferry entrance on right.

INDEX

"Lost Colony," 5

M

McKee's Pier, 105
Mad Inlet, 130
marsh, 10, 25, 29, 37, 60, 62, 68, 72, 76,
  94, 98, 105, 108, 109, 110, 121, 122
  filling, 62, 99, 104, 127
  Spartina, 29
Masonboro
  Inlet, 30-31, 114
  Island, 1, 23-24, 30, 59, 114, 115
Mercer's Pier, 114
Miami Bqch, 10, 43, 45, 50-51
migration, barrier island (*see* barrier
  island: migration)
military occupation, islands, 9, 103,
  104, 118
mobile homes (*see* buildings: mobile
  homes)
Money Island Beach, 98-99
Monmouth Beach, New Jersey, 45
Moore's Inlet, 112
Morehead City, 7, 39
municipal water system (*see* water
  system, municipal)
Myrtle Beach, South Carolina, 130

N

Nags Head, 7, 9, 73, 77, 79
National Flood Insurance Program, 55,
  135-137, 159
navigation, problems, 60, 67, 97
New Bern, 14
New England coast, ix, 3, 5, 9, 10, 23,
  29, 34, 50, 52
New Hanover County, 110-118
New Inlet, 110
New Jersey coast, ix, 3, 5, 9, 10, 23, 39,
  45, 50, 52
"New Jerseyization," 5, 9-11
New River Inlet, 103, 104-105
Nile River Delta, 25
No Name Island, 59, 109
North Carolina Sand Dune Ordinance,
  89, 138, 161
North Carolina State Highway
  No. 12—84
  No. 50—104
  No. 130—124
  No. 133—121, 122
  No. 210—104-105
  No. 211—121
  No. 904—127

northeasters (*see* storms:
  northeasters)
nourishment, beach (*see* beach:
  replenishment)

O

Oak Island, 55, 121,122
Ocean City Fishing Pier, 106
Ocean Isle Beach, 62, 65, 127
ocean side, island, 7, 21, 24-25, 29, 35,
  37, 39, 75, 78, 79, 94, 98
Ocean View Railroad, 7
O'Connor, Dr. Michael, 37
Ocracoke
  Inlet, 7, 9, 94
  Island, 13, 94
  Lighthouse, 94
  village, 7, 14, 95
Onslow
  Beach, 9, 30, 59, 103
  County, 100-106
ordinance *(see* building: codes; *and*
  North Carolina Sand Dune
  Ordinance)
Oregon Inlet, 60, 74, 77, 86, 87
Outer Banks, 1, 21, 27, 39, 59, 69, 77,
  79, 93, 96
  development history, 5-11
overgrazing, 30, 57, 59
  deposition, 27, 45, 59
  fans, 23-24, 27, 29, 59
  passes, 23
  zones, 23, 55, 56, 59, 62, 68, 75, 76,
    78, 79, 87, 89, 90, 92, 93, 94, 98,
    99, 100, 104, 105, 109, 112, 114,
    116, 121, 123, 127

P

Padre Island, Texas, x, 23
Pamlico Sound, 37, 95
Paradise Fishing Pier, 105
Park Service, National (*see* National
  Park Service)
park, state, 99, 118
Pea Island, 69, 74-75
peat, 56, 105, 122, 123
Pender County, 106-109
pier, fishing, 118, 127, 130
piers, building, 152
piles, 152, 159
Pine Knoll Shores, 1, 99
pollution, 10, 65, 99, 104, 106, 108,
  109, 137, 140

Portsmouth
Island, 9, 96, 97
town, 7, 8, 9, 96
posts, 152

Q

R

Raleigh, Sir Walter, 5
recreation, 74, 99, 103
renourishment, beach (*see* beach: replenishment)
replenishment, beach (*see* beach: replenishment)
resorts, 7, 9, 46-47, 77, 110
restoration, beach (*see* beach: replenishment)
retreat, shoreline (*see* barrier island: migration; *and* shoreline: erosion)
Rice Path, 7, 62
Rich's Inlet, 110
ridge, beach, 19-20, 33
ridge and runnel system, 33-35, 36
Riggs, Dr. Stanley, 37
Roanoke
Inlet, 11, 83
Island, 11, 83
Rodanthe, 89
Romans, ix, 51
roof (*see* house, construction of: roof)
runnel (*see* ridge and runnel system)

S

Salter Path, 99
salt marsh (*see* marsh)
Salvo, 77
sand
bluff, 37
fixation, 94
longshore drift, 33, 35, 43, 115
movement (*see also* dune: movement; *and* sand: longshore drift), 23, 25, 30, 31-33, 43, 55, 57, 59, 75, 79, 116
supply, 23, 27, 29, 30, 31-32, 33-35, 40, 45, 48, 50-51, 103, 115, 116
sanitation (*see* waste disposal; septic system; *and* sewage)
scarp, dune (*see* dune: scarp)
sea-level changes (*see also* storm-surge flooding), 17-22, 25, 35-36, 53-55, 149-150
seawall, 10, 33, 43-45

septic (tank) system, 62, 63, 65, 68, 106, 108, 137, 140
setback requirements (*see also* North Carolina Sand Dune Ordinance), 57
sewage, 10, 65, 104, 108, 137
Shacklefoot Island, 100, 103
Shackleford Banks, 23, 27, 33, 62, 97, 98
Shallotte Inlet, 127
Shell Island, 112, 114
shells, sea, 21, 35, 56, 100, 124
shelter, storm (*see* house, construction of)
shoreline
engineering, 10, 39-52, 79, 84, 86, 112, 114, 116
erosion (*see also* barrier island: migration; *and* beach: shape), 19-21, 25, 30, 31-33, 35-37, 39, 40, 43, 45, 46, 79, 84, 87, 89, 90, 92, 94-98, 100, 103, 104, 105, 108, 109, 110, 114, 115, 116, 121, 122, 123, 124
migration (*see* barrier island: migration; beach; shape; *and* shoreline: erosion)
retreat (*see* barrier island: migration; beach; shape; *and* shoreline: erosion)
stabilization (*see* shoreline: engineering)
shrubs (*see* vegetation)
site safety (*see* building: site safety)
soil profile, 56
Smith Island (*see* Bald Head Island)
sound, 21, 25, 27, 40, 59, 90, 105
sound side, island, 5-6, 21, 24-25, 37, 40, 55, 60, 62, 77, 78, 83, 108, 124, 127
erosion, 27, 29, 37, 76, 92, 108
South Carolina, 11, 118
Spartina marsh (*see* marsh, *Spartina*)
storms (*see also* hurricane), 11-15, 59, 75, 83, 84, 89, 90, 93, 96, 104, 114, 115
Ash Wednesday, 86, 92
northeasters, 74, 76, 94, 96, 98
storm-surge flooding (*see also* sealevel changes), 45, 53-55, 59-60, 68, 79, 84, 87, 90, 92, 93, 94, 96, 98, 99, 100, 105, 116, 135-137, 138, 141, 149-151, 158-164
level, 54-55, 59-60, 104, 105, 110, 116, 135-137, 149-150, 158-164
waves, 31, 55, 59-60, 127, 149, 150
Sunset Beach, 58, 59, 65, 66, 127, 130

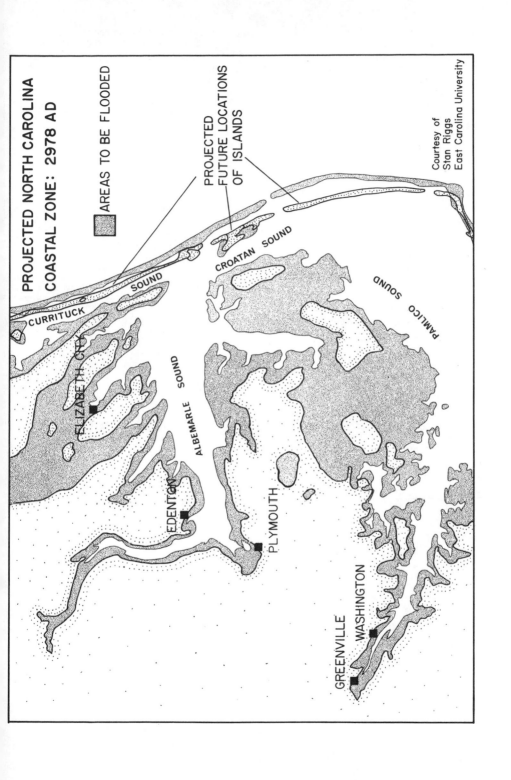

PROJECTED NORTH CAROLINA
COASTAL ZONE: 2978 AD

▨ AREAS TO BE FLOODED

PROJECTED
FUTURE LOCATIONS
OF ISLANDS

CURRITUCK

SOUND

ELIZABETH CITY

ALBEMARLE SOUND

EDENTON

PLYMOUTH

CROATAN SOUND

PAMLICO SOUND

GREENVILLE

WASHINGTON

Courtesy of
Stan Riggs
East Carolina University